The Best of
Charles Jayne

Charles Jayne

Copyright 1995 by American Federation of Astrologers, Inc.
All rights reserved.

No part of this book may be reproduced or transmitted in any form or by any means, electronic or mechanical, including photocopying or recording, or by any information storage and retrieval system, without written permission from the author and publisher. Requests and inquiries may be mailed to: American Federation of Astrologers, Inc., 6535 S. Rural Road, Tempe, AZ 85283.

ISBN-10: 0-86690-449-2
ISBN-13: 978-0-86690-449-0

Cover Design: Jack Cipolla

Current Printing: 2009

Published by:
American Federation of Astrologers, Inc.
6535 S. Rural Road
Tempe, AZ 85285-2040

www.astrologers.com

Printed in the United States of America

Contents

Foreword ... v

Horoscope Interpretation Outlined

Preface to the Second Edition ... 3
Preface ... 4
Introduction ... 5
The Chart As A Whole ... 7
The Main Components ... 11
The Lights and Angles and Their Relationships ... 17
The Pivotal and Singular Factors ... 29
Addendum ... 33

Introduction to Locality Astrology

Preface ... 41
Shifting the Chart ... 43
Locality Charts ... 53

Parallels: Their Hidden Meaning

Preface ... 83
Parallels: The Key ... 87
Types of Parallels ... 91
Orbs of Parallels ... 95
How Parallels Modify A Chart ... 99
Transits in Declination ... 103
Parallels by Progression ... 107
Declination Arc Directions ... 111
Parallels in Synastry ... 115

The Technique of Rectification

Introduction ... 137
The Tools ... 137
The Technique of Rectification ... 141
Rectification Process ... 149
Additional Examples ... 153
Unknown Birth Times ... 163
Horoscope Validation ... 169

Foreword

When the American Federation of Astrologers suggested that we put four of Charles' most important books in one volume, I jumped at the opportunity—and here are the wonderful results!

Charles first had the idea to publish his own (and some other's) books when he did a first draft of *Horoscope Interpretation Outlined* and published it in 1970 under the auspices of our Astrological Bureau. People showed a real interest in this book and so he was encouraged to think of other books that he said needed to be written.

In 1975 there was a new printing of *Horoscope Interpretation Outlined* and in this book he added an appendix listing books in English or translated into English which he felt had superior merit. He stated in the preface that he may have inadvertently omitted a few important books, for which he begged the pardon of the authors.

He believed that one of the main problems of astrology at that time was it had begun to be buried under a sea of mediocrity. Many books that were being published were merely an endeavor to exploit a currently popular field. The books that he listed are limited to interpretation and to the basic components of a chart, and since this is the subject of his book *Horoscope Interpretation Outlined*, the reader was obviously obtaining the book to learn more about such matters.

In 1975 there was yet to be any adequate treatment in book form of the Vertex, the ``third angle'' of any chart, of Pluto, or of the houses. He did include Dane Rudhyar's book on the houses as he thought it was the best material we had on the subject, although it does not attempt to deal with the thorny question of which house system is the best!

Many students of astrology seem to examine a horoscope in a piecemeal way and having gathered bits of information, they then try to put them all together, but usually find that it is really impossible. In Charles' method you start with the chart as a whole, and from there gradually work to the chart in particular. Charles states that the outline attempts to include the worthy contributions of other astrologers and is therefore not limited to just his approach. It was very important to him that due credit be given to other astrologers since no one astrologer is so nearly perfect that he or she cannot learn from others.

He initially lays out a simple skeleton outline to be easily followed. He felt that one could think of horoscope interpretation as the use of a series of filter techniques, each of which may tell us something useful, although it may not do so. For instance, if there is equal weight to all four elements, we learn nothing from any potential deficit or preponderance, in which case we simply pass on to the next filter.

The reader will certainly find that to be completely systematic is advisable and will produce a clear analysis of any horoscope, instead of a fuzzy combination of his or her beliefs.

You will probably be delighted to see that he has included the seven chart patterns that were introduced to astrology by Marc Edmund Jones, as well as an important sector on major configurations and their deeper meaning. For instance, he includes the grand hexagon's meaning (very rare), the cradle, and the cradle with hood, along with the octagon or double square, the pentagram, and the mystic rectangle to name a few extraordinarily revealing configurations when found in the horoscope. He gives illuminating interpretations of these configurations (some very rare).

There is a special section on the lights, the Sun and Moon, which includes the lunation cycle phases and the eight lunation types (from Rudhyar) with Charles' own interpretation of these.

For a number of years he had been concerned about the problem of rectifying a horoscope to its exact time of day, since without an accurate time the Midheaven and Ascendant and their respective aspects to other bodies was a major consideration. No matter how good you were at interpretation, you could not render a meaningful horoscope depicting the characteristics and outer conditions of any given person and his or her life unless you had the planets and lights in the right houses, as well as aspects to the angles (which he was to discover were the main factors showing a person's career and personal projection in life).

So, he decided to write a book on the technique of rectification. This book grew in stages and finally reached a point of completion that satisfied Charles in 1974. In the beginning of this book he again repeats that it is really impossible to emphasize too much the importance of careful and rigorous examination of the placement of the Ascendant and of the planets in the houses before one uses any arcs of direction. He stresses rigorous consistency in interpretations and uses the test that at least eight major directions to or by the angles must fit, not only as to time but also as to correct meaning before one may consider that the angles are probably right. Also, he stated that some similar minimum number of factors must fit not only as to directions and events, but also as to their radical static pattern of relationships of houses and angles to lights and planets.

In his book *Technique of Rectification,* he gives the tools to work with, which, of course, include his methods of direction, including declination arcs and directions for finding the Vertex in any chart. (Now, most computer calculation programs include the accurate position of the Vertex for the chart.)

To rectify a chart one must have a good knowledge of all the main phases of astrology (from Charles): the meaning of the signs, houses, planets, aspects, the ability to interpret, to see the chart as a whole and to pick out the focal features, the ability to cast the chart correctly, the ability to interpret the chart dynamically as well as statically. Charles felt that the best test of astrological competence was the ability to rectify charts, but he thought that nearly all astrologers, except a very small handful, would fail if this were made the criterion for their permission to practice professionally.

In this book too, he starts with the larger factors such as: Are the planets and lights in the right houses? Does the sign on the Ascendant fit the first impression you get from the person whose chart is being rectified? He also points out that one should really have a good case history from the client and one that is accurate as to the time events occurred. This can often be a problem if the client does not want to look up the accurate dates of all the difficult events that occurred in his life. But you cannot expect accurate timing for the future without it.

Much of the book is devoted to examples, which are real eye openers and virtually a complete course in astrology. Each example has actual events and the client's psychological characteristics, in addition to an explanation of how and why they fit beautifully with the client's chart.

This is a book that should be on every astrologer's shelf. It will probably be used for years as a reference manual.

Parallels, Their Hidden Meaning also is included in this volume and focuses on the major ways in which planets in a horoscope are related to each other through parallels of declination.

Fairly frequently a horoscope is dominated by some major configuration. Failure to recognize such a configuration results in failure to interpret the chart correctly. A major configuration may be of three types. A grand cross, grand trine, or similar transversal and aspectual combination is a well-known type that is widely recognized. A second type is a major planetary picture, so that if one knows nothing about midpoints, it is possible to completely miss the boat with certain horoscopes where there is no apparent dominant combination in longitude and declination.

The third type is based on a powerful configuration in declination. Charles cites cases where failure to examine the parallels and the contraparallels would have resulted in a failure to find the main meaning of that horoscope. In one of his examples—Walt Disney—he defies anyone to have forecast Disney's uniqueness and impact on the world if the remarkable configuration in declination was not looked for and used. The bodies in his chart from the Sun to Venus, except for Mars, are a stellium in declination, as they are all parallel each other and Neptune is contraparallel all of them. This creates a fanhandle in declination, with all the great potential of the stellium pouring out through his Neptune to charm and amaze the world.

After learning about such declination configurations, you will wonder how you ever achieved a good chart interpretation without checking the declinations.

Charles also wrote and published an introductory text on locality astrology. In it he includes shifting any natal, or other, horoscope to a different locality. This shifts the angles of the chart which can put all of the radical bodies into different houses.

In the second conventional type of shift, one moves so as to place a radical body on one of the three local planes: Meridian, Horizon, or Prime Vertical. One may have Jupiter on the upper Meridian (Midheaven) while having Mars on or near the horizon. While they may have no aspect *in zodiaco*, these two planets are then in paran square to each other.

The third type of shift moves all bodies backward and forward in the zodiac and not merely in the houses along the equator in right ascension. He gives clear and simple explanations of how to make these three shifts with examples you can follow and execute on your own charts.

He also goes into the matter of casting a birth locality or Johndro chart. He mentions the fact that in the June 1950 issue of *Modern Astrology* magazine, Johndro repudiated his earlier work. In his book *Earth in the Heaven* published in 1929, Johndro brought the zodiac to Earth and in so doing established a baseline which very slowly inched westward. In 1950, after twenty years of checking, he found that the moving baseline was only correct fifty percent of the time, and recommended that a fixed baseline be used which equates the Greenwich Meridian to zero degrees Aries of the tropical zodiac.

The horoscope of Jacqueline Onassis is used as an example of using the Johndro BL (baseline) and BL′ chart. He also uses Marilyn Monroe's horoscope and shows how in having the Moon close to the

Los Angeles Ascendant indicates the importance of her impact on that area. The closeness of the Moon to Athen's Midheaven is indicative of Jacqueline's impact on Greece through her marriage to an outstanding and very wealthy citizen. Charles felt these examples were certainly partial proof of the validity of the new Johndro baseline.

Of course, in this age of computers, most astrologers have easy access to many different locality shifts and charts and therefore don't need to do any calculations by hand. Yet with this first-hand knowledge, you can shift and set up locality charts even if you are far from your computer! An understanding of how this is done can certainly add to your arsenal of tools to use in your astrological practice.

With this volume, which is really four books in one, you have an overall complete course in astrology which you can use as a reference book for all your questions on astrology.

Vivia Jayne
Monroe, New York
May 1995

Horoscope Interpretation Outlined

Dedication

To Dane Rudhyar. All his contemporaries and those who will follow owe much increased awareness to his profound and luminous sights into man's potential.

Preface to the Second Edition

In this second edition I have added a special section at the back of the book on additional techniques in interpretation. The material is very condensed. There are three parts:

One-at-a-time: Planetary and Lunar Nodes.

Two-at-a-time: Transversal—harmonics and parans; Orthogonal—parallels of altitude* and parallels of amplitude*.

Three-at-a-time: *In zodiaco*—planetary pictures; *in mundo*—Arabic Parts*.

Under planetary nodes are included those on the equator that the Church of Light has studied. The planetary nodes are otherwise *in zodiaco* or on the ecliptic, but are heliocentric since I agree with Carl Payne Tobey that in the sense usually meant the geocentric nodes are invalid, despite the claims of the Dobyns and Jones. To the parans, revived in astrology by the late Cyril Fagan, are added aspects taken along the prime vertical in zenith distance* in Campanus houses, as outlined by him; and taken along the horizon in azimuth* in horizontal houses, as outlined by Friedrich Sieggruen, Witte's associate, in his Zenithscope. These last two have hardly been investigated as is even truer of the parallels and contraparallels in altitude* (my preliminary studies of them indicate their importance) and in amplitude* (distance north and south of the prime vertical). All starred (*) factors depend also on an accurately rectified horoscope.

The Arabic Parts* were developed by the Arabic and Hellenic classical astrologers. As George Noonan has shown, they were only calculated *in mundo*, i.e. in right ascension and thus along the equator and not along the ecliptic in longitude (celestial) as all modern astrologers mistakenly do! Jones, in his work with them, does suggest that they are a phenomena of the houses, which does indicate they are not ecliptical.

The importance of planetary pictures (via midpoints) is now widely recognized. Harmonics and the harmonic charts of John Addey are beginning to be appreciated. Since the heliocentric planetary nodes are easy to do, they should be studied by us all, following the lead of Tobey and Erlewine. The brilliant work of Blackwell, Hand, and Kahila on the parans suggests they may have great unrecognized value, natally as well as by transit and direction. They are very much house phenomena, but do not require, fortunately, a rectified horoscope.

It is quite probable that astrology as most of us know it is quite incomplete. Most astrologers have good imaginations and read things into and out of charts that are not there! The addition of missing relationships should make this quite unnecessary.

Charles A. Jayne
February 11, 1977

Preface

In this new printing I have added in an appendix a list of books in English, or translated into English, which have superior merit. It may be that I have inadvertently omitted a few important books, for which I beg pardon of the authors. The main problem of astrology today is that we have commenced to be buried under a sea of mediocrity. Many books that are being published are merely an endeavor to exploit a currently popular field. That is to say that they are largely derivative, i.e. copies of their predecessors. The books I have had the temerity to recommend are not all of equal merit. Some have been included since there is no other book on that particular subject. The books are limited to interpretation and to the basic components of a chart. Timing and specialties have been omitted.

As yet there has been no adequate treatment in book form of the Vertex, the third angle of any chart, of Pluto, or of the houses. Dane Rudhyar's book on the houses has been included since it is the best material we have on the subject, but he does not attempt to deal with the thorny question of which house system is the best! Lewi's book on the 144 Sun sign and Moon sign combinations is a real classic. This is also true of the books by Pagan and Sampson on the zodiac (tropical), yet the latter's book is not widely known. There is no adequate book on the stars and the sidereal zodiac. This is bound to infuriate the fanatical siderealists of the occident, but much of great value in the work of Fagan and Bradley was flawed by their opinionatedness and the incorrect ayanamsa they insisted on. Johndro's first class *The Stars: How and Where They Influence* has to do with timing.

Charles A. Jayne
February 21, 1975
Monroe, New York

Introduction

Too many student astrologers examine a horoscope in a piecemeal manner. Having collected a large number of small bits of information, they try to put them together but find that this is really impossible. The following outline is an attempt to correct this widespread and serious fallacy.

We start with the chart as a whole, and from there work gradually to the chart in particular. This is just the opposite of the usual way of doing it. Two of our most outstanding astrologers, Marc Edmund Jones and Dane Rudhyar, have strongly emphasized this gestalt concept. Gestalt psychology has shown us that we always see the whole at first and only afterward the special parts.

The outline attempts to include the contributions to the interpretation of any horoscope of a number of astrologers and is, therefore, not limited to my own approach. Indeed, I find that one serious flaw of many astrologers is that they seldom pay attention to or give credit to the work of others. Actually, no one astrologer is so nearly perfect that he or she cannot learn from others. In fact, few astrologers have actually made new contributions to the field, and so derive much of what they know from their predecessors and colleagues.

As the outlined method of attack on a horoscope unfolds, I shall recommend books you might read in order to round out your knowledge of different phases of interpretation. This outline is the basis of my course in general horoscope interpretation and is used by my students as a supplement to my course. It presupposes knowledge of the fundamentals: signs, houses, planets, and aspects. The latter should include parallels of declination, but too often does not.

The Skeletal Outline

I. The Chart as A Whole
    A. Preponderance and deficits
        1. By quadruplicity
        2. By element
        3. By polarity
        4. By house
    B. The seven main chart patterns (from Dr. Jones)

II. The Main Components of the Horoscope Structure
   A. The major configurations—bidimensional (grand crosses, grand trines, stellia, T-crosses, etc.)
   B. The major configurations (continued)—tridimensional (when parallels and contraparallels of declination are added to give "solidity" to the structure)
III. The Lights and Angles and Their Relationships
   A. The lights (Sun and Moon)
      1. The lunation cycle phase (from Rudhyar)
      2. The Sun (sign, house, aspects)
      3. The Moon (sign, house, aspects)
   B. The relations of the lights to the angles
      1. By hemisphere
      2. By sextant
   C. The angles (Ascendant, Midheaven and Vertex)
      1. The Ascendant (sign and aspects)
      2. The Midheaven (sign and aspects)
      3. The Vertex (sign and aspects)
IV. The Pivotal and Singular Factors
   A. Traditional techniques
      1. Essentially dignified
      2. Accidentally dignified
      3. Planetary ruler (of Ascendant)
   B. Jones Techniques
      1. The dynamic focus
      2. The vocational indicator
      3. Leading planet (in a locomotive or bowl pattern) and singleton planet (in a bucket)
   C. The pivot
   D. Eclipse energization (from Johndro)
V. The Meaning of Planets by Sign, House and Aspect (This part is important but is not covered in the course I give since time does not admit of such complete coverage.)

One may think of horoscope interpretation as the use of a series of filter techniques, each of which may tell us something useful. Thus, if there is equal weight in all four elements, we learn nothing from any potential deficit or preponderance. In that case, we simply pass on to the next filter. Let me add that in learning interpretation, it is advisable to be systematic since so many astrologers are loose and fuzzy (Neptunian). Later, after the student has acquired knowledge, it will be unnecessary to be so systematic because, after all, interpretation is an art rather than a science.

1

The Chart As A Whole

In order to maintain perspective and to give proper weight to the manifold factors in a horoscope, it is essential to never lose sight of the whole chart. The integrated weight of the whole chart can and does outweigh even the most pivotal part.

It is the mark of the experienced and competent astrologer to maintain this whole view. Thus, if a chart has broad strength in the earth signs and in the fixed ones too, along with heavily accented counter-indications (such as a potent T-cross in mutable signs, which includes Neptune square Mars and opposition Moon—heavy water accent), it must not be given greater weight than the ``pull'' of the whole chart. That pull can be like the keel of a boat, giving balance and stability to what would otherwise be dangerously one-sided.

Initially, it is unnecessary to be concerned with which body is which since a general impression is being obtained. But extra weight will be given to the main significators: the two lights—Sun and Moon—and two angles—Ascendant and Midheaven. To each of these four will be given a weight of two, but only one each to the eight planets. The total weight is then sixteen points.

Preponderance and Deficit of Weight by Quadruplicity, Polarity, and House

Quadruplicity. Since there are three quadruplicities (cardinal, fixed, and mutable), the mean weight will be 16/3 = 5 1/3. A count of five or six will be normal or average. Under five will be a deficit and over six will be a preponderance. Three or four will be a moderate deficit, while zero, one, or two will be a large deficit. Seven or eight will be a moderate preponderance; above eight will be a large one.

A preponderance of any quadruplicity means the person is strongly:

- Cardinal—active, with initiative, and preferring projects to people or ideas or values.
- Fixed—fixed and concerned with one's own values and ideas.
- Mutable—diversified, flexible, and interested in people.

A deficit or lack of any quadruplicity means the person will unconsciously accent what is lacking, i.e. make an extra effort to be cardinal just because it is needed. However, lacking it, the person will be less than successful in contrast to the preponderantly cardinal person who is that way with ease and little effort (and may be too much that way).

Element. The four elements are fire, earth, air, and water. If sixteen is divided by four (number of elements), four is the normal or mean count per element. Three is a small deficit, two a moderate one and zero or one a large deficit. Five is a small preponderance, six is a moderate one, and seven or more is a large one.

Those with a preponderance of earth tend to be down to earth and notably practical with comparative ease. On the other hand, a marked lack of fire means a lack of self-sufficiency and some lack of surety, but there is an effort to offset this by trying to be self-sufficient and spirited (fire). Water gives not only much emotionalism and intuition, but also an all-enveloping tendency. For air, communication and relationship are always extra important and natural. Their heads rule their hearts!

Polarity. Polarity is defined as active vs. passive. The fire and air signs are active and the earth and water signs are passive. A normal or average count is then eight each. A deficit must be six or fewer to be significant and a preponderance must be ten or more. A strong preponderance of active signs (twelve or more) gives a positive person, while a large deficit of such signs (four or fewer) gives one who is passive and usually must be pushed in order to do anything.

House. Houses are angular, succedent, or cadent. Since the Ascendant and Midheaven are no longer included, the total count is reduced from sixteen to twelve so that on an average the normal count will be: four angular, four succedent, and four cadent. The angular houses are the first, fourth, seventh, and tenth; the succedent houses are the second, fifth, eighth, and eleventh; the remaining houses are cadent and are the third, sixth, ninth, and twelfth.

When there is a preponderance of planets (more than five) in angular houses, the person projects and comes across with his or her personality, ideas, etc. The emotions (fifth and eleventh houses) and the strong sense of values (second and eighth houses) of the succedent houses is evidenced when they are preponderant. More inward and mental are the cadent houses, which are not by any means less important than the other ones.

Luise Rainier has a grand cardinal cross in cadent houses so that when you meet her she does not have an unusual or striking personality projection, but on the stage (she won two Oscars) she is extraordinary as there she brings through her cardinality.

Again, a deficit can cause a significant attempt to compensate. Marc Edmund Jones has made us all realize the importance of what is lacking in the horoscope and that in interpretation it is as vital as preponderance.

The Seven Chart Patterns

These were introduced into astrology by Marc Edmund Jones in his *Guide to Horoscope Interpretation*. The lights and planets (ten factors) were found by him to fall into seven patterns.

The Splash. The ten factors are rather evenly distributed around the wheel and as a result the person tends to go off in too many directions. On the other hand, the person never suffers from the fault of being one-sided, having the potential of being truly universal and well-rounded.

The Bundle. All the planets are within about one-third (trine) of the circle. There is definite one-sidedness, but often unusual ability along one line. On the other hand, there is some narrowness, the price one pays for concentrating the psychic energy. This pattern is rather uncommon.

The Locomotive. Here the ten factors tend to be evenly distributed except for one-third of the circle, which is empty. Thus, this person has the pattern of the driving wheel of a locomotive and strong executive drive. The leading planet is of marked importance. If one imagines the ten factors revolving backward (due to the earth's daily rotation), the one of the precession of ten that first rises over the Ascendant is the leading planet. This type also can be quite opportunistic.

The Bowl. The next three types are based on the opposition just as the last two are based on the trine. In the Bowl type, all the planets lie within about 180 degrees so that half the wheel is empty. They are quite self-contained, and must always relate what they have to larger matters since they lack any factor in one-half of the wheel. They tend to be advocates of a cause and interested in the meanings of experience. The leading planet is important but less so than with a locomotive.

The Bucket. Nine factors lie within one-third (the Bundle) to one-half (the Bowl) of the circle in opposition to a single body. As a result, this single factor takes on marked importance as the "handle" of the bucket. This type adjusts to conditions and thus has more external orientation than the Bowl type does. Such a type moves people, whether as teacher, leader, or agitator. As Jones says, ``he or she dips deeply into life and pours forth the materials of experience with unremitting zeal.'' The handle planet must be at least sixty degrees from the nearest planet.

A note on the Bucket and Bowl: If the leading planet in the Bowl is rising, these people scoop up and start things; if it sets, they capture and end things. If the handle of the Bucket is nearer the leading planet (not vital in the Bucket) than the trailing planet, it is said to ``lean back,'' thus showing a tendency for self-preservation and being overly conservative. If the "lean" is the other way (forward), the tendency is to be somewhat rash and self-expending.

The See-Saw. Two planets are opposed by eight, or three by seven, or four by six, or five by five. On one side at least ninety degrees must separate the two groups, while on the other side at least sixty degrees must separate them. This individual, most of the time, lives in terms of opposing forces in relationships and interests. The problem is to keep the two different areas of experience in balance.

The Splay. What you can't classify may be a splay. As Jones describes it, "strong and sharp aggregations of the planets at irregular points" are revealed. The individual is highly individualistic and not easy to classify. It often has a ray-like character in the relations of the planetary groupings to each other. As Jones says, the splay is "particular and impersonal in its interests, in contrast to the universal-impersonal set of the splash, and the particular-personal set of the bundle type."

In some cases a chart may have to be described as a cross between two types, with one of them possibly dominant. This presents no problem in interpretation.

Note: In his *Guide to Horoscope Interpretation*, Jones divides the planets into certain bi-polar departments: Sun-Moon (vitality), Jupiter-Saturn (personality, soul), Mars-Venus (efficiency), and Uranus-Neptune (culture); Mercury is linked with Mars-Venus and Pluto supernumerary.

2

The Main Components

After studying the chart as a whole, its main components must be considered. The main components are the major planetary configurations in two dimensions and in three dimensions when declinations are added.

In this section the discussion will be limited to the major planetary configurations, which, if alone, tend to dominate the horoscope. If there are two and they are not linked, then the life problem can be the attempt to prevent being pulled apart in two different directions.

To be a major configuration it should have a count of at least four or five with the lights and angles, as usual, counted double. The simplest grand trine or T-cross of three planets has a count of only three so it must be considered a secondary configuration, important but hardly dominant. On the other hand, if such a secondary configuration is the strongest single configuration in a chart its importance increases.

At this point in the analysis of the horoscope we are examining its major structural features, and are still far from details. Having left the whole chart for this level, already there is a much greater variety of possible combinations.

There are twelve factors when the two angles are included, and a large number of ways in which they can appear in a three-factor configuration such as a grand trine or T-cross. Indeed, there are 220 such combinations (twelve taken three at a time). Normal orbs are used for such major configurations, although they may be larger than usual at times due to the combined effect of several bodies and the "translation of light." The configurations mentioned first are those that are connected with various kinds of preponderance.

The Major Configurations in Longitude Only

Grand Cross or Square. This usually falls only in signs of a single quadruplicity, thus giving preponderance in that quadruplicity. If the grand cross falls across the cusps of signs so that is in more than one quadruplicity, it is weakened. A grand cross has great strength of resistance and inner power. Since the four arms of the cross point in four directions, there is a diffusive tendency. This is a static configuration, full of strong inner tensions. Resolving trines and sextiles can ease some of the frustrations and make creative release of energy possible.

Grand Trine. The grand trine usually falls in the signs of a single element, thus giving preponderance in that element. This, too, is a diffusive configuration in its effects, which are not good unless it serves to resolve squares and oppositions in the total pattern, or it is given some dynamism by reason of squares or oppositions to its bodies. By itself it is rather weak and lazy. Individuals may coast on the momentum of their luck, taking the easiest way.

Grand Hexagon, Cradle, and Cradle with Hood. The grand hexagon is rare; the cradle is more common. Both are major configurations that consist mainly of trines and sextiles, thus usually falling only in either active or passive signs. The cradle is half of a hexagon (six-sided figure) and shows immaturity and dependency since it is always easy to obtain assistance when needed. It is composed of three sextiles and two trines, plus one opposition; the latter provides the bounds of the figure. The cradle with hood adds one more sextile, one more trine, and one more opposition. It is similar in nature.

Octagon or Double Square. This is very rare, quite diffusive in nature, and composed of oppositions, squares, sesquiquadrates, and semisquares. The inner tensions can be frustrating unless they have an avenue of release, but the native has much strength and is capable of much breadth.

Pentagram. Also fairly rare, the Pentagram is composed of five quintiles (72 degrees). It gives unusual talent (quintile) and creative potential, but interest and effort would be diffused.

Note: With the exception of the two lesser forms of the hexagon (cradle and cradle with hood), all the configurations thus far mentioned have been perfectly symmetrical. Those that follow are partially symmetrical and tend to be less balanced, less diffusive, and more focused.

Mystic Rectangle. This is composed of two oppositions which are trine and sextile each other so that each opposition "resolves" the other one. A nearly even combination of the hard aspects—oppositions, squares, semisquares, and sesquiquadrates—with the soft aspects—trines and sextiles—is generally desirable for real balance. With two oppositions, two trines, and two sextiles, this configuration tends to approach this desired end. It lacks only squares. This configuration with its two oppositions does emphasize challenges and confrontations, which always tend to increase awareness. Due to the resolving aspects there will be external assistance and opportunities and internal capabilities that will make possible effective solutions to the problems posed by the oppositions.

Hard Rectangle. The hard rectangle is composed of two oppositions which are linked, not by trines and sextiles, but by sesquiquadrates (135 degrees) and semisquares (45 degrees). This has some similarity to the grand cross but is less diffusive, emphasizing balance to a degree. The two oppositions again accent the individual being compelled to confront things as well as balancing them. There is considerable tension since no easy (sextiles and trines) aspects characterize this figure, but there also is considerable strength.

Kite. The kite is a grand trine which has a fourth point occupied at the middle of one side, opposite one corner of the triangle and sextile the other two corners. It contains three trines, two sextiles, and one opposition (a little like the cradle with three sextiles, two trines, and one opposition, but more symmetrical). Or one may look at it as a single opposition doubly resolved by trines and sextiles somewhat like the stronger mystic rectangle. It is somewhat diffusive and lazy, but is capable of creative awareness.

The next group of configurations is generally asymmetrical. They are much less diffusive and all-embracing, being more dynamic with a one-sided tendency.

Pythagorean Figure. This configuration is so-named because it is based on the numbers three, four, and five, as is the right triangle of the same name. It is an irregular triangle composed of a square (three signs), a trine (four signs), and a quincunx (five signs). Thus, a body at zero degrees Aries is square one at zero degrees Cancer, which is trine one at zero degrees Scorpio, which is quincunx a body at zero degrees Aries. It is connected with a sense of humor, with a sense of the incongruous, and with a constant and compelling need to adjust to what is out of kilter. Arthur Young studied this and found it important in humor.

T-Cross. This is the four-armed cross with one arm absent. It is a common and important configuration. And due to its very imbalance it is quite dynamic, giving drive. A person who stays on his feet after tripping while running is an example of the principle. The area of the missing arm is important in that one seeks to find balance there. The arm without an opposition is crucial as the fulcrum.

Stellium (or Satellitum). This configuration is a close clustering of at least four bodies; if the Sun, Mercury, and Venus are included, there must be at least five since Venus and Mercury, especially the latter, never get very far form the Sun. Ideally, this should fall in the same sign and house and is weakened if it does not (there is great emphasis in the house and/or sign). There can be genius due to the great potential of this rare configuration. Things are very pointed and single track. A square may be needed to give it spark.

Fanhandle. The Fanhandle is a stellium opposed by a single planet. All the unusual energy of the stellium cluster thrusts out through the single planet as through a nozzle. This makes the planet highly focal. Note also a balancing tendency due to the opposition nature of this configuration. There is greatly heightened awareness, but narrowed down to a sharp point.

Multiple Opposition. This should be composed of at least two bodies opposite two others; if there are three oppositions, it tends to act like the fanhandle, though it does not quite qualify. Just as a stellium is, in principle, like a bundle and a fanhandle is like a bucket, the multiple opposition is like a see-saw. This configuration has a teeter-totter effect, a tendency toward confrontation and challenge which increases objectivity and awareness.

It is impossible to describe these configurations except in general terms because the nature of the planets involved is obviously of the utmost importance and will particularize what must otherwise be general. Thus, if in a T-Cross, Venus is opposition Mars (they are a natural "polar pair") with Saturn in square to them, the effect is very different from what would be if Saturn were to be replaced by, for example, Neptune. Saturn would tend to inhibit, frustrate, and interfere in a "damping" manner with the emotional impulses of Venus opposition Mars. Were Neptune in the fulcrum position, there would be no restraint and a markedly increased tendency to romanticism and colorful fantasies.

Therefore, in trying to assess the meanings of any of these major configurations it is important to first define their meanings one aspect at a time. In the case of the Venus-Mars-Saturn T-cross, one first would evaluate and interpret Venus opposite Mars, then Saturn square Venus (business and necessity interfering with pleasure) and finally Saturn square Mars, which gives the tendency to blow hot (Mars) and cold (Saturn). From this one can reach a synthesized meaning of the total configuration. Indeed, this is one of the important way to learn astrology. Mere memorization of what a configuration means will teach you little. If you break it down, interpret the component aspects, synthesize them, and then compare your interpretation with what you observe about the person. You will learn in a first-hand way what it really means.

The Declination Factor in Major Configurations

A horoscope is presented as two-dimensional. The places of the planets are projected onto the plane of the ecliptic and their distance in arc is then given along that two-dimensional plane from zero degrees Aries from where the ecliptic crosses above the equator. But space is three-dimensional and bodies in space are distributed in those three dimensions. Therefore, a horoscope without the third dimension is simply incomplete. At times this can be seriously misleading. The celestial longitude along the ecliptic is the transverse component of the polar coordinate system we employ; the orthogonal component, at right angles to the ecliptic, is termed celestial latitude. With the exception of Pluto in part of its orbit, the other bodies do not stray overly far in latitude from the ecliptic.

But there is another important polar coordinate system which is used to define the positions of bodies in space: the equator. The positions of the planets can be projected perpendicularly onto that plane, after which the distance from the equatorial intercept to zero degrees Aries along the equator is measured. This is called right ascension. Here the orthogonal component is the distance in arc that a body is above or below the equator, which is termed its declination. The Moon at times reaches a declination above (north) or below (south) the equator of nearly twenty-nine degrees. Two bodies that have the same declination north (+) are said to be in parallel; this is also true of two bodies the same distance south (-) in declination. But, if one is above the equator and the other is below at the same distance, they act as though they are in opposition; this is termed a contraparallel. Bodies that are in parallel act as though they are in conjunction; those in contraparallel act as though in opposition.

Most bodies that are conjunct in longitude are also within orb of a parallel of declination, thus giving most conjunctions double strength. In like manner, most bodies that are in opposition in longitude are also within orb of a contraparallel. While most astrologers do not know it, this is why they consider the conjunction and opposition aspects as the strongest ones! It happens fairly often that bodies are parallel without being conjunct; they also can be contraparallel without being in opposition.

If we deal only with the ecliptic-intercepts of bodies, we can measure the declination of the ecliptic-intercept of the body instead of the declination of the body itself. For example, suppose Mars is at nineteen degrees Gemini and we wish to find the declination of nineteen degrees Gemini, i.e. without celestial latitude. We bring the Sun there since it never has any celestial latitude and find that its declination is twenty-three degrees north of the ecliptic-intercept of Mars, whose bodily declination is 23°24'. But there is a symmetry principle because if the Sun were at eleven degrees Cancer it would also be at twenty-three degrees north. In other words, the point on the ecliptic at nineteen degrees Gemini is parallel to the point on the ecliptic at eleven degrees Cancer. This is so since they are equidistant on either side of zero degrees Cancer. Indeed, the point at eleven degrees Cancer is called the antiscion of Mars. It is what might also be termed a solar parallel since the parallel of nineteen degrees Gemini to eleven degrees Cancer is solely via the Sun's plane or ecliptic.

It is easy to find the antiscion of any ecliptic point. First, memorize this:

Cancer is parallel Gemini, and Capricorn is parallel Sagittarius
Leo is parallel Taurus, and Aquarius is parallel Scorpio
Virgo is parallel Aries, and Pisces is parallel Libra

Note that since Aries is parallel Virgo, it must be contraparallel Pisces. Thus, nineteen degrees Gemini is contrascion eleven degrees Capricorn.

How is the degree of an antiscion or contrascion found? What is the antiscion of, for example, 13 Aries 49? Virgo is parallel Aries, and to find the degrees and minutes of Virgo that are the antiscion of 13 Aries 49, all that is necessary is to subtract the 13°49′ from 29°60′ (equivalent to 30°00′). This gives an answer of 16 Virgo 11. The contrascion (like an opposition) of 13 Aries 49 would then be opposite the antiscion at 16 Pisces 11. Antiscia and contrascia are not as strong as bodily parallels and contraparallels, but they are as strong as trines and should not be overlooked. They are used in the late Alfred Witte's Uranian system.

Why are declinations important to major configurations? One may have an imperfect T-cross or grand cross or any other major configuration in which the orb of a conjunction or opposition is too wide to be valid. However, in some instances the conjunction is replaced by a parallel and the opposition by a contraparallel so that what appears to be an imperfect configuration is found valid after all. This can be crucially important in many horoscopes.

One striking case of a fanhandle by declination occurs in the chart of Walt Disney. He has a stellium below the horizon in Sagittarius and Capricorn, mainly due to parallels of declination. The Sun and Uranus are both conjunct in the third house in Sagittarius and parallel each other and Jupiter, Saturn, and Venus in Capricorn. Jupiter and Saturn are in the fourth house conjunct Mars, and Venus is in the fifth house. They are all contraparallel to Neptune in Cancer in the tenth house of career. Without these declination aspects the genius of Disney is inexplicable. All the potential of his linked Sun-Uranus-Mars-Jupiter-Saturn-Venus stellium came bursting out through the "nozzle" of his elevated Neptune, planet of illusion, film, and fantasy. Enough said!

As the Earth rotates daily along the equator the planets move along their parallels of declination, i.e. parallel to the equator. Thus, if Pluto is twenty degrees north and another body is also about twenty degrees north in another part of the zodiac, Pluto is swept across the other body by the earth's rotation, which is a kind of conjunction! In like manner, bodies in contraparallel tend to oppose each other. Thus, we use declination rather than celestial latitude to obtain effects similar to conjunctions and oppositions. Everyone should make full use of parallels, contraparallels, antiscia, and contrascia in tracing out relationships in a chart which otherwise would go undetected.

How are the orbs of such aspects measured? Traditionally an orb of plus or minus one degree of declination has been used, but this is quite wrong. Suppose two planets are at 0 Cancer 00 and 7 Cancer 30, well within a reasonable orb for a conjunction or opposition. The declinations are 23°27′ and

23°15' north, a difference of orb of only 0°12'. At the other extreme, place two planets at 0 Aries 00 and 7 Aries 30; its declinations are 0°00' and 2°59' north. Here the declination orb for the same seven and a half degree longitude orb is 2°59'. Thus, we are confronted with a sliding scale. How then can we get around it? It can be done by turning any declination of 23°27' or less into an equivalent ecliptic longitude. Having done so the aspect is then measured in longitude (conjunction or opposition of two such equivalent longitudes) instead of in declination.

Note the diagram that illustrates the reading of orbs of declination and the various types of declination aspects. The straight line at the bottom is the equator and the curved line is the ecliptic which intersects the equator at zero degrees Aries and zero degrees Libra. The planet is at D, where it is projected on the ecliptic at C, its south latitude below the ecliptic being 5°14' south. At C it has a celestial longitude of 13 Taurus 51. A line is drawn from C to A. A is the antiscion of D and is at 16 Leo 09. The line CA is parallel to the equator and has a declination of sixteen degrees north. A body whose ecliptic-intercept would be at C would be conjunct D, while at A it would be antiscion D.

A second line has been drawn parallel to the equator through D, i.e. the parallel of its declination, which is 11°00' north. It intersects the ecliptic at two places: P_1 and P_2 or at 28 Aries 40 and 1 Virgo 20; these points are parallel to D and are its equivalent longitudes. Point B is shown on P_1DP_2 extended, which means that B is in bodily parallel to D. Point E is shown on the line CA, which means C is in ecliptic parallel to D, i.e. its body is parallel to D's ecliptic-intercept at C. Thus there are three kinds of parallel: B (bodily, conventional, strongest), E (just described), and A (antiscion type).

Now let us assume that the Sun is at 28 Aries 40. It is 15°11' from C and, therefore, from a conjunction to D, but it is at P_1 so is parallel (bodily) D. Another body, F, has a north declination of 8°35' (latitude 2°00' north) and a longitude of 17 Aries 10. Is this parallel to D? The Sun at 8°35' north has a longitude of 22 Aries 00 (also 8 Virgo 00). This is 6°40' from the ecliptic-equivalent of D at P_1 (28°40'). They are within orb of a conjunction and the two bodies are in parallel.

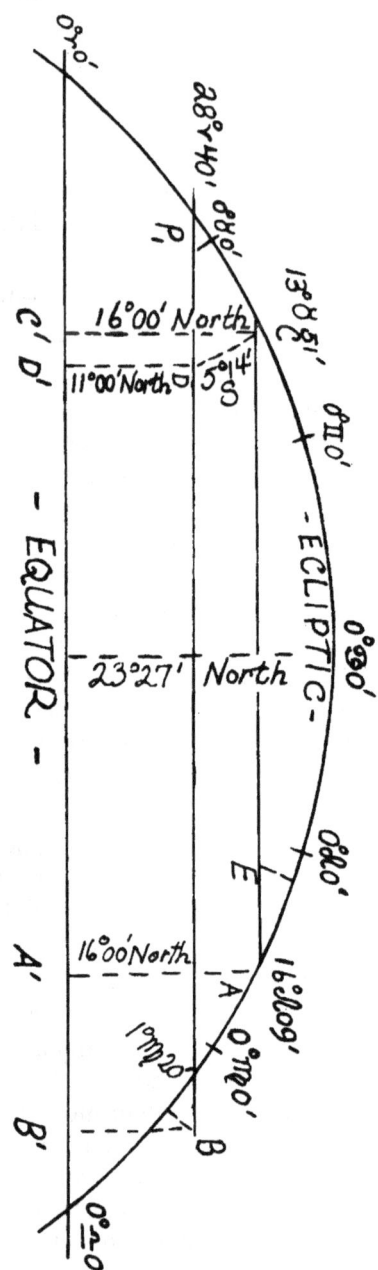

3

The Lights and Angles and Their Relationships

There are seven factors in any human horoscope that are always important: The Earth at the center, the three angles, the two lights, and the one planet that is the key planet. In a birth chart the key planet is always Saturn, in a conception chart it is always Uranus, and in an animation chart (or quickening, when the soul enters the vehicle as the Buddhists say) the key planet is Neptune. Thus, special importance is always given to Saturn in any natal horoscope. This is probably why Grant Lewi found the transit of that planet to be especially significant in all natal charts. The (birth) chart occurs at one's entry into the dense physical world, which is so much the nature of Saturn.

The third angle, the Vertex, and how to find it will be discussed later. Suffice it to say that since space has three dimensions there are three local planes and not just the two that are normally mentioned: the meridian and the horizon. The prime vertical is, like the meridian, perpendicular to the horizon; the meridian runs north and south and the prime vertical is perpendicular to the meridian and runs east and west. For this reason all horoscopes have not just four quadrants, but actually six main divisions, or sextants.

First, the two lights, which are basic to all life on earth and whose apparent size is nearly equal, will be considered. Some of the best work on the Sun and Moon and their relationship has been done by Dane Rudhyar, and the reader is encouraged to peruse *The Lunation Cycle*. The eight types he has identified will be explored as the phases of that cycle are considered.

The Lights

The Sun shows one's vital interests, which are conscious and not apparent since the Sun does not stand for the apparent. The fluctuating Moon, much more changeable than the Sun, is more apparent. It has to do with publicity, the public and the like, but is less conscious paradoxically. One tends to take for granted what the Moon signifies. It has to do with the subconscious and the senses. The Sun is fiery, stable, positive, and masculine, while the Moon is watery, variable, passive, and feminine. They are natural polar opposites.

At one level the Sun stands for the man in his own chart, while in a woman's chart it shows the man (or men) in her life and her relationship with same. In a woman's chart the Moon signifies herself, while in a man's chart the Moon shows the woman (women) in his life and his relations to same. The Moon is more important when people are young than when they are older, and can mean boys as well as girls. The Sun increases in importance when people are older, and in the chart of a woman who is over thirty, active in a career, and in competition with men, she may respond to it directly. This is all at one level.

At another level, the Sun stands for the life energy and the Moon for the vehicle that contains and holds it. Thus, the conception and birth charts are lunar and refer to the inception and birth of the physical vehicle. On the other hand, the animation chart and ego chart, four and seven months after conception, refer to the in-dwelling soul and are solar. At the Animation Epoch, the soul enters the vehicle, and at the E Epoch the ordinary ego-consciousness is separated from the higher consciousness. Thus, the Sun and Moon are profoundly meaningful at several levels. Their ever-changing dance of relationships is of utmost importance and determines many features of life.

The Lunation Cycle Phases

It takes the Sun one year to pass through all the signs and return to its starting point, while it takes twenty-seven and one-third days for the more rapid Moon to do the same. Imagine the two bodies beginning together, i.e. a New Moon. At the end of twenty-seven and one-third days the Moon will have completed what is termed its sidereal cycle, but in that time the Sun will have advanced about twenty-seven degrees in its longer sidereal cycle. Therefore, the Moon must travel for an additional two and one-sixth days to catch up to the Sun and again conjunct it.

This return to the same relationship (or aspect) is termed a synodic cycle, which, in the case of the Sun and Moon is called the lunation period of twenty-nine and one-half days. The return to the same position in the zodiac is the sidereal cycle. Therefore, positions in the constellations, signs, or houses are essentially due to sidereal cycles, whereas aspects are phases in the synodic cycles of bodies with each other, something that Rudhyar has pointed out more clearly than anyone else.

For instance, Mars square Saturn is a phase or stage in the two-year Mars-Saturn synodic cycle. When considering the aspects to the rotating angles, the synodic cycles of the planets and lights with regard to the earth's diurnal cycle shall be considered; the places of the planets and lights in the houses will be of the nature of sidereal cycles. It is difficult to make a sharp line of discrimination between the two types of cycle since nothing ever returns to exactly the same place, but it will help in understanding aspects as contrasted with places in the houses, signs, and constellations if one recognizes they are phases in two different kinds of cycles. A recurrence cycle is both a sidereal and a synodic one. Thus, as the end of the nineteen year metonic cycle, the Sun and Moon return to the same position in the zodiac and to the same aspect almost exactly (in between there are 254 lunar sidereal cycles and 235 lunations).

A waxing Moon (in light) occurs when the Moon passes from the New Moon, when it is conjunct the Sun, to the Full Moon, when it is in opposition to the Sun. A waning Moon (in light) occurs on the return of the Full Moon to the New Moon. The lunation cycle is first divided into the waxing and waning types (two kinds), then into the four quarters, and finally into the eight octants. Those born under a waxing Moon exemplify organic and instinctual growth and the building of structures broadly interpreted. Those born during a waning Moon accent the search for meanings and if the new meaning is at odds with existing structures they may try to destroy them.

The Eight Lunation Types

New Moon Type. The Moon is less than forty-five degrees past the New Moon. This type is highly subjective and rather impetuous. These individuals are self-absorbed, have little objectivity, and little ability to see others as actually separate from themselves (similar to a baby). They are self-projecting and can be so very strongly.

Crescent Type. The Moon is located anywhere from forty-five degrees (semisquare) past the New Moon to the second quarter. They tend to be assertive and feel self-confidence is very important. They may have a sense of inner mission in dealing with the external world and its potential obstacles. In short, there is an tendency to be outgoing, but still no great objectivity.

Second Quarter Type. The Moon is located anywhere from the first square of the Moon to the Sun to 135 degrees (sesquiquadrate) past the Sun. This is the builder who is active in an energetic manner and who is more objective about the realities to be dealt with than were the two prior phases. There is a potential for managerial ability.

Gibbous Type. This type of Moon ranges from 135 degrees past the Sun to the Full Moon. A New Moon is dark and invisible, a crescent Moon is a thin sliver, a quarter Moon is half visible, a gibbous Moon is about three-fourths visible, and a Full Moon is entirely visible. These people are concerned with their own growth and want to know the why of things. They seek understanding and Rudhyar finds they have an important goal in view. They can give or attract devotion. The accent as the Moon nears the Full Moon is already more on meaning than on building structures.

Full Moon Type. This Moon extends from the Full Moon to 135 degrees behind the Sun. This is the first of the four waning types. There is a strong emphasis on relationships with others, at both the individual and collective level, and on clear seeing and understanding. The New Moon type is the most subjective, while the Full Moon type the most objective. Clear understanding is now possible since symbolically the light of the Full Moon is a maximum. Rudhyar speaks of a possible negative development, a duality or split, i.e. divorced from reality or being against oneself.

Disseminating Type. The Moon is located anywhere from 135 degrees behind the Sun to the last quarter. This is again a gibbous Moon, but now reversed. These individuals try to show what they know or have learned. They can be popularizers, people with a cause. The projection is not of the self, as in the opposing phase (crescent) but of one's ideas and beliefs, which are more objective than subjective.

Last Quarter Type. The Moon ranges from the quarter Moon to forty-five degrees behind the Sun. Conflicts involving consciousness, principles, and concrete beliefs and ideas tend to be of major importance. Rudhyar finds they tend to force these issues and may be rather rigid. They often see themselves as pioneers.

Balsamic Type. This Moon extends from forty-five degrees behind the Sun to the New Moon. This is the inverted crescent type and can be amoral. They are future oriented and may martyr themselves in the conviction of serving that which is greater than the self. Since the lunation cycle is in its final phase, these individuals are bringing many things to an end. There is little objectivity and much concentration on individual ends and aims.

The Sun

I shall not attempt to describe the meanings of the Sun and Moon in the twelve signs since this is the kind of material given in any good course on fundamentals. Nor should it be necessary to speak of the Sun and Moon in the twelve houses. Many horoscopes which are not rectified have incorrect house positions, and there is also the problem of which house system is the correct one! I advocate that the divisions between the houses, except at the angles, be regarded as bands rather than sharp lines, thus enabling many house systems to be molded together. As Charles Carter said, the house positions of bodies in general are probably twice as important as they are in the signs. The aspects to the lights are even more vital and will be referred to here.

The Sun in an angular house causes a strong personality projection, most strongly in the first and then in the tenth house. The house in which the Sun is located is vital to the native and consciously so.

The Sun in the fourth house shows a vital phase late in life since the fourth house rules the end of things. Life values, not necessarily only those of a pecuniary nature, are emphasized as vital with the Sun in the second or eighth houses. These are those peculiar succedent houses. The emphasis is on emotional factors when the Sun is in the eleventh and fifth houses, the other succedent houses. As Cyril Fagan noted, there are curious dead spots, strongly static, in the middle of the houses. Death is a special meaning of the eighth house and life (births of children) in the creative fifth house, i.e. for the Sun.

There has been a tendency to downgrade the cadent houses, which are certainly as important as the other houses. It is true that in terms of extroversion and vitality the Sun is weak in the twelfth and sixth houses, less so in the mental third and ninth houses. Those with twelfth house Suns tend to operate behind the scenes, sometimes in institutions. Ninth house Suns do not signify travel (shown by the Moon and Uranus), but do often mean that the individuals will move and settle down a long distance from the birth place. The ninth house accents philosophical interests too. Quite a few writers have third house Suns, or male relatives have extra importance. The house in which the Sun falls is of major importance, which can be immediately seen on looking at a horoscope.

The planetary aspects to the Sun are even more important. Pay particular attention to the most potent aspects: conjunction, opposition, parallel, contraparallel, square, and trine (although the trine is not as strong as the others). A really close conjunction of the Sun and Mercury gives a one-track mind, and a close conjunction of the Sun and Venus can mean the world will be lost for love, i.e. when the person falls in love he or she falls hard. An individual is colored and qualified by close potent aspects to the Sun, although. since the Sun is not very extroverted, this may not be easily apparent. In a man's chart, Pluto-Sun combinations show extra close ties with a woman (often the mother, as Pluto is the planet of the mother), while Neptune aspects increased sensitivity, imagination, emotionalism, and idealistic impracticality. Indeed, Sun-Neptune afflictions can give the delusion that the native is a "chosen" being. Uranus, of course, makes the native independent, erratic, ornery, enterprising, and hard to classify; Saturn aspecting the Sun tends to make the native put up a defensive wall, while increasing responsibility, seriousness, propensity for hard work, and a strong emphasis on practical realism. Jupiter conjunct, parallel or trine the Sun is protective (an aspect often seen in charts that are exceptionally difficult so that it compensates); the squares, oppositions, and contraparallels tend to make the individual overly expansive and enthusiastic, expecting or promising too much and in general not using good judgment. Mars-Sun aspects, except the trine, which is a lazy influence, give drive, energy, and aggressiveness. It all comes to the fact that planetary-Sun aspects, if major and close, are very important.

Again, I emphasize that whether the Sun or Moon is in a male or female horoscope makes important differences in interpretation. This should be kept in mind in particular in connection with the aspects to these lights. Mars square the Sun is not the same in a woman's chart as in a man's. In a woman's, it shows her relationship with men and a strong animus (Mars) figure in the unconscious—the animus figure being the image of the opposite (male) sex in the unconscious of a woman from the psychology of Jung. A strong animus figure gives a strong sex drive. In the case of a man, Venus signifies the anima figure in the unconscious, the ideal female image. The proper identification of these ``images'' is taken from the work of Margaret Morrell, one of the best astrologers and students of Jung. If this structure as to the importance of the sex of the native is not kept in mind, I find that one may misinterpret the chart in a major manner.

The Moon

The Moon in the twelve houses has a similar significance to the Sun in those houses, i.e. it puts important emphasis on the house. Of course, if three or more planets are in a given house, that also will put a major emphasis on that house. But the Moon's house, while important, is much more likely to be taken for granted than if it were the Sun's house. On the other hand, the Moon is far more extroverted in nature than the Sun. Thus the Moon in the tenth house gives publicity (good or bad depending on the aspects to that Moon), whereas the Sun elevated in that same house gives authority, but not necessarily being known to the public.

If the Moon is angular in the first house, there is a tendency to deal with the public and women (Moon) in a personal (first house) face-to-face way. The Moon in the fourth house usually means frequent changes in the home, sometimes in the first part of the life more than later.

Remember that the Moon is far more changeable than the Sun and this affects the affairs of the house in which it falls. Partnerships with women are accented with a seventh house Moon (whereas the Sun there would make them with men). The Moon tends to mean many, whereas the Sun refers to a few, but those that are vital and major. If the Moon is in the eleventh house there should be many acquaintances and participation in group activities.

Second and eighth house Moons accent money and that which one values, but also changes in such matters. A well-aspected eighth house Moon shows that one is likely to inherit, but through a woman rather than via a man.

One's daughters are more accented than are sons when the Moon is in the fifth house. And, of course, with the Moon in the third or ninth houses, there will be much travel unless afflicting aspects from Saturn or Pluto deny the same. The third shows many short trips and the ninth indicates long ones. But the Moon in the third house also stresses female relatives and sisters.

Of course, if either light is in the sixth or twelfth house and is afflicted, there will be problems with illness (and/or employment in the case of the sixth house). An afflicted Moon in the sixth house of a man shows not his own illness, but those of one or more women in his life; if in a woman's chart it would be likely to refer to her. Positions of the lights in either the sixth or twelfth house also can mean that service occupations are important for the individual.

The aspects of the Moon are just as important as those of the Sun. Rudhyar has suggested a new way of relating the lunation cycle to the planets. For example, suppose the individual is a waxing Moon type (Moon between a New and a Full Moon). The planets that lie between the Sun and Moon have already been made an integral part of the self, whereas those between the Moon and where it will be when it reaches full are those bodies the individual must learn to deal with and make part of the self in this life. I think I would modify this excellent idea.

By primary direction bodies move about one degree a year. In 91 years they move ninety degrees or through two lunation phases, and in forty-five and a half years they move forty-five degrees or one phase. Not many people live past ninety-one years.

Because the current average life span is about forty years (for the whole world) it might be assumed that those born at the beginning of a phase might live to the end of the next one or that one born at the end of a phase is likely to live to the end of the next one. This suggests to me that one should take the planets that lie after the Moon in the phase it is in and the planets lying in the next phase as those which the person must meet with and embody in this life. The arc in which these planets lie will be from forty-five degrees to ninety degrees and on an average will be sixty-seven and a half degrees long, equivalent by direction to about sixty-eight years or the probable length of life in an area of high technology.

Let us consider my chart where the Sun is at 15 Libra 43 and the Moon at 11 Taurus 28. The Full Moon prior to birth occurred at 28 Virgo 23. Two more phases after this brings us to the last quarter with the Moon at 20 Cancer 30. In passing from its natal position to this place in Cancer, the Moon will be conjunct Saturn, then Mars, and finally Pluto, which lie in the eleventh and twelfth houses. These will then have a special significance in my life. One always starts prenatally with the start of the phase in which one is born.

It should not be necessary to give the aspects of the planets to the Moon in detail. In a man's horoscope, difficult aspects to the Moon show difficult and unsatisfactory relationships with women in general; in a woman's chart they show many life problems, but this can give her much strength of character. Even the so-called difficult aspects (opposition, contraparallel, and square) or Mars to the Sun can be carried by the Sun without much trouble. Indeed, the Sun conjunct or parallel Saturn is not a very difficult combination, but a conjunction of the Moon to Saturn or difficult aspects of Mars to the Moon are trying for the Moon because these two planets are the traditional malefics. I always assume that the aspects that one has are essential and can be used constructively with the right understanding.

Pluto-Moon aspects (other than the trine, which is no problem) may be less trying than Pluto-Sun aspects, since Pluto and the Moon have something in common. Pluto-Moon aspects in a man's chart show psychological ties with women on the part of women in his life; in a woman's chart such ties are shown for herself. But Neptune-Moon aspects, except the trine, are very hard to handle since they are delusional. One needs a good Saturn to offset the fantasies and lack of reality that such Neptune-Moon aspects impart.

The Sun square Moon is difficult for all male-female relationships, especially in the horoscopes of women. Uranus-Moon aspects, except the felicitous trine, give much erratic behavior, instability, unpredictability, and ups and downs. The aspects of Mercury-Venus-Jupiter, even under the hard aspects (oppositions and square), cause little that is any real problem. Conjunctions, parallels, and trines of the Moon and Venus in a man's chart are the best auguries of happy relationships with the air sex. Venus is a planet of love, affection, and friendship, rather than of sexual passion, unless combined with other bodies such as Mars and Pluto, in particular.

The Relationship of the Lights to the Angles

One of the most vitally important things in a horoscope is the relationship of the lights to the angles, which is another way of saying to the local planes. This is probably most obvious when two lights are on the same side of such a plane. Thus, if both the Sun and Moon rise they are both east of the meridian plane; if they both set they are west of it. Or both may be above the horizon or both may be below it. This is what is termed hemisphere emphasis.

Actually, when one also uses the prime vertical plane, perpendicular to the horizon and running due east and west, both lights can be south of that plane or both can be north of it. These three local planes, by way of the three angles that they create, actually divide space into six divisions called sextants. The lights may be distributed in a number of ways in these sextants. First to be considered are the three angles.

In cutting the meridian, the plane of the ecliptic creates an axis or line of interception which lies in the meridian, the upper end pointing south in the northern hemisphere (Midheaven) and the lower end pointing north (IC).

In cutting the horizon, the plane of the ecliptic creates an axis or line of interception which lies in the horizon's plane. One end, which can be due east but seldom is, is the Ascendant, where the Sun first appears above the horizon; the opposite end is the Descendant, where the Sun sets below the horizon. But the ecliptic plane also cuts the prime vertical, its line of interception creating an axis that lies in the plane of the prime vertical. The most significant end is always due west (above or below the horizon), the other end being due east.

It is easy to find this Vertex angle, provided the birth occurred more than thirty degrees from the equator, by using a tables of houses and doing two things: Use the IC as though it were the Midheaven in the tables of houses, and use the co-latitude instead of the latitude (the co-latitude always equals ninety degrees, the terrestrial latitude). The resulting "Ascendant" is the Vertex and it is always on the setting side of the chart and due west.

Rising and setting bodies are separated form one another on a chart by the Midheaven-IC axis. Day bodies (above the horizon) are separated from night bodies (below the horizon) by the Ascendant-Descendant line. Finally, the Vertex-Antivertex line separates the southern bodies (in the six signs following the Vertex) from the northern ones (in the six signs preceding the Vertex).

This is also the way in which the sextants are created. If the Midheaven is at zero degrees Cancer, then the Ascendant at zero degrees Libra opposes the Vertex at zero degrees Aries. If the Midheaven is at zero degrees Capricorn, then the Ascendant at zero degrees Aries opposes the Vertex at zero degrees Libra. These two special cases are so, no matter what the terrestrial latitude may be, and only in these two special cases, so the six sextants reduce to four quadrants.

If both lights are rising (east of the meridian) the individual has choices to make, is relatively free of others (unless there are many planets setting), and is making more new karma rather than working out old karma. But if both lights are setting (west of the meridian) the native is largely at the disposal of others in working out past karma, and what is done by one's own efforts is always subject to others.

Both lights above the horizon or on the day side accent that which is public and a life lived in connection with public affairs. With both lights below the horizon on the night side, the emphasis is on the private side of life (but not secret) and that is the type of life that will be led, unless there is an unusual clustering of planets above the horizon to offset these lights.

When the lights are in the six signs after the Vertex they are on the side of the direction of the equator, thus underlining collective and social interests. If in the six signs preceding the Vertex, the lights are in the direction of the pole (whether the northern or southern hemisphere) and individual values and aims will be paramount. The diagrams on the next page show the horoscope divided into six parts (the sextants) by the three angles and what each sextant means. Of the three descriptive terms, the most vital one is in capital letters. Note that there are two possible relations of the Ascendant and Vertex; thus, two diagrams.

The Angles

The Ascendant is the one angle given a disproportionate emphasis by most astrologers. The Midheaven is just as significant, although in a different way. I reject the equal house system, which relegates the Midheaven-IC axis to a minor role.

It is a serious question whether the houses and signs (or constellations) should be ``read'' in the same chart. Separate, purely mundane charts are possible wherein the planets are projected and positioned on the purely local and thus mundane prime vertical plane (Cyril Fagan's Mundoscope) and/or the purely local and thus mundane horizontal plane (the Zenith Chart of Witte's associate Friedrich Sieggruen). Little or no attention is paid to the Descendant of the horizontal house system, the Vertex, which was discovered many years ago by Johndro and me. All three angles are important, although one must have a rectified chart to be sure of their accuracy. Certainly these three angles rank in importance with the two lights, albeit they are more external in nature and role. For it is through the three angles that the individual projects the self into the skein of circumstances and concrete conditions.

The Ascendant. The importance of the Ascendant in the twelve signs is well known and will not be covered here since it belongs in an elementary course and text. But the relations of the planets to the Ascendant are very important and not so well understood since the Ascendant must be quite accurate before one may be sure of an aspect to it.

It is recognized that a planet rising conjunct the Ascendant modifies the Ascendant and thus the

Horoscope Interpretation Outlined/25

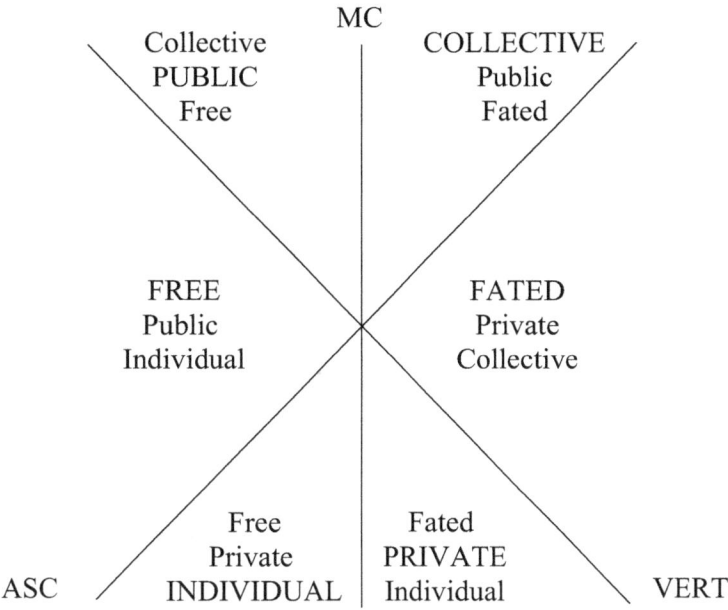

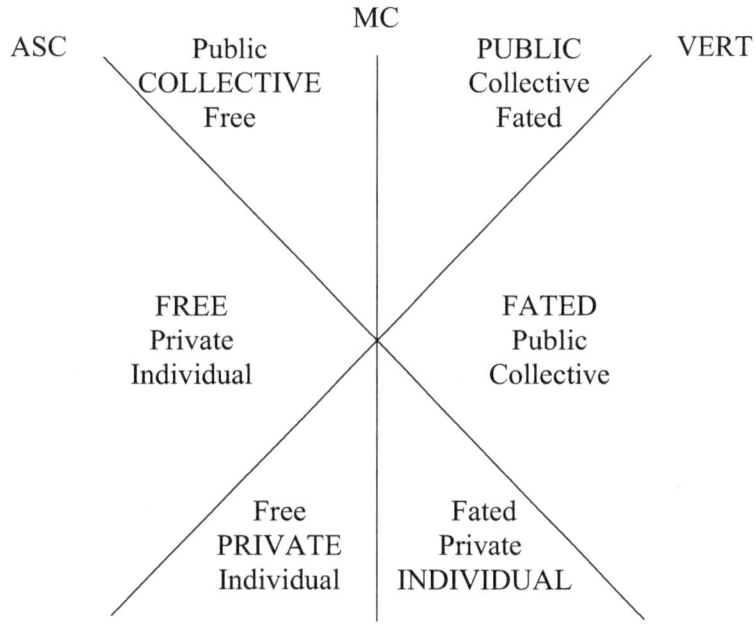

personality projection, physical appearance, and what one attracts to oneself in the way of personal relationships. The Ascendant has a magnetic quality as was pointed out by Johndro; the Vertex is electrical in nature. Mars conjunct the Ascendant can give a person some of the action and aggression of that planet, and also attract martian experiences or relationships, and thus violence, to the person. But the Ascendant can be modified by other powerful aspects in addition to the conjunction, i.e. parallel, contraparallel, opposition, square. This is not generally recognized to be true by most astrologers. After 21 years spent in rectifying charts, I have found that these other aspects must be taken into account.

The Sun aspecting the Ascendant gives a solar and vital quality. Mercury's aspects accent the ability (or inability) to communicate, while Venus adds not only to the charm but also the beauty of the appearance. Jupiter gives some breeziness, enthusiasm, and bounce (its extroverted side), and protects one against trouble at the last moment.

It is difficult to be born under afflicting aspects of Saturn, especially the conjunction (Nicholas DeVore found this produced "blue babies"). In addition, it inhibits and makes one more cautious. I recall a lady with an Aries Ascendant who seemed atypical of Aries since she had Saturn opposite the Ascendant.

Uranus adds to eccentricity in the temperament, abruptness, and sudden changes, and makes one tall if rising.

These are only the simplest of cases, since a person may have the Moon conjunct the Ascendant (moody, changeable, and tending to travel and deal with many people personally) and Neptune squaring it so that the Ascendant is modified by both bodies. The Neptune makes the constitution less strong and more sensitive (psychically as well as physically), and increases sentimentality and the inability to be discriminating or practical (may be parasitical).

Pluto, if conjunct the Ascendant and unafflicted, is usually well-placed since it gives depth of psychological penetration—x-ray vision into the secrets of others and personal investigative ability. But in other aspects (squares, oppositions, contraparallels), there can be serious problems due to one's psychological ties or the ties of others (often the mother or mother-in-law).

Of course, oppositions to the Ascendant have a profound effect on the personal relations with others in general and on partners and spouses in particular. This is also true of contraparallels to the Ascendant from the seventh house.

If the Ascendant is in the last three degrees of a sign it is already partly under the influence of the next sign and if in the first three degrees of a sign it is still partly under the influence of the last sign. The importance of the decanates (division of the signs into three parts of ten degrees each) has been vastly overdone; it is probable that any such division belongs to the sidereal zodiac. Rather, if each sign is mainly divided into two halves, it gives twenty-four semisigns. In general, as with the first signs of the zodiac, the first part of any sign is more direct, primitive, and simpler than is true of the last part. In this respect, the last part is like the last signs of the zodiac, too, as was pointed out by Charles Carter and Walter Sampson. This should be kept in mind in placing Ascendants in any sign, but a full discussion of this belongs to a discussion of rectification. Just realize that usually the first thing a person sees about someone is the Ascendant, then the Moon, and finally the least obvious part, the Sun. If the individual is what Dr. Jones called a Sun type, the Sun may be more important than the

Moon or Ascendant, but it is not necessarily more apparent or extroverted.

The Midheaven. Just as the Sun rises over the horizon at the Ascendant, so it crosses the upper meridian at the Midheaven at true noon each day, and crosses the lower meridian at the IC at true (rather than mean) midnight each night. The Midheaven has to do with status—not just the physical location (where one ``stands''), but also social status, reputation, and authority. The IC end of the axis (fourth house cusp), signifies home, family relations, and one's foundation. It is more impersonal in nature than the Ascendant-Descendant axis, but is certainly every bit as important.

An individual projects the self as much through the Midheaven as through the Ascendant, although this is never stated. When people speak of their reputation, their ``public image,'' their fame, their authority, etc., they are referring to their Midheaven. For people who consider career to be everything, the Midheaven is more important to them than the Ascendant. And one could correlate the Moon more closely with the Ascendant than the Midheaven, and the Sun more closely with the Midheaven than the Ascendant. Indeed, the Midheaven is the main factor in any horoscope that refers to career matters. Planetary aspects to the Midheaven are more vital for career than sixth house positions or Dr. Jones' vocational indicator, but again the chart must be rectified.

Little is ever said about the sign the Midheaven falls in. An Aries Midheaven is suitable for any kind of pioneering, while a Taurus one is fine where great fixity and determination are required and also in dealing with tangible items. A Gemini Midheaven gives considerable variety, adaptability, and flexibility in career matters. Those with a Cancer Midheaven often have the capacity to deal with the public and can sense its mood. Leo Midheavens are best for careers where color and drama are called for, whereas one in Virgo gives the capacity for handling details or that which requires some analytical ability. I once rectified a chart for a male auditor and accountant for the U.S. Army. He had a Leo Midheaven if his given time was correct, whereas a Virgo Midheaven fit his career much better. Of course, other factors had to fit also.

A Libra Midheaven gives a good sense of strategy and the ability to be a mediator or go-between. Scorpio Midheavens give some of the dramatic sense of Leo, but also depth and strong determination in the execution of career aims. This contrasts with the adjustability of a mutable Sagittarius Midheaven and its quality of directness in business pursuits. Capricorn at the Midheaven is, of course, long on practicality and organizational ability and, like all cardinal signs, makes for much activity. If Aquarius is on the Midheaven, the individual is likely to be less conservative than a Capricorn Midheaven and more progressive and independent. Pisces on the Midheaven gives, as do all the water signs, an intuitive and emotional quality in business affairs, plus much changeability. The foregoing is brief and rather general, needing much to be qualified by aspects to the Midheaven by the lights and planets.

Squares, oppositions, and contraparallels to the Midheaven show career problems and obstacles, so that one looks to the conjunctions, parallels, trines, and quincunx aspects to evaluate career potential. Pluto aspecting the Midheaven gives marked detective and research ability, but in conjunction or parallel also shows the mother as dominant. If Neptune aspects the Midheaven there can be prophetic ability with most of the benefits intangible in nature and with enhanced imagination in career. Uranus with the Midheaven accents the ability for the individual to operate as a freelancer and with a minimum of supervision; this favors electronics, transportation, and fresh enterprises and originality.

Saturn stabilizes one's career, holds one strictly accountable, makes for greater responsibility and hard work, and favors the things of Saturn: real estate, farming, mining, and that which is old. Jupiter with the Midheaven can bring fame, honor, a good income, and superior social or professional status, and is linked with the law, banking, and publishing. Mars to the Midheaven gives extra energy (in conjunction and parallel), can involve one in public fights, gives executive ability, and encourages occupations requiring physical strength and courage.

Venus in aspect to the Midheaven enables one to make a living from modeling, cosmetics, women's clothes and adornments, selling in general, and that which requires artistic taste and a color sense. Mercury, of course, favors writing, public speaking, and all forms of communication. The Moon brings fame and dealings with the public or women or both, and changes or travel in connection with the career. The Sun favors authority, dealings with those in authority, government, and important men.

Squares, oppositions and contraparallels of the same bodies show problems of the same nature as the above aspects show opportunities.

The Vertex. Much less is known about the Vertex than about the other two angles. Each angle is single-ended, which means that a body at the Descendant acts not like a conjunction to the cusp of the seventh house, but rather like an opposition to the Ascendant. In like manner, the Sun at the Midheaven is conjunct it but opposite the cusp of the fourth house. The significant end of the Vertex is on the setting side of the chart and so is west. This makes it the most fated of the three angles and it appears to be even more impersonal than the Midheaven.

The Sun at the Ascendant (sunrise) gives a strong personal approach to life. The Sun at the Midheaven (noon) gives authority and positions at the head of organizations, whereas the sunrise type steers clear of them. The Sun conjunct the Vertex (sunwest) gives an individual who is key in a group or collective situation and one very much subject to fated conditions, whereas the suneast (sun in opposition to the Vertex) person has something to say about the same sort of situations since the Sun is on the rising side of the chart.

If the Ascendant refers to one's personal inclination and the Midheaven to one's status, then the Vertex may refer to one's role. One's role or the part one plays is not a matter of personal choice but is fated or destined, being determined by one's part in various social and collective situations. In this respect it is much like the actor who asks for a part in a play, usually taking the part he or she can get. The part was not written by the actor so the actor is at the mercy of the playwright or director.

Planets which are strongly linked by aspect to the Vertex are therefore bound up with the fated part of life. One cannot really change the things signified by that which is involved with the Vertex since it has to do with one's lot in life, actually determined by one's past and thus peculiarly karmic. The Vertex is the Descendant of the never used and neglected horizontal house system. The only two completely symmetrical house systems spatially are the Campanus and horizontal. The Vertex and Ascendant both move when the Midheaven does, but nearly always at different rates to it and each other so that both are important in directions. The Vertex of the birth chart determines the Moon on the conception chart, by conjunction or opposition, in the case of seven-month children. The Vertex appears to be even more important in mundane astrology.

4

The Pivotal and Singular Factors

In working from the chart as a whole to the particular parts the first single factors considered were the lights and angles. The Moon's Nodes and the equinoxes also should have been mentioned since they are, like the angles, axes created by the intersection of two planes. Unfortunately, only the mean longitude of the Moon's Node is usually given. One needs Stayl's book on sidereal astrology for the formula that enables one to turn mean into true longitude of the Node. It is an important factor not only as to connections with others, but also since all eclipses of the Sun ad Moon must occur near one Node or the other.

Zero degrees Aries and Libra, the equinoctial points, are also important and are used in the Uranian system. They signify the world in general and our relationship to it. Thus, to the three local angles must be added to these more general and universal axes or nodes. The true Node can be as far as 1°46′ from the mean Node given in most ephemerides so that aspects by direction should never be taken to the mean Node.

Any one of the eight known planets may be picked out as of extra importance, thus making it focal or pivotal in some one of several ways. The lights, angles, Moon's Node and equinoxes are always of special importance, whereas the other bodies may be, but often are not.

Traditional Techniques

Essentially Dignified. This refers to the extra qualitative strength given to any body located in a sign that it rules. The list is well-known: Mars-Aries, Venus-Taurus, Mercury-Gemini, Moon-Cancer, Sun-Leo, Mercury-Virgo, Venus-Libra, Pluto-Scorpio, Jupiter-Sagittarius, Saturn-Capricorn, Uranus-Aquarius, and Neptune-Pisces. One can give extra significance to any body if it is in its own sign.

Accidentally Dignified. Traditionally, a body conjunct the Ascendant or Midheaven was said to be accidentally dignified. I should add that bodies within orb of an opposition to the angles should also be termed so dignified. And bodies conjunct or opposite the Vertex should also be included. In this case I would exclude parallels and contraparallels. Essentially, such bodies are given extra weight due to being strongly angular, although not having the qualitative superiority they have when essentially dignified. I think extra weight should be given to any body which is conjunct a cardinal point (zero degrees Aries, Cancer, Libra, or Capricorn). The orbs should not be large for any real effectiveness and should not exceed five degrees. Some extra weight can also be given to any body conjunct either of the Moon's Nodes, although I would give less weight than for the cardinal points. In all these cases, such a body is really on or very near two planes.

Planetary Ruler. The planet ruling the sign on the Ascendant has been long termed the ruling planet, but this is too strong a statement. Nonetheless any planet which rules the ascending sign should be given extra weight. And the sign this ruler is in qualifies it, this being especially significant in the case of the Moon.

Jones' Techniques

The Dynamic Focus. Find the closest natal square and the closest natal opposition. If of these two (assuming there are two) the square is closer, the person is more practical than theoretical (unless Neptune is part of the square); if the closer one is an opposition, the person is more theoretical than practical (unless Saturn is involved). One then finds the dynamic focal body to be that which must be moved ahead in the zodiac to make the aspect exact. The other body is the sustaining one. The dynamic focal body should be given high weight. It is through it that the native operates and functions to a great degree. Jones has renamed it the body of dynamic aptness.

The Vocational Indicator. The vocational indicators are Moon, Mercury, Venus, and Mars. The one that is closest to the Sun but behind it in the zodiac, and thus rising before the Sun, is the vocational indicator. If it is Mercury, the person has technical ability which may be in one of many fields. Venus as the vocational indicator accents refinement and taste in one's vocation and thus artistry, understood broadly as applicable in many ways and walks of life. Mars gives a one-pointed driving effort such as pioneer, mechanizer, promoter, builder, engineer, or advertiser. When the Moon is the indicator, Jones says "his role in life is to stimulate others to the effort from which both those others and he himself will profit, rather than to carry some particular enterprise on to success through his own devices." He is a good tutor or coach and an inspirer of others.

Leading Planet, Singleton Planet, Trigger

In discussing the bowl and locomotive patterns I spoke of the leading planets in those patterns. Jones now terms them the cutting planets and has added the bundle, i.e. one may also use the cutting (leading) planet in that pattern. He terms cutting planets as high focus. The singleton planet in a bucket pattern is the handle body and is also considered to have high focus importance. Finally, in the irregular splay pattern a body often stands off from the others and is described by him as the reins planet, i.e. "holding the reins in" (self-discipline). Remember that a splay usually has a sort of tripod arrangement. This body is also high focus. He considers that a high focus body is of extreme importance in the interpretation of a chart, although not all charts have such a focal body. Only the see-saw and splash patterns have not been mentioned as having high focus bodies. But, at times, focal planets may be found in them by other means. Thus, exceptional extra weight should be given to such high focus bodies.

The closest square to a high focus body is what he terms the trigger. A pure trigger is a simple square and not part of a T-cross (composed of squares that offset each other) or grand cross. Jones uses these orbs: Sun, 17°; Moon, 12°30'; planets, 10° (applying to major aspects only). I consider them too wide and use instead: Sun, 10°; Moon, 10°; planets, 7°30'.

Consider whether the high focus body applies or separates in the trigger. Both here and in his dynamic aptness (focus) cases, applying means it must be moved ahead in the zodiac to make the aspect exact, no matter whether it is retrograde or direct, or whether in the usual sense it applies or separates. The trigger is considered by him to be of utmost importance. If the high focus body separates, the nature of it is practical, distributive, and outgoing; if it is applying, it is the more self-centered of the two and represents an inward tendency which sustains the whole process.

But there are other focalizing factors. A singleton planet, by reason of being the sole body above or below the horizon, or rising or setting (which need not be the handle planet of a bucket pattern) is highly focal and important. Likewise, if all bodies lie on the same side of either the meridian or horizon (or Vertex) there is a most powerful emphasis on that hemisphere. One has here a bundle or bowl which gains additional importance by its house position.

The Pivot

I emphasize this form of emphasis although it is not very original. A pivot is a body which is part of two (or more) major configurations and which leads to the integration of the chart. Such a body is quite important and there can be more than one. If two bodies which are pivots are in aspect, this is highly significant. They then make a kind of hinge, linking two major configurations.

Eclipse Energization

Solar or lunar eclipses occurring up to one year after or before the chart affect the bodies in it via conjunctions and oppositions with a maximum orb of plus or minus three degrees. The best source for data on eclipses is *Encyclopedia of Astrology* by Nicholas DeVore. It includes a table of penumbral eclipses of the Moon (appulses) which are just as important as partial solar eclipses and which are not elsewhere available. Natal bodies in conjunction or opposition (I would include parallel and contraparallel with orbs of declination equivalent to three degrees by longitude; see earlier discussion of declination orbs), such eclipses have considerable extra energy and are thus rendered focal in still another and final way.

Those who wish to learn more of Jones' methods should read *Essentials of Astrological Analysis*.

The Meaning of the Planets by Sign, House and Aspect

There is not enough space to cover this material here and my main objective was to present an outline with the accent on the major factors. This sort of information can be found in many of the better textbooks. Margaret Hone's *Modern Astrology* is one of the best general texts, although it is not very original. Evangeline Adams' *Astrology: Your Place in the Stars* is quite good for giving the meanings of the lights and planets in the twelve signs. All of Charles Carter's books are excellent and are worth reading, too.

Addendum

The term *in zodiaco* means that the measurement of position or aspect has been made along the ecliptic from zero degrees Aries in celestial or zodiacal longitude. The term *in mundo* refers to measurements along the celestial equator in right ascension from zero degrees Taurus or along one of the two local planes: the horizon or prime vertical. Astronomers mainly use right ascension. I term the arc of distance along the prime vertical the zenith distance as measured from the zenith, which is the point directly over one's head. The azimuth is measured from the north point of the horizon and along the horizon towards the east. The belief held by many astrologers that only *in zodiaco* positions or aspects ought to be used is a major error.

A nodical axis is formed by the intersection of two planes which may be considered to be without bound. Such an axis is then infinitely long. Being of indefinite length, its direction in space does not vary whether one is standing on the Sun or on the Earth. This is why a heliocentric planetary Node through the Sun has the same position even if observed geocentrically. If the Node were at a finite distance, then its geocentric position would indeed differ from its heliocentric one, especially in the case of Mercury, Venus, and Mars.

In like manner, if the Moon's nodical axis is of infinite length, there can be no difference between its geocentric and its barycentric positions. The Earth-Moon barycenter, about 3,000 miles from the Earth's center, is the only center through which the lunar nodical axis always passes. As the Earth and Moon revolve in twenty-seven and a third days about this barycenter, and always on opposite sides of it, the Earth's center is only on that nodical axis twice in that time, i.e. when the Moon is at its true North or South Node. If instead of the infinite barycentric Nodes, the geocentric Lunar Nodes were used at a finite distance, then when the Moon was square its true Nodes they would be about 1°24′ from an opposition to each other.

One-at-a-Time

There is no concern with hypothetical bodies of asteroids in this discussion. Astrology deals only with Nodes and planets, including the Sun, Moon, and stars. Node means Ascendant, Midheaven, Vertex, zero degrees Aries (tropical) and the other Nodes of the Moon and planets. Therefore, the reference here is not to extra bodies but to extra Nodes. A body which is in conjunction, opposition, or square (other aspects are less potent) a heliocentric planetary Node, or an angle which is in conjunction or opposition to one acts as though the body itself were there. This has been confirmed by a quarter of a century of study by Carl Payne Tobey and later by Michael Erlewine.

I suggest an orb of three degrees for conjunctions, oppositions, and squares; smaller for other aspects. If the Sun, for instance, is conjunct the North or South Node of Jupiter at ten degrees Cancer or Capricorn, it is as though the Sun is conjunct Jupiter.

Two-at-a-Time

Mars square Saturn or Mercury parallel Neptune are examples of combinations taken two at a time. Aspects and positions along and on the ecliptic or equator, prime vertical, or horizon are transversal. Those on either side of such planes are orthogonal (right angles). Conventional aspects are transversal and *in zodiaco*.

The same is true of harmonics. In conventional aspects the 360 degree circle is divided by numbers from one (conjunction) to two (opposition) to three (trine) to four (square) to six (sextile), these being the Ptolemaic aspects. Thirty degrees (division by twelve) and 150° (five-twelfths) were not Ptolemaic, nor were the semisquare (one-eighth or 45°) nor the sesquiquadrate (three-eighths or 135°) aspects. Harmonics or mini-aspects are based on the division of the circle by larger numbers. In this sense, the quintile (one-fifth or 72° and two-fifths or 144°) and the septile (one-seventh, 51°26′; two-sevenths, 102°51′; and three-sevenths, 154°17′) are in the mini-aspect category, although long used by Jones, Rudhyar, and Koch.

The work of John M. Addey and others has proven that these harmonics are highly significant. In some instances the proof is statistical. Those with many septiles are ministers, as those interested in the beyond. The absence of standard aspects or a subnormal number of them may mean that there are an unusual number of mini-aspects (failure to use them will result in a misinterpretation of the chart). Some of the harmonics were found to be significant by John Nelson in his heliocentric studies of the Sun's effects on radio propagation. I strongly recommend *Harmonics in Astrology* by Addey. It is one of the most important of the 20th century. An entire chart may be based on a single harmonic such as the navamsa or ninth harmonic chart, which in India is given nearly equal importance with the natal chart. Of course, the higher the harmonic, the smaller the orb that must be used.

If the Midheaven is projected along the meridian to the zenith and the Ascendant projected along the horizon to the East Point, then their distance apart along the prime vertical east-west plane (perpendicular to the horizon and meridian) must always be a right angle of ninety degrees. Many house system chart forms show the Midheaven and Ascendant as a right angle, even though in high terrestrial latitudes they are often far from ninety degrees apart along the ecliptic. If the Sun is just on the horizon at sunrise and the Moon is just crossing the upper meridian, then they are in mundane square to each other even though they may be trine ecliptically. This is what the ancients termed a parantellonta relationship, or paran for short.

A paran is a bodily conjunction, opposition, or square as to the three local planes. If they both rise over the eastern horizon at the same time—a conjunction in oblique ascension, set on the western horizon at the same time—a conjunction in oblique descension, or are conjunct on the upper or lower meridian at the same time, they are in paran conjunction, but are probably not exactly conjunct in longitude.

The conjunctions on the meridian are in right ascension. They may be opposite in right ascension, or opposite in oblique ascension to oblique descension. Finally, a right ascension conjunction to the upper or lower meridian may be in square to the oblique ascension or oblique descension of the second body—a paran square. These are basically *in mundo* and house aspects of the second and fourth harmonics only. It has been found that if during the prior or following day two bodies have this relationship, even if they are not on those local planes now, they still act in a paran manner.

When Jimmy Carter was sworn in as president on January 20, 1977 in Washington, D.C. close to Noon Eastern Standard Time, Pluto was about twenty-seven degrees earlier in the zodiac than was Uranus. Uranus was opposite the Taurus Ascendant and thus early on the western horizon, as was

Pluto bodily. They had nearly the same oblique descension, so were in paran conjunction opposite the Ascendant in mundo. This will prove to be vitally important to the Carter Administration and the opposition it must meet.

The work of Robert Hand on paran transits at major events of stress indicates that they may be more potent than conventional *in zodiaco* aspects. Since he has written an authoritative book on transits, his suggestions have much weight.

In my natal chart the *in zodiaco* quintile of Neptune to Moon (0°17' from exactitude) and the quintile of Neptune to Mercury (exact to the minute) are both paran squares within less than two degrees. The psychological potential of the natal quintiles must express itself through *in mundo* squares. Indeed, unless they had such aspects, or had aspects to the angles (Midheaven, Ascendant, and Vertex) or were part of planetary pictures that included one or more angles, that potential might only express outwardly with very great difficulty.

As parans are much affected by terrestrial altitude, were I to move far north or south, they would no longer be in paran square in my subsidiary locality chart and thus those two quintiles and the Moon-Mercury biquintile would be less effective.

The fourth harmonic quality of these parans is a strong indication as to their external and circumstantial nature, for the number four has that nature as Addey and others have noted. This is one reason why extra weight is given to conjunctions, oppositions, and squares, all of which belong to the one, two, and four series harmonically. Thus, Tobey finds that the only powerful aspects of the Sun to the Moon's North Node are conjunctions, oppositions, and squares—the semisquare is minimal in strength (the eighth harmonic). This is his lunar wobble, which has much to do with psychological instability. I suggest that the orb of paran aspects might be limited to plus or minus three degrees.

To find the natal parans, find the right ascensions, oblique ascensions, and oblique descensions of the Sun, Moon and eight planets, which requires one to make the same speculum that would be used for primary directions and for locality shifts. Right ascensions can be found from a right ascension longitude table such as in my *Progressions and Directions*. DeLuce's *Complete Method of Prediction* has an ascensional difference table, which makes it possible to turn right ascension into oblique ascension and oblique descension. Parans also may be calculated based on bodies being on the plane of the prime vertical.

Assuming that a chart has been rectified, one can measure the exact house (Campanus) positions in degree and minute along the prime vertical—the zenith distance in Fagan's Mundoscope. A change of locality changes all such positions. One can do likewise as to exact positions in the seldom used horizontal houses, in azimuth along the horizon. The Vertex is the Descendant of this house system. If born at least thirty degrees from the equator, one may use the same technique as one does in any tables of houses in finding the Vertex to find the horizontal house cusps from a Campanus table, i.e. use the IC in place of the Midheaven and the co-latitude in place of the terrestrial latitude, provided one realizes that the eleventh house cusp will show up as the fifth, the twelfth as the sixth and so on. House positions are more vital than sign positions so that the foregoing deserves to be researched.

Along this same line of inquiry one can study bodies having the same or opposite altitudes, above or below the horizon. One can also, using an altitude-azimuth table (see Progressions and Directions), find the distance the two bodies are from the prime vertical plane to see if they are parallel or contraparallel in this way, i.e. in amplitude.

This is the symmetry principle since any two bodies equidistant orthogonally on either side of a plane—equator in declination, horizon in altitude, and prime vertical in amplitude—are symmetrical relative to that plane. William Davidson suggested many years ago that synastry based on house rather than on sign positions might be quite important. This is why the neglected Mundoscope of Fagan and Zenithscope of Sieggruen may be considerably more useful to astrologers than realized.

Three-at-a-Time

We come now to the relationship of three factors at a time instead of just the conventional two. Let factor A be at zero degrees Aries and factor B as far away from A as possible at zero degrees Libra (an opposition). Then zero degrees Cancer is one of the two midpoints between A and B (term it M), and zero degrees Capricorn is the other one (call it N). There must always be two midpoints.

The MN axis is the midpoint axis and the axis of symmetry. Note that AB and MN make a cross or fourth harmonic figure. Planetary pictures are based on the second, fourth, and eighth harmonics only. If a body is at M, then A/B = M, which translates as the midpoint between A and B (A/B), is on the MN axis of symmetry, this being a direct planetary picture. In an indirect one, the third factor is square to MN or, less potent, is semisquare or sesquiquadrate to it. Thus the = stands for conjunction, opposition, square, semisquare, or sesquiquadrate MN. No sextiles, trines, or other aspects are used for any planetary picture. Of course if a fourth factor were at N, opposition M, then it could be written A/B = M/N—the midpoint of A and B is square to the midpoint of M and N. Still more complex combinations are possible They are significant in timing as well as radically. They were developed by the late Alfred Witte and then copied by Reinhold Ebertin in his cosmobiology. Witte's complete system is the Uranian system or the Hamburg School. I don't like systems since they exclude what doesn't belong to the system. Of all such systems known to me, the Uranian system is the best.

Bodies and nodes are transversely in aspect to each other or orthogonally equidistance from a plane (one and two are two-at-a-time) or are related by the formula A/B = M (three is three at a time; two and three display the symmetry principle). These are the sole ways in which bodies and nodes appear to be related to each other.

One-at-a-time: the formula is n/1. Here n is the number of factors; the Sun, Moon, and eight planets only, or many more. 1 mans factorial 1. Two-at-a-time: the formula is n x (–1)/2. Factorial 2 means 1 x 2; factorial 3 means 1 x 2 x 3, and so on. Three-at-a-time: n x (–1) x (–2)/3.

Let us assume that we have a rectified horoscope and so may use the three angles plus the Moon's Node plus zero degrees Aries. To these five is added the lights and planets so that n = 15. Two at a time is 15 x 14/2. This gives 105 combinations. Three-at-a-time gives 15 x 14 x 13/3. This gives 495 combinations. Thus, there are more than five times as many taken three-at-a-time as there are two-at-a-time. That is why the orb for planetary pictures is seldom over a degree and a half; if no light or angle is involved, it usually is not over one degree. Four-at-a-time yields 1,365 combinations or three times as many as taken three-at-a-time. Planetary pictures are , in general, not as potent as close major aspects (two-at-a-time), but they are considerably more specific in what they mean. For now, a Mars to Venus aspect may be modified by the Sun, Moon, six planets, three angles, zero degrees Aries, and the Moon's Node—some thirteen different variations on a theme, the Mars-Venus theme.

As Hans Niggeman, innovator of the Uranian system in the U.S. has said, a planetary picture is only major if it involves the personal points, i.e. the angles or lights. One must bear this in mind in adding midpoints to the armory of the techniques of horoscope interpretation. The use of a ninety degree or forty-five degree dial considerably facilitates the finding of the planetary pictures in any horoscope. I recommend Jacobsen's *Introduction to the Uranian System*.

A close relationship of the old Arabic Parts to the new planetary pictures can be shown. Consider the widely used Part of Fortune. It is a point which has the same distance form the Ascendant that the Moon has from the Sun, i.e. Moon - Sun + Ascendant = Part of Fortune. This may be rewritten as Moon/Ascendant = Sun/Pars Fortuna. If there is a body at the place of Fortuna, then we have a complete fourfold planetary picture. It may, of course, be completed temporarily by either progression or transit.

The work of George Noonan has shown that modern astrologer do not calculate the many parts in the same way as the classical astrologers who discovered and developed them did.

The parts must be calculated not *in zodiaco* but *in mundo*, i.e. in right ascension only. From the right ascension of the Moon one subtracts the right ascension of the Sun. The resulting arc of right ascension is then added to the right ascension of the Ascendant to gain the right ascension of Fortuna. It is assumed to be on the equator, without any declination.

Using a right ascension-longitude table, one converts the right ascension of Fortuna back to ecliptic longitude. There can be a difference of several degrees between this correct way of finding the parts and the current, wholly incorrect way. The only reason the latter has any validity in some cases is that, as already shown, it may be thought of as a fourfold planetary picture. Modern astrologers are monomaniacs about two things: The ecliptic is the sole significant plane in space, and the moment of birth is the sole significant moment for putting up a chart. As Jones noted, the parts are phenomena of the houses—a change of the Ascendant two hours later usually keeps the parts in the same houses, although the positions would shift forward *in zodiaco*. Thus the parts are really house, *in mundo*, and right ascension in nature.

I hope that three little used techniques that do not require the use of a rectified chart will be much more widely used in the future: the lunar and planetary Nodes, paran aspects, and harmonics and harmonic charts. Only when there is use of all techniques will a complete and non-fanciful reading of a horoscope be possible.

Recommended Books on Horoscope Interpretation

Charles E.O. Carter, *The Astrological Aspects*, *The Foundations of Astrology*, *Some Principles of Horoscope Delineation*
Nicholas DeVore, *Encyclopedia of Astrology*
Zipporah Dobyns and Nancy Roof, *The Astrologer's Casebook*
Margaret Hone, *The Modern Textbook of Astrology*
Vivia Jayne, *Aspects to Horoscope Angles*
L. Edward Johndro, *The Astrological Dictionary*
Marc Edmund Jones, *Astrology, How and Why It Works*, *Guide to Horoscope Interpretation*
Grant Lewi, *Heaven Knows What*

Isabelle Pagan, *From Pioneer to Poet*
Dane Rudhyar, *The Astrological Houses*, *The Lunation Cycle*
Walter Sampson, *The Zodiac: A Life-Epitome*
Carl Payne Tobey, *Neptune*
Barbara H. Watters, *Horary Astrology and the Judgment of Events*
Alfred Witte, *Lexicon*, *Rules for Planetary Pictures*

Introduction to
Locality Astrology

Preface

This is a condensed introduction to the main features of locality astrology. In moving from the place of birth to another locality there are changes in the horoscope. This does not mean that a locality chart replaces the natal one, but only that it modifies it, as does, for instance, the progressed chart. One might even consider that such a locality chart is a kind of progression in space instead of in time.

Actually, there is more than one way to deal with the effects of other localities. Dodson has written a most useful book, *Horoscopes of the United States and Cities*, on the horoscopes of nations, states, towns, etc. One may then compare a radical chart with such charts in order to find out how the individual will relate to a city, for example. In this book I shall not be concerned with this approach while fully recognizing its value.

It may be argued that the horoscope of a city would be especially vital if one were dealing with the city, such as doing business with its administration. There is reason to believe that if one merely lives there and does not deal with the corporate entity of the city, he or she would nonetheless be affected by the locality. One effect would be a general one that would be the same for anyone living there. That is to say that every particular place has its own Midheaven, Ascendant, and Vertex angles, this being based on bringing the zodiac to Earth as Johndro and others did. I will deal with this in Chapter 2.

In the first chapter of this book I plan to deal with the effects of shifting any natal, or other, horoscope to a different locality. The first kind of shift is the conventional one of shifting the angles, which can put all the radical bodies into different houses. Their positions in the zodiac remain the same.

In the second kind, one moves so as to place a radical body on one of the three local planes: meridian, horizon, or prime vertical. There are places where an individual may have Jupiter on the upper meridian, i.e. at the Midheaven, while at the same time another body such as Mars may be on the horizon or very near it, so that it is rising. While they may have no aspect *in zodiaco*, they are in a paran square to each other *in mundo* since the meridian and horizon are always in a mundane square to each other.

The third kind of shift actually moves all bodies, backward or forward, in the zodiac and not merely in the houses. While there are three ways of doing this, as developed by Edward Johndro, I shall only deal with the simplest one of the three: the shift along the equator in right ascension. Use of the other two shifts along the prime vertical and the horizon in azimuth is more complex and calls for a rather accurate birth time. I shall deal with this shift before the paran type.

In the back of the book is a table which enables one to find the right ascension (R.A.) of any body from its radical celestial longitude and celestial latitude. Mention will also be made of Fagan's Mundoscope and Sieggruen's Zenithscope.

Since this book is only an introductory text I have not tried to give the methods of doing the second and third of Johndro's two shifts in the zodiac. They are especially crucial if the move is a long one or if there is a major shift in terrestrial latitude. This type of locality service, as well as the right ascension one and the Mundoscope and Zenithscope, can be obtained from a chart calculation service.

Charles A. Jayne
July 3, 1978
Monroe, New York

1

Shifting the Chart

The Conventional Shift

A meridian is a plane perpendicular to the Earth's surface that runs north and south from pole to pole. On any map these are seen as north-south lines. The zero degree one passes through Greenwich, England. The western one stretches to 180 degrees in the mid-Pacific. And the eastern one stretches the other way around the Earth to the 180 degree International Date Line in the central Pacific.

If John Jones, for example, were born in Camden, New Jersey on the 75th meridian at 7:00 a.m. Eastern Standard Time, the addition of five hours would make noon the Greenwich Time of his birth. Suppose his birth place was 40 degrees north latitude and he moved west along that parallel of latitude to 40 degrees north and 105 degrees west (105th meridian). How can this shift be shown?

The 105th meridian is the central one of the Mountain Standard Time Zone and is, therefore, seven hours earlier than Greenwich Time. Therefore, he was born, in the new locality, at 5:00 a.m. Mountain Standard Time. If a chart is erected for this time it will be one valid form of a locality chart. Each fifteen degrees of terrestrial longitude (celestial longitude is in the zodiac; terrestrial longitude is on Earth and is equivalent to right ascension in space) is equal to a change of one hour. Any place west is earlier in time. Any place east is later in time. Don't phone a friend in London from Chicago at 10:00 p.m. Central Standard Time!

The thirty degree westward shift that he made is also a backward shift of his Midheaven of thirty degrees of right ascension. And the two-hour shift in his time of birth is also a shift decrease of two hours of sidereal time. *Since the Universal or Greenwich Time of birth is unchanged the planets stay in the same degrees of the same signs.* But, as the Midheaven moved back about thirty degrees of celestial longitude (not exactly the same as thirty degrees of right ascension), nearly all of the planets will have moved one house later. If the Sun was in the twelfth house at the natal locality, it probably will now be in the first house because the cusp of that house has moved approximately one sign or thirty degrees earlier in the zodiac.

Suppose you wish to shift a chart from Los Angeles, California to Stockholm, Sweden. From a table of latitudes and longitudes in the United States find the local mean time (LMT) difference from Los Angeles to the Greenwich meridian. It is usually in the last column of such a table and in this case is seven hours, fifty-three minutes, zero seconds. Then, from a table of latitudes and longitudes in the world, find the LMT distance of Stockholm, Sweden from Greenwich (in this case, one hour, twelve minutes, twelve seconds). Then add these two figures to find the time difference between Stockholm and Los Angles: nine hours, five minutes, twelve seconds. Since the shift is eastward, add this to the natal sidereal time to find the sidereal time of the locality chart. Had the move been from Stockholm to Los Angeles, this would have been subtracted as the move would have been westward.

Suppose the move is from Los Angeles to New York City. Since both places are on the same side of the Greenwich meridian, take the difference between the LMT values for the two cities. In the case of Stockholm, as it is on the other (east) side of the Greenwich meridian from Los Angeles (west), their two LMT values were added. The LMT value for New York City is four hours, fifty-five minutes, forty-eight seconds. When this is subtracted from Los Angeles' seven hours, fifty-three minutes, zero seconds, the result is two hours, fifty-eight minutes, twelve seconds. This figure is then used to change the sidereal time at Los Angles to that of New York City, or vice versa.

Of course when the chart is set up in the new locality, the terrestrial latitude of the new place is used instead of the natal or radical latitude. The geographic latitude of Los Angeles is 34N03, while that of Stockholm is 59N20.

This mode of locality shift is relatively easy to do and has much merit. It ought to be used even more widely than it is by professionals and students. The locality chart is a secondary one, but can be quite important because everyone knows how major changes of locality can affect lives.

It should be realized that very short moves will not be very significant with any of the locality shifts described in this book. If one moves about ninety miles, that is equal to only about one and a half degrees.

A second consideration is how long a time one is in a place which may be far from the place of birth. If one is there for a short time, the full effect of the locality will not be experienced.

Essentially, timing factors are stronger than locality ones so that even if one is in a favorable locality, this will not completely offset the effects of major problematic transits or progressions. This is very important. On the other hand, the effects of most timing influences are limited to how long they affect an individual, whereas a given place will always have the same meaning due to its nature. Therefore, if one is in a special locality for some time, it can be quite potent in its influence.

The Right Ascension Shift

Let me repeat the word of caution about the planets on the local planes. They are most vital but the time of birth must be quite accurate. An error of only four minutes will throw the natal and shifted Midheaven off by a full degree or about sixty miles! Therefore, for most people, this first one of the three unpublished and new Johndro shifts is much more likely to be practical as errors in the time of birth will only affect the angles, and the Moon somewhat.

In the right ascension shift, one turns all natal or radical positions into their right ascension first.

Then one makes the shift—backward if west of where the chart occurred, and forward if east of where it took place. Finally, one converts the right ascensions back to ecliptic longitudes in order to read their aspects to the radical chart.

A great circle drawn through the north and south poles of the Earth that passes through a planet cuts the equator at a right angle, thus projecting the planet onto the equator. That place on the equator is the right ascension place and its distance along the equator from zero Aries, where the ecliptic crosses the equator, is the right ascension arc.

The right ascension of any planet in any ephemeris can be found using the table in the back of this book. This requires doing the same double interpolation that must be done to find the exact Ascendant if given the Midheaven and the terrestrial latitude. The table extends to six degrees of celestial latitude north and south. Rarely does a planet have a latitude greater than this. Mars can reach 6°30' and Venus about nine degrees on occasion, but one can interpolate far beyond these tabular limits to reach these values. From 1902 until 1951, Pluto's latitude had not exceeded nine degrees north or south so the table can be used for it, too, with interpolation.

A speculum will be created to be used later for the shifting of the planets to the local planes (see page 46). It is valuable thing and is used when doing primary directions. The celestial longitudes of all bodies and angles are listed in the second column and the celestial latitudes in the third column. These are simply copied from the chart and/or from the ephemeris. Then, using the data in these two columns, find the right ascensions from the table and list them in column four. The declinations are placed in column five.

This method of right ascension shifting can be used even if the time of the chart is fairly uncertain. If it is uncertain, one will be unable to use the angles (Midheaven, Ascendant and Vertex). The ascensional differences (arcs between the right ascensions and the oblique ascensions or oblique descensions) can be added in columns seven and eight. Column six gives the distance in right ascension from a planet to the upper (U) or lower (L) meridian and is termed the meridian distance (MD). This will be essential when planets are later brought to the upper or lower meridian. Column one has, of course, the names of the angles and lights and planets.

The latitude of San Diego is 32N43 and the longitude is 117W10. Therefore, to find the extent of the west shift from my place of birth, calculate the difference between 117W10 and 75W08 (natal longitude), which equals 42W02. Then subtract this value from the right ascensions of all the bodies in the chart and from the RAMC (column four). The results are listed in column nine. Remember, right ascension is measured along the celestial equator in space and terrestrial longitude is measured along the same equator on Earth so that they are equivalent.

The right ascensions for the San Diego meridian are shown in the speculum in column nine. To convert these values back to celestial longitude (column ten), go to the table and look at the column with zero degrees latitude. Using that column and doing a single interpolation, the celestial longitude for San Diego and for all other places on that same north-south meridian are found. The final step is to take the aspects from the locality positions to the natal angles, lights, and planets. Note that in finding the Ascendant and Vertex in San Diego, its latitude is used instead of the natal one. I use geocentric latitude (instead of the conventional geographic), which for San Diego is 32N33 (it is always less than the geographic latitude). Geocentric latitude is used in this speculum (natal latitude is 39N54).

Speculum

Charles A. Jayne, October 9, 1911, 10:39:30 p.m. EST, 75W08, 54N50:06

Bodies 1	Long. S 2	Lat. S 3	R.A.s 4	Decl. S 5	M.D.s 6	A.D.s 7	O.A.s 8	R.A.s 9	Long. S 10
MC	27 PI 09	0:00	357:23	-1:08	-	-	-	315:21	12 AQ 53
ASC	16 CN 14	0:00	(107:36)	+22:28	-	-20:13	87:23	-	1 GE 14
Vertex	2 SG 36	0:00	(240:32)	-20:42	-	-	-	-	29 LI 17
Sun	15 LI 43	0:00	194:29	-6:11:30	17:06L	-5:12	189:17	152:27	0 VI 23
Moon	11 TA 26	+0:57	38:42	+16:11	41:19u	-14:03	24:39	356:40	26 PI 22
Mercury	5 LI 44	+1:50	185:59	-0:36	-	-	-	143:57	21 LE 34
Venus	13 VI 36	-4:54	163:00	+1:55	-14:23L	-1:36	161:24	120:58	28 CN 50
Mars	10 GE 31	-0:57	69:03	+21:06	+71:40u	-	-	27:01	29 AR 04
Jupiter	16 SC 40	+0:50	224:27	-16:02	-	-	-	182:25	2 LI 38
Saturn	19 TA 03	-2:32	48:18	-15:03	-	-13:00	34:18	6:16	6 TA 38
Uranus	25 CP 25	-0:38	297:29	-21:36	-	-	-	255:27	16 SG 36
Neptune	23 CN 44	-0:35	115:28	+20:48	-	-	-	73:26	14 GE 44
Pluto	28 GE 59	-6:27	88:57	+17:00	-	-	-	46:55	19 TA 22

L is the abbreviation for a locality position and N the abbreviation for a natal position. The LMC at 12 Aquarius 53 is 1°22′ from a trine to N Mars, but this is really too wide as it is equivalent to about eighty-two miles. To be exact it would have to be eighty-two miles further west and thus in the Pacific Ocean! The aspects are:

        L Moon Conjunct N MC 47′E
        L Jupiter Antiscion N MC 13′E
        L MC Antiscion N Jupiter 27′E
        L Uranus Sextile N Sun 53′W
        L Neptune Trine N Sun 59′E
        L Pluto Conjunct N Saturn 20′W

        L Vertex Opposition L Mars 13′
        L Vertex Contraparallel L Sun 20′

The antiscion is a form of parallel and similar to a conjunction in which the ecliptic intercepts of the two bodies are in parallel. In addition they are equidistant from zero degrees Cancer and zero degrees Capricorn. The E. is for east and means that the aspect would be exact that distance east of San Diego or about the same number of miles. W is for west and has the same meaning. Since the Midheaven and Jupiter are doubly in antiscion I would enjoy prestige and some success in that area.

This is strongly reinforced by the conjunction of the locality Moon to the natal Midheaven. As that Moon comes from the eleventh house there would be good friendships, group affiliations, and public

Introduction to Locality Astrology/47

relations. Since my closest natal aspect is the opposition of Uranus to Neptune, the sextile and trine they make to the natal Sun is a resolving influence for a problematic opposition affecting my personal relationships as Neptune is in my natal first house and Uranus is in the seventh house.

The Pluto-Saturn conjunction also accents the eleventh house in which Saturn is found at birth, and matters of binding security. Natally, as the speculum shows, the two bodies are in a parallel so that this reinforces a natal tendency.

At the bottom of the list are two aspects between locality factors that are not true of the natal chart: L Vertex Opposition L Mars, and L Vertex Contraparallel L Sun. As the Vertex is the most karmic and impersonal of the three angles, I would become karmically involved with key men (Sun-Vertex) and some Martian conditions there. Fortunately, my natal Sun and Mars are trine. From this, one would have to assume this is a good locality.

Almost overlooked is the parallel of the L Ascendant to the L Venus. The L Ascendant at 1 Gemini 14 is the same distance in back of 0 Cancer 00 as 28 Cancer 46 is after it! Thus this is only four minutes from being exact to Venus and still another augury of good personal relationships. Those who are conservative may wish to limit any antiscion orbs to thirty minutes instead of one degree, but this is not necessary when a light or an angle is involved as in every case here. Before leaving the right ascension shift, which is generally unknown and very valuable, let's ask where I might have some especially favorable aspects. When the time of birth is uncertain, one tries to aspect the lights (Sun and Moon) to the traditional benefics (Jupiter and Venus).

It so happens my Sun is nearly midway between Venus and Jupiter. I can't move thirty degrees east without going into the Atlantic Ocean. So I move 29°46' west.

	R.A.s	*Long. S.*	*Aspects to Natal Places*
MC	321:37	25 Aquarius 21	
ASC		19 Gemini 14	
Vertex		11 Scorpio 02	Opposition Moon 24E
Sun	164:43	13 Virgo 23	Conjunction Venus 13E (but natal conpar.)
Moon	8:56	9 Aries 43	Sextile Mars 48E
Mercury	156:13	4 Virgo 20	
Venus	133:14	10 Leo 47	Square Moon 49E (but natal trine))
Mars	39:17	11 Taurus 54	Conjunction Moon 28W
Jupiter	194:41	15 Libra 56	Conjunction Sun 13W
Saturn	18:32	20 Aries 15	
Uranus	267:43	27 Sagittarius 54	Square MC 45W (but natal sextile)
Neptune	85:42	26 Gemini 03	Square MC 66E (but natal trine)
Pluto	59:11	1 Gemini 19	

I have arbitrarily placed the conjunction of the Sun and Venus the same distance from the exact aspect (13 minutes east) as is Jupiter conjunct the Sun (13 minutes west). The natal contraparallel of Venus to the Sun is not too bad as they are both benefics. The squares of Uranus and Neptune to the

MC involve a natal sextile and a natal trine. The square of Venus to the Moon involves a natal trine, too. Nor did I have room for the antiscion of Venus to natal Saturn (10 minutes east), which also involves a natal trine. The sole problematic aspect would be L Mars Conjunct N Moon, bringing some friction with women friends.

This meridian—29W46 - 75W08 = 104W54—is only five miles west of Denver, Colorado with a latitude of 39N54 geographic (I use 39N43 geocentric). The Ascendant and Vertex are given for that geocentric latitude. The opposition of the Moon to the Vertex is indicative that fated and karmic conditions involving women and groups would occur there. The Moon stands out as having the sole aspect of stress in the whole locality pattern. If I moved south on this meridian to about thirty-four or thirty-five degrees north latitude, the locality Ascendant would move backward into a trine with the natal Sun. And the Vertex would shift backward until out of orb of the opposition to the natal Moon. Santa Fe, New Mexico is 35N30 (geocentric) and 105W57. Other lesser places in that state would be even better.

This right ascension shift is a marvelous tool and we owe much to Johndro for its development. Of the aspects in the last example, six did not involve the angles and therefore would have been useful even if the time of birth had been uncertain. Next, placing the natal bodies on the local planes will be explored. This does require some accuracy in the time of the chart, which is why I have mentioned it last.

Shifting to the Local Planes and the Parans

I have already mentioned the meridian plane. In a horoscope the upper meridian is represented by the Midheaven and the lower meridian is represented by the IC or cusp of the fourth house. The Midheaven and IC are the intersections of the ecliptic with the upper and the lower meridian.

The Ascendant is the intersection of the ecliptic with the eastern horizon and the Descendant (seventh house cusp) is the intersection of the ecliptic or plane of the zodiac, with the western horizon. The horizon is like the floor of a room—a plane tangent to the Earth's surface, while the meridian is like a north-south wall of that same room. Imagine you are in a corner of the room where floor (horizon), a north-south wall (meridian) and an east-west wall (the prime vertical or the third local plane) all meet. This helps in visualizing these three very vital local planes. The ecliptic also cuts that east-west wall or prime vertical to create the Vertex (always due west) and opposing the antivertex (always due east).

Astrologers have found that if a planet is bodily on one of these three local planes it is especially effective. If the Sun is at one of the three angles by conjunction or opposition, it is on one of these planes as it never has any appreciable celestial latitude. Figure 1 shows how Pluto can be conjunct the Midheaven and still be far from the upper meridian plane due to its high celestial latitude. The circle represents the horizon. The vertical line stands for the upper meridian. The horizontal line is that of the prime vertical, marked E and W at its two ends for east and west. Similarly, the meridian is S at one end, at the south point of the horizon, and N at the other end, for the north point. The prime vertical and meridian cross at the center of the circle at the zenith (Z), which is directly over the locality. The curved line halfway from S to Z is the equator which intersects SZ at M. The terrestrial latitude of the place is forty-five degrees north, this being the arc from M to Z. The ecliptic is the dashed line that also cuts the meridian at M, the horizon at A (Ascendant) and at D (Descendant). The equator always crosses the meridian at a right angle, this being the reason for the term right ascension. The ecliptic usually does not cross the meridian at a right angle, except at zero degrees Cancer and zero degrees Capricorn.

On October 5, 1971, Pluto's longitude was 0 Libra 00, so it was conjunct the Midheaven (M), but as its celestial latitude was 15N39, it was far from being bodily on the meridian plane. On July 28, 1969, its right ascension was 180 degrees so that when the Midheaven was 0 Libra 00 it was then bodily on the upper meridian. But its longitude was only 23 Virgo 12, making it seem too far away to be conjunct the Midheaven from the ninth house. This is an extreme case as no other planet ever attains such high latitudes as Pluto does, but it illustrates our point. If we wish to bring any body other than the Sun to the meridian, right ascension must be used.

In the speculum it can be seen that Mars has a right ascension of 69°03' and that the RAMC is 357°23'. The arc from the upper meridian to a planet in right ascension is termed the meridian distance (MD). Adding 360 degrees to Mars' right ascension gives 429°03'. This is done so that the RAMC may be subtracted from it to obtain the MD of +71°40'. It is given a plus sign as it is on the rising or left side of the chart. That plus also means that if Mars is to be on the upper meridian, movement must be east (+) to bring it there. And the arc that must be moved through is the meridian distance (MD) of +71°40'. At the top of the speculum is the terrestrial longitude and latitude of my birth place: 40N05 (geographic) and 75W08. since I was born in the western hemisphere and west of the zero degree Greenwich meridian, the terrestrial longitude should be written as -75°08'. Then if +71°40' is added to -75°08', the result is -3°28', which is west as it is still minus.

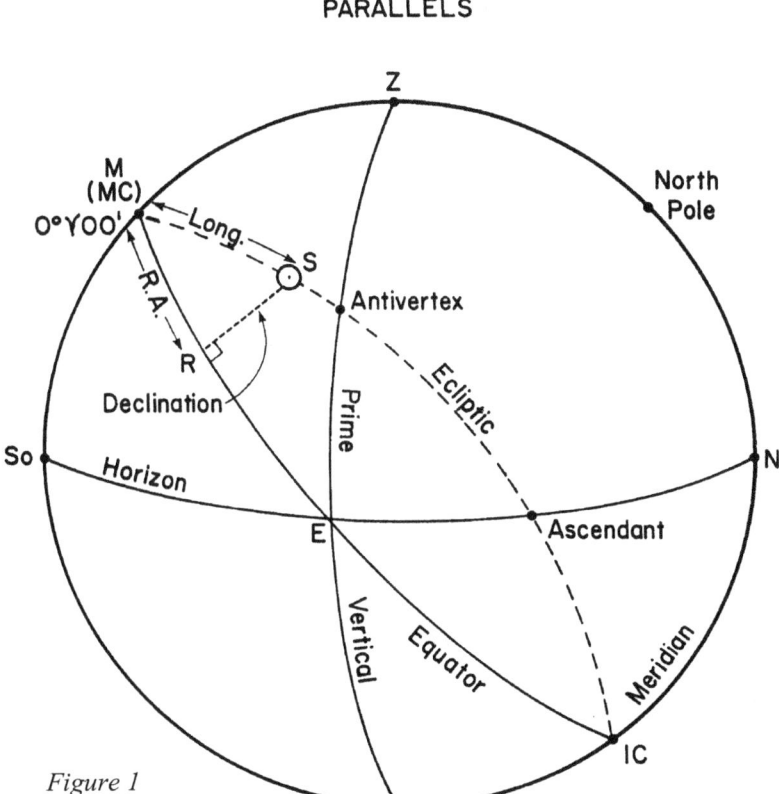

Figure 1

Anywhere along that meridian Mars will be at the upper meridian whether it be in the northern or the southern hemisphere. I used this method of locality-shifting during the year and a half that I wrote "Planets and You" for *Horoscope* magazine. Along that meridian Mars would be accented in my life, especially in career matters. Edinburgh, Scotland is 3W11, which is 0°17′ east of this meridian (-3°28′ - 3°11′). As each minute of arc is about one mile, this is a permissible orb. The meridian passes through West Africa and Spain. Madrid is 3W41. So these two cities are potentially important to me in a Martian way. Once the right ascensions of the natal planets have been found, along with the distance from the meridian (upper or lower) it is easy to do this type of shift. However, if the time of birth is only approximate, this will not be a dependable technique. I recommend no more than one degree of orb.

For those who wish to carry matters a step further, there are two extra columns for Venus. If a great circle is passed through the north and south points of the horizon (see Figure 1), it cuts the prime vertical (at V) in a right angle and the equator at 0. V is the place of the planet Pluto on the prime vertical in Fagan's Mundoscope. 0 is the oblique ascension place of the planet Pluto on the equator. If on the setting or right side of the chart, it is the oblique descension (OD) place. R is Pluto's right ascension position on the equator. The difference between oblique ascension and right ascension, or oblique descension and right ascension is the ascensional difference. If a planet is bodily on the horizon it must have the same oblique ascension or oblique descension as the Ascendant or its opposite point. It is very easy to find the oblique ascension of the Ascendant as it is always the RAMC plus ninety degrees. In my case, when ninety degrees is added to my RAMC of 357°23′, an oblique ascension of the Ascendant of 87°23′ is obtained.

Conversely, if the oblique ascension of a body rising on the eastern horizon is known, all that is necessary to find the RAMC of that place is to subtract ninety degrees from the oblique ascension. The ascensional differences (ADs) depend on two things: the declination of the planet in column five and the terrestrial latitude of the place. Let us look at my Venus in Edinburgh, where the latitude is 55N57. From column four the declination of Venus is 1N55. The sine AD = tan declination times tan terrestrial latitude. For Venus tan 1°55′ times tan 55°57′ = sine AD. AD is 2°50′. Is it subtracted from or added to Venus' right ascension, which form column four is 163:00? The simple laws for ascensional difference in the northern hemisphere are:

>**Rising Planets** (to find the OA): If declination is north, subtract AD from RA; if declination is north, add AD to RA.
>**Setting Planets** (to find the OD): If declination is south, add AD to RA; if declination is south, subtract AD from RA.
>If one is dealing with the southern hemisphere, all the arithmetic signs given above are reversed.

I was born in the northern hemisphere, where Edinburgh and Madrid also are located. The declination of Venus is somewhat north, so the AD of 2°50′ must be subtracted from its right ascension of 163°00′ since Venus is on the rising side of the chart. Thus, as column seven shows, its oblique ascension is 160°10′. The next task is to find the RAMC of the place where Venus will have this oblique ascension and rise, so ninety degrees is subtracted from 160°10′, which gives 70°10′ as the RAMC and it is +70°10′ as Venus is rising. From 357°23′ (natal RAMC) to +70°10′ equals 72°47′ as the MD. As my natal terrestrial longitude is -75°08', 72°47' is added to -75°08', which gives -2°21' west or about fifty miles east of Edinburgh. Since Venus is rising and Mars is culminating very close to Edinburgh, this is a paran or *in mundo* square. I have never visited that city but clearly my emotional life would be a stormy one in and near it. The two planets are zodiacally square at birth (orb of 3°07'), but they are in cadent houses—Venus in the third house and Mars in the twelfth house—so the square would be a much more powerful part of my pattern in that area. As Fagan has pointed out, such *in mundo* squares, oppositions, and conjunctions of two bodies are, in abbreviated form, parans. Some specialists in locality astrology do use *in mundo* aspects in locating people.

In order to try the experiment of putting planets on the prime vertical instead of the horizon, it is necessary to find a second kind of AD, or A'Å. It is based on the declination of the planet and the co-latitude of the birth place instead of the latitude. The co-latitude is ninety degrees minus the latitude. In the case of Madrid, which is 40N25, it would be -49°35'. Sine A'Å = tan declination + tan co-latitude. Sine A'Å = tan 1°55' + tan -49°35', which is 2°15'. One follows the rules of the southern hemisphere. Since the AD was subtracted from Venus' right ascension, the A'Å is now added, which gives 165°15', the OA'. Again, ninety degrees is subtracted from this to find the RAMC of +75°15' to have Venus on the prime vertical. Measured from the natal RAMC this gives an MD of +77°52'. As the terrestrial longitude is -75°08', the difference is +2°44'. Because it is +, the locality is 2E44.

In order to find where Venus will be due west instead of east, subtract the A'Å from the right ascension to obtain the OD', which in this is 160°45'. Then add the ninety degrees to find the RAMC, which is 250°45'. To reach this, the Midheaven would have to be moved backward or west, i.e. 357°23' - 250°45' = 106°38', and it would be minus since it is westward. Finally, -75°08' - 106°38' = -181°46' west or +178°14' east in the central Pacific.

2

Locality Charts

The Johndro Chart

In this chapter the matter of casting a birth locality (BL) or Johndro chart will be discussed.

In June 1950 in Margaret Morrell's *Modern Astrology* magazine, Edward Johndro repudiated his earlier work. His important book, *The Earth in the Heavens* was published in 1929 and has since been reprinted. In this book he brought the zodiac to Earth and in so doing established a baseline which was equivalent to zero degrees Aries. He used a moving baseline which very slowly inched westward. In the 1950 article he stated that after a further twenty years of checking, the moving baseline was only correct fifty percent of the time. He then recommended that a fixed baseline be used which equates the Greenwich Meridian to zero degrees Aries of the tropical zodiac. This had been earlier suggested by Sepharial and others. I have tested this new baseline and find it, as he did, far better than the old one.

Certain astrologers have disregarded this change and insist on using his old baseline. Two of them claim that he went back to the old one just before he died in November 1951 within half an hour of his wife. W. Kenneth Brown, one of my closest friends and his partner for fifteen years, survived him until February 1958. Never at any time in that period did he speak of Johndro as having gone back to his old baseline, so I feel it is up to those who claim otherwise to prove their allegations. Their problem is that they are not as willing to recant as Johndro was. It took a lot of courage on his part to admit he was wrong.

The June 1950 article was the first of a series, the rest of them being devoted to his electrical or E Ascendant, which is the same as my Antivertex. He thought the failure to use it was another reason for the trouble with any baseline.

Oddly enough, a fixed baseline is equivalent to a tropical zodiac correlation. In the case of his earlier moving baseline, it effectively kept the same stars overhead, other than for their very minute proper motions, at the same localities! As of 1930, the ayanamsa in right ascension between the moving and the fixed Greenwich baseline was 29°10′. In longitude the difference was larger, being slightly over thirty-one degrees.

While this is not the place for an extended discussion, it is my view that the correct equinoctial ayanamsa was fairly close to the values he gave. As the vernal and autumnal equinoxes lead the polar precession, the polar ayanamsa is roughly three and a half degrees less—something that the fanatical followers of Fagan and Bradley are quite unaware of! Therefore, it is possible that there is a valid moving baseline that correlates to a sidereal zodiac, although I surmise that his value was a little too large for the differences between the two baselines and the two zodiacs. I recall one test I made of his new baseline that shows that transiting Uranus was opposite the locality Midheaven of Los Alamos at the time the first atomic device was exploded. I use an equinoctial ayanamsa of about thirty degrees as of 2000 A.D.

Is there any justification for the use of the Greenwich meridian other than its curious relationship to the Great Pyramid, which Johndro discovered? Philosophically, I am convinced that such a widely used baseline as the Greenwich meridian is not just arbitrary although it may appear to be so. If the Earth is divided into two hemispheres or halves such that in one there is the most water and the least land and in the other the most land and the least water, it results in an interesting division of the Earth. The one with the most land is termed the principal hemisphere. The center of it, i.e. its pole, is a little over forty-seven degrees north latitude and is near to Nantes, France, and thus quite close to the Greenwich meridian. This strongly suggests that this may be the underlying *raison d'etre* for the Greenwich meridian. Until and unless there is major geological and continental rising and subsidence, this pole would not shift appreciably. The assumption can be made, therefore, that there is good reason to employ the Greenwich meridian as the baseline for bringing the heavens down to Earth.

A BL chart may be cast even when the time of birth is unknown, and thus is most useful for such difficult cases. It is also significant even if the time is known because it gives still another orientation to the usual horoscope. If an individual was born along the Greenwich meridian at the beginning of spring in the northern hemisphere, i.e. the Sun being at zero degrees Aries, then the BL Midheaven is zero degrees Aries. Suppose, though, that the individual was born with the Sun at zero degrees Aries, but ninety degrees west of Greenwich. The ninety degrees of right ascension (or six hours of sidereal time) is then subtracted from the zero degrees Aries of Greenwich and its zero hours of sidereal time, which equals zero degrees or 360 degrees of right ascension. This gives the place ninety degrees west a locality RAMC of 270 degrees, which is equal to zero degrees Capricorn. Since the native's Sun is at zero degrees Aries, his or her BL Midheaven will also be zero degrees Capricorn.

Suppose that birth occurred along the Greenwich zero degree meridian at the commencement of summer with the Sun at zero degrees Cancer. It is also known that the locality Midheaven is zero degree Aries, and that the natal Sun is ninety degrees later than zero degrees Aries. As a result, the BL Midheaven is ninety degrees plus zero degrees Aries to equal zero degrees Cancer. If the native had been born ninety degrees west of Greenwich with a locality Midheaven of zero degrees Capricorn, then the zero degree Cancer Sun would add ninety degrees to the locality Midheaven to give a BL Midheaven of zero degrees Aries.

Locality Midheaven means the fixed Midheaven of the place and has nothing to do with the individual. To that locality Midheaven one adds the distance the Sun is from zero degrees Aries in longitude to find the individual locality or BL Midheaven. This is one of the two ways and the easiest way for doing it. With the BL Midheaven found in this way one may use solar arc directions in longitude for aspects to or by it—and they work.

A second, or BL', Midheaven is found by right ascension for which one uses solar arc directions in right ascension that also work as Johndro indicated. I will use my chart as an example of these two ways of doing a Johndro chart. The time of day is disregarded for any BL or BL' chart.

My natal terrestrial longitude is -75°08', being minus since it is west. Therefore, first subtract that value from the zero degree or 360 degree RAMC of the Greenwich meridian. The result is a RAMC of 284°52' as the RAMC of the birth place, Jenkintown, Pennsylvania.

In longitude (using the table in the back of this book at zero degrees celestial latitude) this gives a Midheaven longitude of 13 Capricorn 41. My natal Sun is 15 Libra 43 or 195°43' from zero degrees Aries. This is added to that locality Midheaven's longitude: 13 Capricorn 41 plus 195°43' equals 29 Cancer 24. One uses, of course, the terrestrial latitude and co-latitude of the birth place to find the BL Ascendant and the BL Vertex, and all of the house cusps. If the time of birth is unknown, one assumes noon local time, so as to reduce the error in the BL Midheaven to plus or minus thirty minutes at most. An error in the birth time of twenty-four minutes is equal to about one minute in the Sun's motion so that the birth locality Midheaven will be quite accurate.

When my BL Midheaven by solar arc trined Uranus at 25 Capricorn 25 at the end of the third house, it set off the natal opposition. This happened at the beginning of August 1969 at the time I was laid off from a job at a Wall Street firm. I am using Uranus as usually the most accurate of all planets. When the twelfth house Sun at 15 Libra 43 trined the Midheaven by solar arc in late spring 1955, I had just formed an important career link with an important man. When the Midheaven by solar arc trined the Moon at 11°26' in the eighth house, ruling Cancer in the ninth house, there was a long trip and visit with an important woman within a month.

There is a second way to find the Johndro Midheaven (termed the BL' Midheaven), which is found solely by right ascension. One finds the arc of right ascension from zero degrees Aries to the natal Sun, which for me is 194°29'. This is added to the RAMC of the BL Midheaven, which as earlier specified was 284°52' (360° - 75°08'). These numbers are added: 194°29' plus 284°52' equals 479°21'. Then subtract the circle (360 degrees) to find the BL' Midheaven has a right ascension of 119°21' (equivalent to 27 Cancer 15). But its longitude will not be used; only its right ascension.

Suppose the goal is to bring this Midheaven to a trine of natal Uranus, setting off, as was done before with longitude, the natal opposition. Uranus' right ascension is 297°29' so subtract the trine (120 degrees) from this for a result of 177°29' of right ascension or the progressed Midheaven. From 119°21' to this value is 58°08'. These are primary directions or the equatorial (true) arcs of DeLuce, Wagner and others. Add this 58°08' to the natal right ascension of the Sun: 194°29' + 58°08' = 252°37'.

How can it be determined when the Sun will reach there? This right ascension is equivalent to a longitude of 13 Sagittarius 59. If the adjusted calculation date is used (advisable with right ascension arcs), the Sun reached that degree in late October 1969 near the end of the period of radical change and adjustment in my career (beginning of August 1969 to the end of October 1969). And on this second direction there was an unsuccessful move to New York. In this connection the move was made exactly in late October—Uranus natally at the end of the third house affecting the fourth house—due to career.

These examples of both kinds of timing, i.e. by the conventional solar arc in longitude and the more seldom used true solar arc in right ascension, are cited not as proof but as illustrating how to use the BL-BL' charts.

In the case of Marilyn Monroe, her natal ninth house Venus was brought near to a conjunction to her Midheaven by Ronald C. Davison, who rectified her chart. Her birth locality chart had both Jupiter and the Moon in Aquarius conjunct her Midheaven, an excellent explanation for the great publicity she received after death as well as during her life. Jacqueline Onassis is also attractive and has been the subject of an extraordinary amount of publicity. They are excellent test cases of the birth locality chart and the new baseline.

Natally, Jacqueline Onassis has a late Aries Moon trine the Midheaven at the end of Leo, but that is hardly enough. In her birth locality chart, Venus and Jupiter in the tenth house are parallel to its Midheaven, so both she and Monroe had Moon-Venus-Jupiter aspects to their Midheavens. One may also shift a Johndro chart to another locality. I did this for Onassis and found that in Greece, where she lived with her husband, her shifted birth locality Midheaven was virtually the same as her natal Midheaven in her natal locality. Thus, it may be argued she was indeed fated to live in Greece.

Onassis can be used as another example of the Johndro BL and BL' charts. She was born July 28, 1929 at 2:30 p.m., Eastern Daylight Time in Southampton, Long Island, New York (72W23, 40N54 geographic). Her natal Midheaven is 29 Leo 38, Sun at 5 Leo 09, and Moon at 25 Aries 37. First subtract the -72°23' west longitude from Greenwich, i.e. 359°60' - 72°23' = 284°37' as the right ascension of the locality Midheaven for Southampton. This is equivalent to 16 Capricorn 14. Her Sun is 125°09' from zero degrees Aries so this is added to the locality Midheaven's longitude which gives 21 Taurus 24 as the BL Midheaven. To find the BL Midheaven, look up 5 Leo 09 in the table which gives an equivalent right ascension of 127°31' which is added to the RAMC of Southampton: 127°31' + 287°37' = 415°08'. Then subtract 360 degrees and find that the birth locality Midheaven is 55°08' (equivalent to 27 Taurus 25).

Since parallels of declination are going to prove to be important, the next step is to find the declination of this BL' Midheaven. (Declination and right ascension belong together which is why the declination of the BL' Midheaven is used.) It is 19N30. It is often simpler to read parallel aspects if the celestial longitude of the Sun is located when it has the given declination. Such positions in longitude are termed ecliptic equivalents (EEs). On the next page are the declinations of the relevant bodies and their ecliptic equivalents.

Midpoints in declination have been used by Reinhold Ebertin and Roger Hutcheon. If the maximum orb in longitude is plus or minus 7°30' (for lights or angles; less between planets) then the maximum orb for midpoints should be 2°15' (less between planets). These orbs can be applied to the arc between the ecliptic equivalents as a way of turning declination into the equivalent longitude values since the orb of parallels and contraparallels is not a fixed one.

In these terms she has the Sun, Mercury, Venus, Jupiter, and the Sun/Venus and Sun/Jupiter mid-

Introduction to Locality Astrology/57

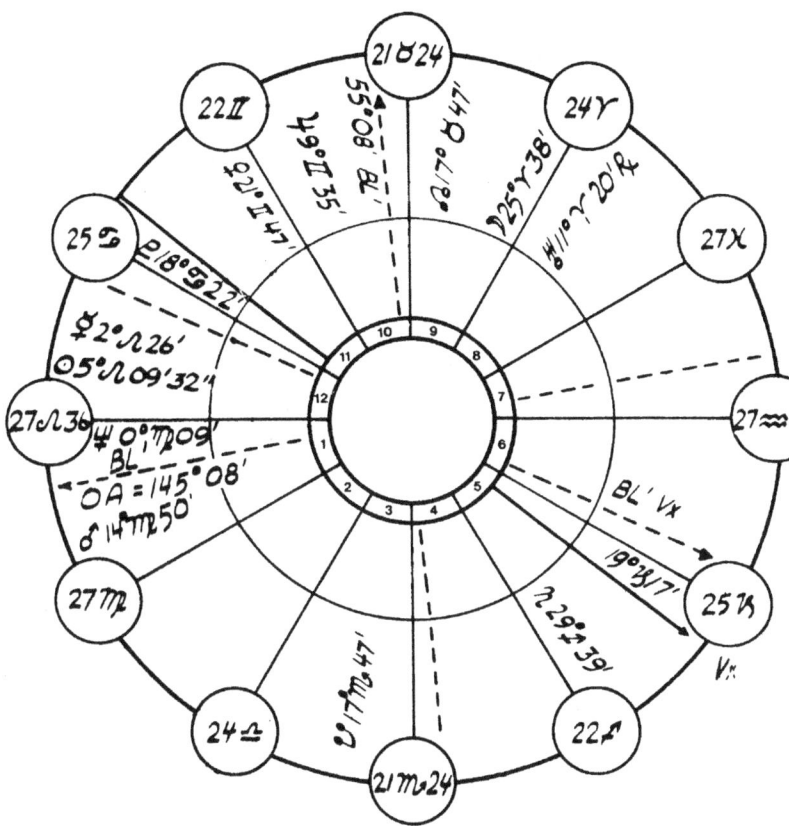

Jacqueline Onassis
July 28, 1929, 2:30 PM EST, Southampton, New York, 40N43, 72W23
Campanus Houses

points (in declination) in some kind of parallel to her BL' Midheaven. I submit this does much to account for the wealth, prestige, and publicity that she has received. The *dolce vita* of ease and affluence is a characteristic of Venus-Jupiter combinations. The accent on the Sun fits with the authority of her two husbands, etc.

She was married in Scorpios, Greece to Aristotle Onassis (nearest coordinates are 20E00 and 39N00). The right ascension of the locality Midheaven for that town is about twenty degrees, which is added to zero degrees of right ascension at Greenwich. This gives a Midheaven of about 21 Aries 47. To this is added the celestial longitude of her Sun or 125°09', which gives about 27 Leo 00 as her birth locality Midheaven. This is only two and a half degrees from her natal Midheaven so that the house cusps there are quite similar to the natal ones. The right ascension of her natal Sun is at 127°31' and this is added to the twenty degrees right ascension of the Scorpios locality Midheaven to result in about 147 degrees as the RAMC of the BL' Midheaven, which is equivalent to about 25 Leo 15.

Body or Angle	Declination	Ecliptic Equivalents
BL MC	+19:35:30	27 Taurus 25
Sun	+18:59	24 Taurus 51 Antiscion
Mercury	+21:08	4 Gemini 57
		27 Taurus 34 Antiscion
Venus	+20:45	2 Gemini 56
Jupiter	+21:09	5 Gemini 02
Sun/Venus	+19:52	28 Taurus 39 Midpoint in declination
Sun/Jupiter	+20:04	29 TA 36 Midpoint in declination

I have noticed that if an individual stands out in some way, a light (Sun or Moon) may make a close major aspect to one of the angles of the place. For instance, the locality Midheaven for Athens is 25 Aries 35, only three minutes from a conjunction to Onassis' Moon. In the case of Marilyn Monroe, the Moon at 19 Aquarius 40 is conjunct the locality Ascendant of Los Angeles where she was born on June 1, 1926 at 9:30 a.m., Pacific Standard Time. The 118W15 longitude of Los Angeles gives the right ascension of its Midheaven as 241°45′, equivalent to 3 Sagittarius 46 on the Midheaven. At the geocentric latitude the Los Angeles Ascendant is then 20 Aquarius 12 conjunct Monroe's Moon at 19 Aquarius 40. It may be a few minutes of arc later due to Davison's rectification of the time of birth and thus even closer to the Ascendant.

As both Monroe and Onassis are women, they are shown by the Moon. The closeness of the Moon to the Los Angeles Ascendant shows the importance of Monroe to that area; the closeness of the Moon to the Athens Midheaven is indicative of her impact on Greece through her marriage to an outstanding and very wealthy citizen. All of this also is partial proof of the validity of the new Johndro baseline.

The Johndro Article Excerpt

. . . Repudiation of the Greenwich base suggested in the 1929 text does not imply repudiation of that book in other respects. Its electrophysical groundwork has been established and greatly extended. The complete unification of Newton's and Maxwell's laws is the goal of physics today. These laws, properly related, are now the testing ground for every old and new astrological concept—a sure guide to progress, a sure detector of error.

Now if Greenwich cannot be soundly pinned to 1 Taurus 15 on the zodiacal dial, what are we to do? Accept some one of the several alternative notions that our text incubated in other noggins since 1929? Not at all! The way out of this jungle of confusion is quite simple. Return Greenwich to the current vernal equinox, as per Sepharial and other earlier advocates, and retain this coordination regardless of the westward shifting of the equinox. This means the Midheaven and Ascendant of any place remain fixed in the receding signs, circling the sidereal heavens in the precessional cycle.

Why did some of us depart form this widely taken-for-granted concept? As to others who did, ask them. As for this investigator, departure arose from the fact that when the Ascendants of countries, towns, and event locations were tested down through history on this basis, these Ascendants, so determined, made sense in about fifty percent of checks and failed miserably to tell the other half of history's story. The same was found to hold true of Ascendants based on any other single Greenwich base. This explains why no writer on the subject got more than a 50-50 vote of applause for accuracy. Coincidences score that well. It has not been good enough.

There appeared no sound "out" form this dilemma till other lines of research stumbled upon a concept which the GEM (short for Gravitational-Electro-Magnetic) law would have predicated without ado had we consulted it earlier in the quest. Others had toyed with this concept experimentally on sheer geometrical premises without realizing what correlated laws lie back on this new frame of reference—comparatively new, that is, to astrology, though extensively used by astronomy.

Without at this time going into the deep water of clarifying the GEM law, the nubbin of the answer to this and many more riddles can be stated simply. All electromagnetic fields are in quadrature pairs and both these E and M components are quadrature to their G component, around which they revolve. In astrological lingo this postulates and means just what it says—that for any given place (latitude and longitude) on a charged spherical body, such as our Earth, there is only one G, but there must be an M and an E, both of which must satisfy the stated GEM component relations, and conform to the geometry of their invariable quadratures. In short, the E and M components postulate two Ascendants, not one; one magnetic (M) and one electric (E).

The magnetic Ascendant is defined as the ecliptic point intersected by the east horizontal circle. This is the "usual" Ascendant given in tables of houses.

The electric Ascendant is defined by the ecliptic point intersected by the east-west prime vertical of the place, passing through the latitude of the place and the east and west point on the horizontal circle.

Obviously, when either equinox rises, the M and E Ascendants will coincide on the ecliptic and the one represents the other so that the "one Ascendant" failings would never appear there. But as the horizon departs more and more form the equinoxes and approaches the signs adjacent to the solstices, the increasing declination of the ecliptic forces the M and E Ascendants farther and farther apart, so that they differ in some cases by a whole sign or more. As a consequence, neglect of the E Ascendant led not only to widely divergent views about the Greenwich base, but also to erroneous rectifications of nativities, and even to wrong conclusions as to the true conception date as determined by the Moon's exchange on the magnetic Ascendants of the birth and conception charts.

Since to early astrologers the Ascendant was the horoscope, and indeed does have more bearing on personal status than the rest of the figure, it is obvious that the use of both Ascendants is one of the first of many more technical reforms necessary to replace muddle with system. To ignore the E Ascendant while accepting and using the M Ascendant leaves astrology where physics was under the guidance of Newton's laws prior to Maxwell and Planck. In turn, Maxwell's five equations covering E and M relations were not complete, as they failed to include the G component transformations.

In another article we will present both short-cut and trigonometric methods for obtaining the E Ascendant. We shall also point out the very different natures of the two Ascendants, the why of their psychological and event differences, and incidentally, we hope, bury once and for all the silly, unsettled controversy as to whether planets induce or impel—get set for a bit of shock!

By reconciling Greenwich to the vernal equinox through taking out the blank spots left by neglect to include the E Ascendant as well as its M component, we shall restore our reference system to the same seasonal and horary basis as the astronomical reference works from which our astrological ephemeris stems—measuring longitude and sidereal time from the equinox, while referring horary time to Greenwich.

This in no way disturbs the significance of the fixed stars; it merely shifts the Midheavens and signs together around the constellations and past the stars by turn, instead of retaining the same star on the same location zenith (save for their proper motion) while leaving the zodiacal precession to shift for itself, as changing Greenwich bases presumed. The change is sidereal, not zodiacal. Greenwich recedes as the current zodiac recedes. They have no relative motion in the seasonal sense, only in the diurnal sense. . . .

Mundoscope and Zenithscope Charts

Looking again at Figure 1, note that a great circle through Pluto and the north and south points of the horizon intersects the equator at 0 (the oblique ascension point) and, at a right angle, the prime vertical (west to east) at V. V is the position of Pluto in Cyril Fagan's Mundoscope.

All bodies can be similarly projected onto the prime vertical and are in the Mundoscope. When the prime vertical is divided by similar great circles through the north and south points into twelve equal symmetrical divisions it results in the houses of the Campanus system.

These great circles—of both the planets and house cusps—cross not only the prime vertical and equator, but also the ecliptic. The well-known Campanus cusps on the ecliptic are one result of this. The great circles through the planets cut the ecliptic at what I term their vertical (celestial) longitudes. I have found from tests that these vertical longitude values respond to directions. A Mundoscope of itself has nothing to do with the ecliptic and is a pure house system. A body four degrees, thirty-nine minutes from the eleventh cusp is merely a house position that has nothing to do with the zodiac.

On that same diagram a line from the zenith passes through Pluto and cuts the equator at zero minutes (oblique ascension), the ecliptic at HL and the horizon at AZ. AZ stands for azimuth which is the arc measured along the horizon from the East Point in placing the planets on the horizon in the Zenithscope. Witte's partner Sieggruen used it.

The HL point on the ecliptic is the horizontal longitude and is responsive to directions just as the vertical longitude point is. The positions along the prime vertical are measured from the East Point, also. The great circle that cuts the horizon at a right angle not only passes through the zenith, but also the nadir (not the same as the IC as the Nadir is always directly under one's feet). The house system associated with the azimuth positions is the little-used horizontal house system which has the Vertex as the cusp of its seventh house and the antivertex—Johndro's electrical Ascendant—at the cusp of its first house. This horizontal system is linked with the fated elements in life, like the Vertex angle, and with the direction from the birth place of significant places on Earth as Michael Erlewine has found. The arcs above and below the horizon are known as the altitude (H) arcs. The altitude-azimuth system is used in navigation and surveying. The arcs measuring the distances of bodies on either side of the prime vertical are the amplitude arcs.

As it might be expected, Johndro was the first astrologer to recognize the importance of both the Mundoscope and the Zenithscope. He had marvelous names for them. The Mundoscope, perpendicular to the horizon, was the Ferris wheel with its twelve baskets! Likewise, the Zenithscope was the merry-go-round, whose orientation is horizontal and ninety degrees from the Ferris wheel. As Johndro notes, this ninety degree relationship is that of any magnetic field to its associated electric field. The Vertex-Antivertex axis is electrical; the Ascendant-Descendant axis is magnetic; the Midheaven-IC axis is gravitational—thus, his GEM!

A tables of houses for the Campanus system can be used to find the intermediate house cusps just the way the Vertex is found. The cusps of all the horizontal houses can be found without a special table. In my chart, as an example, subtract the terrestrial latitude form ninety degrees using the natal geocentric latitude of 39N54. This gives a co-latitude of 50S06, which I use in the tables of houses. I use the fourth house cusp as though it were the Midheaven and the tenth house cusp. Then the resulting Ascendant is the Vertex on the setting side of the chart. The eleventh house cusp is actually the fifth house cusp (add six signs), the twelfth house cusp is actually the sixth house cusp (add six signs), etc.

This chapter has dealt not with the shifting of charts but rather with a different orientation a chart can be given due to locality factors. A Johndro chart usually has different angles and house positions than a conventional chart. A Mundoscope and a Zenithscope are projected onto two of the main local planes.

There are three basic ways of presenting planetary positions: In a heliocentric horoscope; in a geocentric one, but without houses; and in a topocentric one where the center is at the place of birth and not the center of the Earth, and where the planets are projected onto one of the local planes.

The third type has been much neglected and may prove to be quite important. Fagan, Johndro, Sieggruen, Blackwell, Hand, Kahila, Erlewine, McCormick, and a few others are opening up this field of study. In these local charts some new aspectual relationships appear that are vital and missing from the conventional chart which is an abortive attempt to combine the second and third types. Hand's pioneer work on ascensional transits is an integral part of this as they are, unlike ordinary transits, affected by terrestrial latitude.

Northern Latitudes

	0	1	2	3	4	5	6
♈	0°00′	359°37′	359°13′	358°49′	358°25′	358°01′	357°37′
1	0 55	0 32	0 08	359 44	359 20	358 56	358 32
2	1 50	1 27	1 03	0 39	0 15	359 51	359 27
3	2 45	2 22	1 58	1 34	1 10	0 46	0 22
4	3 40	3 17	2 53	2 29	2 05	1 41	1 17
5	4 35	4 12	3 48	3 24	3 00	2 36	2 12
6	5 30	5 07	4 43	4 19	3 55	3 31	3 07
7	6 25	6 02	5 38	5 14	4 50	4 26	4 02
8	7 21	6 57	6 33	6 09	5 45	5 21	4 57
9	8 16	7 52	7 28	7 04	6 40	6 16	5 52
10	9 11	8 47	8 23	7 59	7 35	7 11	6 47
11	10 06	9 42	9 18	8 55	8 31	8 07	7 43
12	11 02	10 38	10 14	9 51	9 27	9 03	8 39
13	11 57	11 33	11 09	10 46	10 22	9 58	9 34
14	12 53	12 29	12 05	11 42	11 18	10 54	10 30
15	13 48	13 25	13 01	12 38	12 14	11 50	11 26
16	14 44	14 20	13 57	13 34	13 10	12 46	12 22
17	15 40	15 16	14 53	14 30	14 06	13 42	13 18
18	16 35	16 12	15 49	15 26	15 02	14 39	14 15
19	17 31	17 08	16 45	16 22	15 58	15 35	15 11
20	18 27	18 04	17 41	17 18	16 54	16 31	16 07
21	19 23	19 00	18 37	18 14	17 51	17 28	17 04
22	20 20	19 56	19 33	19 11	18 48	18 25	18 01
23	21 16	20 53	20 30	20 08	19 45	19 22	18 58
24	22 12	21 50	21 27	21 05	20 42	20 19	19 55
25	23 09	22 47	22 24	22 02	21 39	21 16	20 52
26	24 06	23 44	23 21	22 59	22 36	22 13	21 50
27	25 02	24 41	24 19	23 57	23 34	23 11	22 48
28	25 59	25 38	25 16	24 54	24 31	24 09	23 46
29	26 57	26 35	26 13	25 51	25 29	25 07	24 44
♉	27 54	27 33	27 11	26 49	26 27	26 05	25 42
1	28 51	28 30	28 08	27 47	27 25	27 03	26 40
2	29 49	29 27	29 06	28 45	28 23	28 01	27 38
3	30 46	30 25	30 04	29 43	29 21	28 59	28 37
4	31 44	31 23	31 02	30 41	30 19	29 58	29 36
5	32 42	32 21	32 00	31 39	31 18	30 57	30 35
6	33 40	33 20	32 59	32 38	32 17	31 56	31 34
7	34 38	34 18	33 58	33 37	33 16	32 55	32 33
8	35 37	35 17	34 57	34 36	34 15	33 54	33 33
9	36 36	36 16	35 56	35 36	35 15	34 54	34 33

Northern Latitudes

	0	1	2	3	4	5	6
10	37°34′	37°15′	36°55′	36°35′	36°15′	35°54′	35°33′
11	38 33	38 14	37 54	37 35	37 15	36 54	36 33
12	39 33	39 14	38 54	38 35	38 15	37 55	37 34
13	40 32	40 13	39 54	39 35	39 15	38 56	38 35
14	41 31	41 13	40 54	40 35	40 16	39 57	39 36
15	42 31	42 13	41 54	41 36	41 17	40 58	40 38
16	43 31	43 13	42 54	42 36	42 18	41 59	41 39
17	44 31	44 13	43 55	43 37	43 19	43 00	42 40
18	45 31	45 14	44 56	44 38	44 20	44 01	43 42
19	46 32	46 14	45 57	45 39	45 21	45 03	44 44
20	47 32	47 15	46 58	46 40	46 23	46 05	45 49
21	48 38	48 16	47 59	47 42	47 25	47 07	46 49
22	49 34	49 17	49 00	48 44	48 27	48 09	47 52
23	50 35	50 18	50 02	49 46	49 29	49 12	48 55
24	51 36	51 20	51 04	50 48	50 32	50 15	49 58
25	52 38	52 22	52 06	51 51	51 35	51 18	51 02
26	53 40	53 24	53 09	52 54	52 38	52 22	52 06
27	54 42	54 27	54 12	53 57	53 42	53 26	53 10
28	55 44	55 29	55 15	55 00	54 45	54 30	54 14
29	56 46	56 32	56 18	56 03	55 49	55 34	55 18
♊	57 48	57 35	57 21	57 07	56 53	56 38	56 23
1	58 51	58 38	58 24	58 10	57 57	57 42	57 28
2	59 53	59 41	59 27	59 14	59 01	58 47	58 33
3	60 56	60 44	60 31	60 18	60 05	59 52	59 38
4	61 59	61 47	61 35	61 22	61 10	60 57	60 44
5	63 03	62 51	62 39	62 27	62 15	62 02	61 50
6	64 06	63 55	63 43	63 32	63 20	63 08	62 56
7	65 09	64 59	64 47	64 37	64 25	64 13	64 02
8	66 13	66 03	65 52	65 42	65 30	65 19	65 08
9	67 17	67 07	66 57	66 47	66 36	66 25	66 14
10	68 21	68 11	68 02	67 52	67 42	67 31	67 21
11	69 25	69 16	69 07	68 57	68 48	68 38	68 28
12	70 29	70 21	70 12	70 03	69 54	69 45	69 35
13	71 34	71 26	71 17	71 09	71 00	70 51	70 42
14	72 38	72 31	72 22	72 15	72 06	71 58	71 49
15	73 43	73 36	73 28	73 21	73 13	73 05	72 57
16	74 47	74 41	74 33	74 27	74 19	74 12	74 04
17	75 52	75 46	75 39	75 33	75 26	75 19	75 12
18	76 57	76 51	76 45	76 39	76 33	76 27	76 20
19	78 02	77 56	77 51	77 45	77 40	77 34	77 28

Northern Latitudes

	0	1	2	3	4	5	6
20	79°07′	79°02′	78°57′	78°52′	78°47′	78°41′	78°36′
21	80 12	80 08	80 03	79 59	79 54	79 49	79 44
22	81 17	81 13	81 09	81 05	81 01	80 56	80 52
23	82 22	82 18	82 15	82 11	82 08	82 04	82 00
24	83 28	83 24	83 21	83 18	83 15	83 11	83 09
25	84 33	84 30	84 27	84 25	84 22	84 20	84 17
26	85 38	85 36	85 33	85 32	85 29	85 28	85 25
27	86 44	86 42	86 40	86 39	86 37	86 36	86 34
28	87 49	87 48	87 46	87 46	87 44	87 44	87 42
29	88 55	88 54	88 53	88 53	88 52	88 52	88 51
♋	90 00	90 00	90 00	90 00	90 00	90 00	90 00
1	91 05	91 06	91 07	91 07	91 07	91 08	91 09
2	92 11	92 12	92 14	92 14	92 15	92 16	92 18
3	93 16	93 18	93 20	93 21	93 23	93 24	93 26
4	94 22	94 24	94 27	94 28	94 30	94 32	94 35
5	95 27	95 30	95 33	95 35	95 38	95 40	95 43
6	96 32	96 36	96 39	96 42	96 45	96 48	96 51
7	97 38	97 42	97 45	97 49	97 52	97 56	98 00
8	98 43	98 47	98 51	98 55	99 00	99 04	99 08
9	99 48	99 52	99 57	100 01	100 07	100 12	100 16
10	100 53	100 58	101 03	101 08	101 14	101 19	101 24
11	101 58	102 04	102 09	102 15	102 21	102 26	102 32
12	103 03	103 09	103 15	103 21	103 27	103 33	103 40
13	104 08	104 14	104 21	104 27	104 34	104 41	104 48
14	105 13	105 19	105 27	105 33	105 41	105 48	105 56
15	106 17	106 24	106 33	106 39	106 47	106 55	107 03
16	107 22	107 29	107 38	107 45	107 53	108 02	108 11
17	108 26	108 34	108 43	108 53	108 59	109 09	109 18
18	109 31	109 39	109 48	109 57	110 05	110 15	110 25
19	110 35	110 44	110 53	111 03	111 12	111 22	111 32
20	111 39	111 49	111 58	112 08	112 18	112 29	112 39
21	112 43	112 54	113 03	113 13	113 24	113 35	113 46
22	113 47	113 57	114 08	114 18	114 30	114 41	114 52
23	114 51	115 01	115 13	115 23	115 35	115 47	115 58
24	115 54	116 05	116 17	116 28	116 41	116 52	117 04
25	116 57	117 09	117 21	117 33	117 46	117 58	118 10
26	118 01	118 13	118 25	118 38	118 51	119 03	119 16
27	119 04	119 16	119 29	119 42	119 55	120 08	120 22
28	120 07	120 19	120 33	120 46	120 59	121 13	121 27
29	121 09	121 22	121 36	121 50	122 03	122 18	122 32

Northern Latitudes

	0	1	2	3	4	5	6
♌	122°12′	122°25′	122°39′	122°53′	123°07′	123°22′	123°37′
1	123 14	123 28	123 42	123 57	124 11	124 26	124 42
2	124 16	124 31	124 45	125 00	125 15	125 30	125 46
3	125 18	125 33	125 48	126 03	126 18	126 34	126 50
4	126 20	126 36	126 51	127 06	127 22	127 38	127 54
5	127 22	127 38	127 54	128 09	128 25	128 42	128 58
6	128 24	128 40	128 56	129 12	129 28	129 45	130 02
7	129 25	129 42	129 58	130 14	130 31	130 48	131 05
8	130 26	130 43	131 00	131 16	131 33	131 51	132 08
9	131 27	131 44	132 01	132 18	132 35	132 53	133 11
10	132 28	132 45	133 02	133 20	133 37	133 55	134 14
11	133 28	133 46	134 03	134 21	134 39	134 57	135 16
12	134 29	134 47	135 04	135 22	135 40	135 59	136 18
13	135 29	135 47	136 05	136 23	136 41	137 00	137 20
14	136 29	136 47	137 06	137 24	137 42	138 01	138 21
15	137 29	137 47	138 06	138 24	138 43	139 02	139 22
16	138 29	138 47	139 06	139 25	139 44	140 03	140 24
17	139 28	139 47	140 06	140 25	140 45	141 04	141 25
18	140 28	140 46	141 06	141 25	141 45	142 05	142 26
19	141 27	141 46	142 06	142 25	142 45	143 06	143 27
20	142 26	142 45	143 05	143 25	143 45	144 06	144 27
21	143 25	143 44	144 04	144 24	144 45	145 06	145 27
22	144 23	144 43	145 03	145 24	145 45	146 06	146 27
23	145 22	145 42	146 02	146 23	146 44	147 05	147 27
24	146 20	146 40	147 01	147 22	147 43	148 04	148 26
25	147 18	147 39	148 00	148 21	148 42	148 03	149 25
26	148 16	148 37	148 58	149 19	149 41	150 02	150 24
27	149 14	149 35	149 56	150 17	150 39	151 01	151 23
28	150 11	150 33	150 54	151 15	151 37	151 59	152 22
29	151 09	151 30	151 52	152 13	152 35	152 57	153 20
♍	152 06	152 27	152 49	153 11	153 33	153 55	154 18
1	153 04	153 25	153 47	154 09	154 31	154 53	155 16
2	154 01	154 22	154 44	155 06	155 29	155 51	156 14
3	154 58	155 19	155 41	156 03	156 26	156 49	157 12
4	155 54	156 16	156 39	157 01	157 24	157 47	158 10
5	156 51	157 14	157 36	157 58	158 21	158 44	159 08
6	157 48	158 10	158 33	158 55	159 18	159 41	160 05
7	158 44	159 07	159 30	159 51	160 15	160 38	161 02
8	159 40	160 04	160 27	160 49	161 12	161 35	161 59
9	160 37	161 00	161 23	161 46	162 09	162 32	162 56

Northern Latitudes

	0	1	2	3	4	5	6
10	161°33′	161°56′	162°19′	162°42′	163°06′	163°29′	163°53′
11	162 29	162 52	163 15	163 38	164 02	164 25	164 49
12	163 25	163 43	164 11	164 34	164 58	165 21	165 45
13	164 20	164 44	165 07	165 30	165 54	166 18	166 42
14	165 16	165 40	166 03	166 26	166 50	167 14	167 38
15	166 12	166 36	166 59	167 22	167 46	168 10	168 34
16	167 07	167 31	167 55	168 18	168 42	169 06	169 30
17	168 03	168 27	168 51	169 14	169 38	170 02	170 26
18	168 58	169 23	169 46	170 09	170 33	170 57	171 21
19	169 54	170 18	170 42	171 05	171 29	171 53	172 17
20	170 49	171 13	171 37	172 01	172 25	172 49	173 13
21	171 44	172 08	172 32	172 56	173 20	173 44	174 08
22	172 39	173 03	173 27	173 51	174 15	174 39	175 03
23	173 35	173 58	174 22	174 46	175 10	175 34	175 58
24	174 30	174 53	175 17	175 41	176 05	176 29	176 53
25	175 25	175 48	176 12	176 36	177 00	177 24	177 48
26	176 20	176 43	177 07	177 31	177 55	178 19	178 43
27	177 15	177 38	178 02	178 26	178 50	179 14	179 38
28	178 10	178 33	178 57	179 21	179 45	180 09	180 33
29	179 05	179 28	179 52	180 16	180 40	181 04	181 28
♎	180 00	180 23	180 47	181 11	181 35	181 59	182 23
1	180 55	181 18	181 42	182 06	182 30	182 55	183 18
2	181 50	182 13	182 37	183 01	183 25	183 49	184 13
3	182 45	183 08	183 32	183 56	184 20	184 44	185 08
4	183 40	184 03	184 27	184 51	185 15	185 39	186 03
5	184 35	184 58	185 22	185 46	186 10	186 34	186 58
6	185 30	185 54	186 18	186 42	187 06	187 30	187 53
7	186 25	186 49	187 13	187 37	188 01	188 25	188 48
8	187 21	187 44	188 08	188 32	188 56	189 20	189 43
9	188 16	188 39	189 03	189 27	189 51	190 15	190 38
10	189 11	189 34	189 58	190 22	190 46	191 10	191 33
11	190 06	190 29	190 53	191 17	191 41	192 05	192 28
12	191 02	191 25	191 48	192 13	192 36	193 00	193 23
13	191 57	192 20	192 43	193 08	193 31	193 55	194 18
14	192 53	193 16	193 39	194 03	194 26	194 50	195 13
15	193 48	194 12	194 35	194 58	195 21	195 45	196 08
16	194 44	195 07	195 30	195 53	196 16	196 40	197 03
17	195 40	196 02	196 25	196 48	197 11	197 35	197 58
18	196 35	196 58	197 21	197 44	198 07	198 30	198 53
19	197 31	197 54	198 17	198 40	199 02	199 25	199 48

Northern Latitudes

	0	1	2	3	4	5	6
20	198°27′	198°50′	199°13′	199°36′	199°58′	200°21′	200°43′
21	199 23	199 46	200 09	200 32	200 54	201 16	201 39
22	200 20	200 42	201 05	201 28	201 50	202 12	202 34
23	201 16	201 38	202 01	202 24	202 46	203 08	203 30
24	202 12	202 35	202 57	203 20	203 42	204 04	204 26
25	203 09	203 31	203 53	204 16	204 38	205 00	205 21
26	204 06	204 28	204 50	205 12	205 34	205 56	206 17
27	205 02	205 25	205 47	206 09	206 30	206 52	207 13
28	205 59	206 22	206 43	207 05	207 26	207 48	208 09
29	206 57	207 19	207 40	208 01	208 22	208 44	209 05
♏	207 54	208 16	208 37	208 58	209 19	209 40	210 01
1	208 51	209 13	209 34	209 55	210 16	210 37	210 57
2	209 49	210 10	210 31	210 52	211 13	211 34	211 54
3	210 46	211 07	211 28	211 49	212 10	212 31	212 51
4	211 44	212 05	212 25	212 46	213 07	213 27	213 47
5	212 42	213 03	213 23	213 43	214 04	214 24	214 44
6	213 40	214 01	214 21	214 41	215 01	215 21	215 41
7	214 38	214 59	215 19	215 39	215 58	216 18	216 38
8	215 37	215 57	216 17	216 37	216 56	217 15	217 35
9	216 36	216 56	217 15	217 35	217 54	218 13	218 32
10	217 34	217 54	218 13	218 33	218 52	219 11	219 29
11	218 33	218 53	219 12	219 31	219 50	220 09	220 27
12	219 33	219 52	220 11	220 30	220 48	221 07	221 25
13	220 32	220 51	221 10	221 28	221 46	222 05	222 23
14	221 31	221 50	222 09	222 27	222 45	223 03	223 21
15	222 31	222 50	223 08	223 26	223 44	224 02	224 19
16	223 31	223 49	224 07	224 25	224 43	225 00	225 17
17	224 31	224 49	225 06	225 24	225 42	225 59	226 15
18	225 31	225 49	226 06	226 23	226 41	226 58	227 14
19	226 32	226 49	227 06	227 23	227 40	227 57	228 13
20	227 32	227 49	228 06	228 23	228 39	228 56	229 12
21	228 33	228 50	229 06	229 23	229 39	229 55	230 11
22	229 34	229 50	230 06	230 23	230 38	230 54	231 10
23	230 35	230 51	231 06	231 23	231 38	231 53	232 09
24	231 36	231 52	232 07	232 23	232 38	232 53	233 08
25	232 38	232 53	233 08	233 24	233 38	233 53	234 08
26	233 40	233 55	234 09	234 24	234 38	234 53	235 07
27	234 41	234 57	235 11	235 25	235 39	235 53	236 07
28	235 43	235 58	236 12	236 26	236 40	236 54	237 07
29	236 46	237 00	237 14	237 27	237 41	237 54	238 07

Northern Latitudes

	0	1	2	3	4	5	6
♐	237°48′	238°02′	238°15′	238°29′	238°42′	238°55′	239°07′
1	238 51	239 04	239 17	239 30	239 43	239 55	240 07
2	239 53	240 06	240 19	240 31	240 44	240 56	241 08
3	240 56	241 09	241 21	241 33	241 45	241 57	242 09
4	241 59	242 11	242 23	242 35	242 46	242 58	243 09
5	243 03	243 14	243 25	243 37	243 48	243 59	244 10
6	244 06	244 17	244 28	244 39	244 50	245 01	245 11
7	245 09	245 20	245 31	245 41	245 52	246 02	246 12
8	246 13	246 23	246 34	246 44	246 54	247 04	247 13
9	247 17	247 27	247 37	247 47	247 56	248 06	248 15
10	248 21	248 30	248 40	248 49	248 58	249 07	249 16
11	249 25	249 34	249 43	249 52	250 00	250 09	250 17
12	250 29	250 38	250 46	250 55	251 03	251 11	251 19
13	251 34	251 42	251 49	251 58	252 05	252 13	252 21
14	252 38	252 46	252 53	253 01	253 08	253 15	253 23
15	253 43	253 50	253 57	254 04	254 11	254 18	254 25
16	254 47	254 54	255 01	255 07	255 14	255 20	255 27
17	255 52	255 58	256 05	256 11	256 17	256 22	256 29
18	256 57	257 03	257 09	257 15	257 20	257 25	257 31
19	258 02	258 07	258 13	258 18	258 23	258 28	258 33
20	259 07	259 12	259 17	259 21	259 26	259 31	259 35
21	260 12	260 17	260 21	260 25	260 29	260 34	260 38
22	261 17	261 21	261 25	261 28	261 32	261 36	261 40
23	262 22	262 25	262 29	262 32	262 35	262 39	262 42
24	263 28	263 30	263 33	263 36	263 39	263 42	263 45
25	264 33	264 35	264 37	264 40	264 42	264 45	264 47
26	265 38	265 40	265 41	265 44	265 45	265 48	265 49
27	266 44	266 45	266 46	266 48	266 49	266 51	266 52
28	267 49	267 50	267 50	267 52	267 52	267 54	267 54
29	268 55	268 55	268 55	268 56	268 56	268 57	268 57
♑	270 00	270 00	270 00	270 00	270 00	270 00	270 00
1	271 05	271 05	271 05	271 04	271 04	271 03	271 03
2	272 11	272 10	272 10	272 08	272 08	272 06	272 06
3	273 16	273 15	273 14	273 12	273 11	273 09	273 08
4	274 22	274 20	274 19	274 16	274 15	274 12	274 11
5	275 27	275 25	275 23	275 20	275 18	275 15	275 13
6	276 32	276 30	276 27	276 24	276 21	276 18	276 15
7	277 38	277 35	277 31	277 28	277 25	277 21	277 18
8	278 43	278 39	278 35	278 32	278 28	278 24	278 20
9	279 48	279 43	279 39	279 35	279 31	279 26	279 22

Northern Latitudes

	0	1	2	3	4	5	6
10	280°53′	280°48′	280°43′	280°39′	280°34′	280°29′	280°25′
11	281 58	281 53	281 47	281 42	281 37	281 32	281 27
12	283 03	282 57	282 51	282 45	282 40	282 34	282 29
13	284 08	284 02	283 55	283 49	283 43	283 37	283 21
14	285 13	285 06	284 59	284 53	284 46	284 40	284 33
15	286 17	286 10	286 03	285 56	285 49	285 42	285 35
16	287 22	287 14	287 07	286 59	286 52	286 45	286 37
17	288 26	288 18	288 11	288 02	287 55	287 47	287 39
18	289 31	289 22	289 14	289 05	288 57	288 49	288 41
19	290 35	290 26	290 17	290 08	290 00	289 51	289 43
20	291 39	291 30	291 20	291 11	291 02	290 53	290 44
21	292 43	292 33	292 23	292 13	292 04	291 55	291 45
22	293 47	293 37	293 26	293 16	293 06	292 56	292 47
23	294 51	294 40	294 29	294 19	294 08	293 58	293 48
24	295 54	295 43	295 32	295 21	295 10	294 59	294 49
25	296 57	296 46	296 35	296 23	296 12	296 01	295 50
26	298 01	297 49	297 37	297 25	297 14	297 02	296 51
27	299 04	298 51	298 39	298 27	298 15	298 03	297 51
28	300 07	299 54	299 41	299 29	299 16	299 04	298 52
29	301 09	300 56	300 43	300 30	300 17	300 05	299 53
♒	302 12	301 58	301 45	301 31	301 18	301 05	300 53
1	303 14	303 00	302 47	302 33	302 19	302 06	301 53
2	304 16	304 02	303 38	303 34	303 20	303 06	302 53
3	305 18	305 03	304 50	304 35	304 21	304 07	303 53
4	306 20	306 05	305 51	305 36	305 22	305 07	304 53
5	307 22	307 07	306 52	306 36	306 22	306 07	305 52
6	308 24	308 08	307 53	307 37	307 22	307 07	306 52
7	309 25	309 09	308 54	308 37	308 22	308 07	307 51
8	310 26	310 10	309 54	309 37	309 22	309 06	308 50
9	311 27	311 10	310 54	310 37	310 21	310 05	309 49
10	312 28	312 11	311 54	311 37	311 21	311 04	310 48
11	313 28	313 11	312 54	312 37	312 20	312 03	311 47
12	314 29	314 11	313 54	313 37	313 19	313 02	312 46
13	315 29	315 11	314 54	314 36	314 18	314 01	313 44
14	316 29	316 11	315 53	315 35	315 17	315 00	314 43
15	317 29	317 10	316 52	316 34	316 16	315 58	315 41
16	318 29	318 10	317 51	317 33	317 15	316 57	316 39
17	319 29	319 09	318 50	318 32	318 14	317 55	317 37
18	320 28	320 08	319 49	319 30	319 12	318 53	318 35
19	321 27	321 07	320 48	320 29	320 10	319 51	319 33

Northern Latitudes

	0	1	2	3	4	5	6
20	322°26′	322°06′	321°47′	321°27′	321°08′	320°40′	320°31′
21	323 25	323 04	322 45	322 25	322 06	321 47	321 28
22	324 23	324 03	323 43	323 23	323 04	322 45	322 25
23	325 22	325 01	324 41	324 21	324 01	323 42	323 22
24	326 20	325 59	325 39	325 19	324 59	324 39	324 19
25	327 18	326 57	326 37	326 17	325 56	325 36	325 16
26	328 16	327 55	327 35	327 14	326 53	326 33	326 13
27	329 14	328 53	328 32	328 11	327 50	327 30	327 10
28	330 11	329 51	329 29	329 08	328 47	328 27	328 06
29	331 09	330 47	330 26	330 05	329 44	329 25	329 03
♓	332 06	331 44	331 23	331 02	330 41	330 20	329 59
1	333 04	332 41	332 20	331 59	331 38	331 16	330 55
2	334 01	333 38	333 17	332 55	332 34	332 12	331 51
3	334 58	334 35	334 13	333 51	333 30	333 08	332 47
4	335 55	335 32	335 10	334 48	334 26	334 04	333 43
5	336 51	336 29	336 07	335 44	335 22	335 00	334 39
6	337 48	337 25	337 03	336 40	336 18	335 56	335 34
7	338 44	338 22	337 59	337 36	337 14	336 52	336 30
8	339 40	339 18	338 55	338 32	338 10	337 48	337 26
9	340 37	340 14	339 51	339 28	339 06	338 43	338 21
10	341 33	341 10	340 47	340 24	340 02	339 39	339 17
11	342 29	342 06	341 43	341 20	340 58	340 35	340 12
12	343 25	343 02	342 39	342 16	341 53	341 30	341 07
13	344 20	343 58	343 35	343 12	342 49	342 25	342 02
14	345 16	344 53	344 30	344 07	343 44	343 20	342 57
15	346 12	345 48	345 25	345 02	344 39	344 15	343 52
16	347 07	346 44	346 21	345 57	345 34	345 10	344 47
17	348 03	347 40	347 17	346 52	346 29	346 05	345 52
18	348 58	348 35	348 12	347 47	347 24	347 00	346 37
19	349 54	349 31	349 07	348 43	348 19	347 55	347 32
20	350 49	350 26	350 03	349 38	349 14	348 50	348 27
21	351 44	351 21	350 57	350 33	350 09	349 45	349 22
22	352 39	352 16	351 52	351 28	351 04	350 40	350 17
23	353 35	353 11	352 47	352 23	351 59	351 35	351 12
24	354 30	354 06	353 42	353 18	352 54	352 30	352 07
25	355 25	355 01	354 38	354 14	353 50	353 26	353 02
26	356 20	355 57	355 33	355 09	354 45	354 21	353 57
27	357 15	356 52	356 28	356 04	355 40	355 16	354 52
28	358 10	357 47	357 23	356 59	356 35	356 11	355 47
29	359 05	358 42	358 18	357 54	357 30	357 06	355 42

Southern Latitudes

	0	1	2	3	4	5	6
♈	0°00′	0°23′	0°47′	1°11′	1°35′	1°59′	2°23′
1	0 55	1 18	1 42	2 06	2 30	2 54	3 18
2	1 50	2 13	2 37	3 01	3 25	3 49	4 13
3	2 45	3 08	3 32	3 56	4 20	4 44	5 08
4	3 40	4 03	4 27	4 51	5 15	5 39	6 03
5	4 35	4 58	5 22	5 46	6 10	6 34	6 58
6	5 30	5 54	6 18	6 42	7 06	7 30	7 53
7	6 25	6 49	7 13	7 37	8 01	8 25	8 48
8	7 21	7 44	8 08	8 32	8 56	9 20	9 43
9	8 16	8 40	9 04	9 28	9 51	10 15	10 38
10	9 11	9 35	9 59	10 23	10 46	11 10	11 33
11	10 06	10 30	10 54	11 18	11 41	12 05	12 28
12	11 02	11 25	11 49	12 13	12 36	13 00	13 23
13	11 57	12 20	12 44	13 08	13 31	13 55	14 18
14	12 53	13 16	13 39	14 03	14 26	14 50	15 13
15	13 48	14 12	14 35	14 58	15 21	15 45	16 08
16	14 44	15 07	15 30	15 53	16 16	16 40	17 03
17	15 40	16 02	16 25	16 48	17 11	17 35	17 58
18	16 35	16 58	17 21	17 44	18 07	18 30	18 53
19	17 31	17 54	18 17	18 40	19 02	19 25	19 48
20	18 27	18 50	19 13	19 36	19 58	20 21	20 43
21	19 23	19 46	20 09	20 23	20 54	21 17	21 39
22	20 20	20 42	21 05	21 28	21 50	22 12	22 34
23	21 16	21 38	22 01	22 24	22 46	23 08	23 30
24	22 12	22 35	22 57	23 20	23 42	24 04	24 26
25	23 09	23 31	23 53	24 16	24 38	25 00	25 21
26	24 06	24 28	24 50	25 12	25 34	25 55	26 17
27	25 02	25 25	25 47	26 09	26 30	26 52	27 13
28	25 59	26 22	26 43	27 05	27 26	27 48	28 09
29	26 57	27 19	27 40	28 01	28 22	28 44	29 05
♉	27 54	28 16	28 37	28 58	29 19	29 40	30 01
1	28 51	29 13	29 34	29 55	30 16	30 37	30 57
2	29 49	30 10	30 31	30 52	31 13	31 34	31 54
3	30 46	31 07	31 28	31 49	32 10	32 31	32 51
4	31 44	32 05	32 25	32 46	33 07	33 27	33 47
5	32 42	33 03	33 23	33 43	34 04	34 24	34 44
6	33 40	34 01	34 25	34 41	35 01	35 21	35 41
7	34 38	34 59	35 19	35 39	35 58	36 18	36 38
8	35 37	35 57	36 17	36 37	36 56	37 15	37 35
9	36 36	36 56	37 15	37 35	37 54	38 13	38 32

Southern Latitudes

	0	1	2	3	4	5	6
10	37°34′	37°54′	38°13′	38°33′	38°52′	39°11′	39°29′
11	38 33	38 53	39 12	39 31	39 50	40 09	40 27
12	39 33	39 52	40 11	40 30	40 48	41 07	41 25
13	40 32	40 51	41 10	41 28	41 46	42 05	42 23
14	41 31	41 50	42 09	42 27	42 45	43 03	43 21
15	42 31	42 50	43 08	43 26	43 44	44 02	44 19
16	43 31	43 49	44 07	44 25	44 43	45 00	45 17
17	44 31	44 49	45 06	45 24	45 42	45 59	46 15
18	45 31	45 49	46 06	46 23	46 41	46 58	47 14
19	46 32	46 49	47 06	47 23	47 40	47 57	48 13
20	47 32	47 49	48 06	48 23	48 39	48 56	49 12
21	48 33	48 50	49 06	49 23	49 39	49 55	50 11
22	49 34	49 50	50 06	50 23	50 38	50 54	51 10
23	50 35	50 51	51 06	51 23	51 38	51 53	52 09
24	51 36	51 52	52 07	52 23	52 38	52 53	53 08
25	52 38	52 53	53 08	53 24	53 38	53 53	54 08
26	53 40	53 55	54 09	54 24	54 38	54 53	55 07
27	54 42	54 56	55 11	55 25	55 39	55 53	56 07
28	55 44	55 58	56 12	56 26	56 40	56 54	57 07
29	56 46	57 00	57 13	57 27	57 41	57 54	58 07
♊	57 48	58 02	58 15	58 29	58 42	58 55	59 07
1	58 51	59 04	59 17	59 30	59 43	59 55	60 07
2	59 53	60 06	60 19	60 31	60 44	60 56	61 08
3	60 56	61 08	61 21	61 33	61 46	61 57	62 09
4	61 59	62 11	62 23	62 35	62 48	62 58	63 09
5	63 03	63 14	63 25	63 37	63 50	63 59	64 10
6	64 06	64 17	64 28	64 39	64 52	65 01	65 11
7	65 09	65 20	65 31	65 41	65 54	66 02	66 12
8	66 13	66 23	66 34	66 44	66 56	67 04	67 13
9	67 17	67 27	67 37	67 46	67 58	68 06	68 15
10	68 21	68 30	68 40	68 49	68 59	69 07	69 16
11	69 25	69 34	69 43	69 52	70 01	70 09	70 17
12	70 29	70 38	70 46	70 55	71 03	71 11	71 19
13	71 34	71 42	71 49	71 58	72 05	72 13	72 21
14	72 38	72 46	72 53	73 01	73 08	73 15	73 23
15	73 43	73 50	73 57	74 04	74 11	74 18	74 25
16	74 47	74 54	75 01	75 07	75 14	75 20	75 27
17	75 52	75 58	76 05	76 11	76 17	76 22	76 29
18	76 57	77 03	77 09	77 15	77 20	77 25	77 31
19	78 02	78 07	78 13	78 18	78 23	78 28	78 33

Southern Latitudes

	0	1	2	3	4	5	6
20	79°07′	79°12′	79°17′	79°21′	79°26′	79°31′	79°35′
21	80 12	80 17	80 21	80 25	80 29	80 34	80 38
22	81 17	81 21	81 25	81 28	81 32	81 36	81 40
23	82 22	82 25	82 29	82 32	82 35	82 39	82 42
24	83 28	83 30	83 33	83 36	83 39	83 42	83 45
25	84 33	84 35	84 37	84 40	84 42	84 45	84 47
26	85 38	85 40	85 41	85 44	85 45	85 48	85 49
27	86 44	86 45	86 46	86 48	86 49	86 51	86 52
28	87 49	87 50	87 50	87 52	87 52	87 54	87 54
29	88 55	88 55	88 55	88 56	88 56	88 57	88 57
♋	90 00	90 00	90 00	90 00	90 00	90 00	90 00
1	91 05	91 05	91 05	91 04	91 04	91 03	91 03
2	92 11	92 10	92 10	92 08	92 08	92 06	92 06
3	93 16	93 15	93 14	93 12	93 11	93 09	93 08
4	94 22	94 20	94 19	94 16	94 15	94 12	94 11
5	95 27	95 25	95 23	95 20	95 18	95 15	95 13
6	96 32	96 30	96 27	96 24	96 21	96 18	96 15
7	97 38	97 35	97 31	97 28	97 25	97 21	97 18
8	98 43	98 39	98 35	98 32	98 28	98 24	98 20
9	99 48	99 43	99 39	99 35	99 31	99 26	99 22
10	100 53	100 48	100 43	100 39	100 34	100 29	100 25
11	101 58	101 53	101 47	101 42	101 37	101 32	101 27
12	103 03	102 57	102 51	102 45	102 40	102 34	102 29
13	104 08	104 02	103 55	103 49	103 43	103 37	103 31
14	105 13	105 06	104 59	104 52	104 46	104 40	104 33
15	106 17	106 10	106 03	105 56	105 49	105 42	105 35
16	107 22	107 14	107 07	106 59	106 52	106 45	106 37
17	108 26	108 18	108 11	108 02	107 55	107 47	107 39
18	109 31	109 22	109 14	109 05	108 57	108 49	108 41
19	110 35	110 26	110 17	110 08	110 00	109 51	109 43
20	111 39	111 30	111 20	111 11	111 02	110 53	110 44
21	112 43	112 33	112 23	112 13	112 04	111 54	111 45
22	113 47	113 37	113 26	113 16	113 06	112 56	112 47
23	114 51	114 40	114 29	114 19	114 08	113 58	113 48
24	115 54	115 43	115 32	115 21	115 10	114 59	114 49
25	116 57	116 46	116 35	116 23	116 12	116 01	115 50
26	118 01	117 49	117 37	117 25	117 14	117 02	116 51
27	119 04	118 51	118 39	118 27	118 15	118 03	117 52
28	120 07	119 54	119 41	119 29	119 16	119 04	118 52
29	121 09	120 56	120 43	120 30	120 17	120 05	119 53

Southern Latitudes

	0	1	2	3	4	5	6
♌	122°12′	121°58′	121°45′	121°31′	121°18′	121°05′	120°53′
1	123 14	123 00	122 47	122 33	122 19	122 06	121 53
2	124 16	124 02	123 48	123 34	123 20	123 06	122 53
3	125 18	125 03	124 49	124 35	124 21	124 07	123 53
4	126 20	126 05	125 51	125 36	125 22	125 07	124 53
5	127 22	127 07	126 52	126 36	126 22	126 07	125 52
6	128 24	128 08	127 53	127 37	127 22	127 07	126 52
7	129 25	129 09	128 54	128 37	128 22	128 07	127 51
8	130 26	130 10	129 54	129 37	129 22	129 06	128 50
9	131 27	131 10	130 54	130 37	130 21	130 05	129 49
10	132 28	132 11	131 54	131 37	131 21	131 04	130 48
11	133 28	133 11	132 54	132 37	132 20	132 03	131 47
12	134 29	134 11	133 54	133 37	133 19	133 02	132 46
13	135 29	135 11	134 54	134 36	134 18	134 01	133 45
14	136 29	136 11	135 53	135 35	135 17	135 00	134 43
15	137 29	137 10	136 52	136 34	136 16	135 58	135 41
16	138 29	138 10	137 51	137 33	137 15	136 57	136 39
17	139 28	139 09	138 50	138 32	138 14	137 55	137 37
18	140 28	140 08	139 49	139 30	139 13	138 53	138 35
19	141 27	141 07	140 48	140 29	140 10	139 51	139 33
20	142 26	142 06	141 47	141 27	141 08	140 49	140 31
21	143 25	143 04	142 45	142 25	142 06	141 47	141 28
22	144 23	144 03	143 43	143 23	143 04	142 45	142 25
23	145 22	145 01	144 41	144 21	144 02	143 42	143 22
24	146 20	145 59	145 39	145 19	144 59	144 39	144 19
25	147 18	146 57	146 37	146 17	145 56	145 36	145 16
26	148 16	147 55	147 35	147 14	146 53	146 33	146 13
27	149 14	148 53	148 32	148 11	147 50	147 29	147 09
28	150 11	149 50	149 29	149 08	148 47	148 26	148 06
29	151 09	150 47	150 26	150 05	149 44	149 23	149 03
♍	152 06	151 44	151 23	151 02	150 41	150 20	149 59
1	153 04	152 41	152 20	151 59	151 38	151 16	150 55
2	154 01	153 38	153 17	152 55	152 34	152 12	151 51
3	154 58	154 35	154 13	153 51	153 30	153 08	152 47
4	155 54	155 32	155 10	154 58	154 26	154 04	153 43
5	156 51	156 29	156 07	155 54	155 22	155 00	154 39
6	157 48	157 25	157 03	156 40	156 18	155 56	155 34
7	158 44	158 22	157 59	157 36	157 14	156 52	156 30
8	159 40	159 18	158 55	158 32	158 10	157 48	157 26
9	160 37	160 14	159 51	159 28	159 06	158 43	158 21

Southern Latitudes

	0	1	2	3	4	5	6
10	161°33′	161°10′	160°47′	160°24′	160°02′	159°39′	159°17′
11	162 29	162 06	161 43	161 20	160 58	160 35	160 12
12	163 25	163 02	162 39	162 16	161 53	161 30	161 07
13	164 20	163 58	163 35	163 12	162 49	162 25	162 02
14	165 16	164 53	164 30	164 07	163 44	163 20	162 57
15	166 12	165 48	165 25	165 02	164 39	164 15	163 52
16	167 07	166 44	166 21	165 57	165 34	165 10	164 47
17	168 03	167 40	167 17	166 52	166 29	166 05	165 42
18	168 58	168 35	168 12	167 47	167 24	167 00	166 37
19	169 54	169 31	169 07	168 43	168 19	167 55	167 32
20	170 49	170 26	170 02	169 38	169 14	168 50	168 27
21	171 44	171 21	170 57	170 33	170 09	169 45	169 22
22	172 39	172 16	171 52	171 28	171 04	170 40	170 17
23	173 35	173 11	172 47	172 23	171 59	171 35	171 12
24	174 30	174 06	173 42	173 18	172 54	172 30	172 07
25	175 25	175 02	174 38	174 14	173 50	173 26	173 02
26	176 20	175 57	175 33	175 09	174 45	174 21	173 57
27	177 15	176 52	176 28	176 04	175 40	175 16	174 52
28	178 10	177 47	177 23	176 59	176 35	175 11	175 47
29	179 05	178 42	178 18	177 54	177 30	177 06	176 42
♎	180 00	179 37	179 13	178 49	178 25	178 01	177 37
1	180 55	180 32	180 08	179 44	179 20	178 56	178 32
2	181 50	181 27	181 03	180 39	180 15	179 51	179 27
3	182 45	182 22	181 58	181 34	181 10	180 46	180 22
4	183 40	183 17	182 53	182 29	182 05	181 41	181 17
5	184 35	184 12	183 48	183 24	183 00	182 36	182 12
6	185 30	185 07	184 43	184 19	183 55	183 31	183 07
7	186 25	186 02	185 38	185 14	184 50	184 26	184 02
8	187 21	186 57	186 33	186 09	185 45	185 21	184 57
9	188 16	187 52	187 28	187 04	186 40	186 16	185 52
10	189 11	188 47	188 23	187 59	187 35	187 11	186 47
11	190 06	189 42	189 11	188 55	188 31	188 07	187 43
12	191 02	190 38	190 14	189 51	189 27	189 03	188 39
13	191 57	191 33	191 09	190 46	190 22	189 58	189 34
14	192 53	192 29	192 05	191 42	191 18	190 54	190 30
15	193 48	193 25	193 01	192 38	192 14	191 50	191 26
16	194 44	194 20	193 57	193 34	193 10	192 46	192 22
17	195 40	195 16	194 53	194 30	194 06	193 42	193 18
18	196 35	196 12	195 49	195 26	195 02	194 39	194 15
19	197 31	197 08	196 45	196 22	195 58	195 35	195 11

Southern Latitudes

	0	1	2	3	4	5	6
20	198°27′	198°04′	197°41′	197°18′	196°54′	196°31′	196°07′
21	199 23	199 00	198 37	198 14	197 51	197 28	197 04
22	200 20	199 56	199 33	199 11	198 48	198 25	198 01
23	201 16	200 53	200 30	200 08	199 45	199 22	198 58
24	202 12	201 50	201 27	201 05	200 42	200 19	199 55
25	203 09	202 47	202 24	202 02	201 39	201 16	200 52
26	204 06	203 44	203 21	202 59	202 36	202 13	201 50
27	205 02	204 41	204 19	203 57	203 34	203 11	202 48
28	205 59	205 38	205 16	204 54	204 31	204 09	203 46
29	206 57	206 35	206 13	205 51	205 29	205 07	204 44
♏	207 54	207 33	207 11	206 49	206 27	206 05	205 42
1	208 51	208 30	208 08	207 47	207 25	207 03	206 40
2	209 49	209 27	209 06	208 45	208 23	208 01	207 38
3	210 46	210 25	210 04	209 43	209 21	208 59	208 37
4	211 44	211 23	211 02	210 41	210 18	209 58	209 36
5	212 42	212 21	212 00	211 39	211 19	210 57	210 35
6	213 40	213 20	212 59	212 38	212 17	211 56	211 34
7	214 38	214 18	213 58	213 37	213 16	212 55	212 33
8	215 37	215 17	214 57	214 36	214 15	213 54	213 33
9	216 36	216 16	215 56	215 36	215 15	214 54	214 33
10	217 34	217 15	216 55	216 35	216 15	215 54	215 33
11	218 33	218 14	217 55	217 35	217 15	216 54	216 33
12	219 33	219 14	218 54	218 35	218 15	217 55	217 34
13	220 32	220 13	219 54	219 35	219 15	218 56	218 35
14	221 31	221 13	220 54	220 35	220 16	219 57	219 36
15	222 31	222 13	221 54	221 36	221 17	220 58	220 38
16	223 31	223 13	222 54	222 36	222 18	221 59	221 39
17	224 31	224 13	223 55	223 37	223 19	223 00	222 40
18	225 31	225 14	224 56	224 38	224 20	224 01	223 42
19	226 32	226 14	225 57	225 39	225 21	225 03	224 44
20	227 32	227 15	226 58	226 40	226 23	226 05	225 46
21	228 33	228 16	227 59	227 42	227 25	227 07	226 49
22	229 34	229 17	229 00	228 44	228 27	228 09	227 52
23	230 35	230 18	230 02	229 46	229 29	229 12	228 55
24	231 36	231 20	231 04	230 48	230 32	230 15	229 58
25	232 38	232 22	232 06	231 51	231 35	231 18	231 02
26	233 40	233 24	233 09	232 54	232 38	232 22	232 06
27	234 42	234 27	234 12	233 57	233 42	233 26	233 10
28	235 44	235 29	235 15	235 00	234 45	234 30	234 14
29	236 46	236 32	236 18	236 03	235 49	235 34	235 18

Southern Latitudes

	0	1	2	3	4	5	6
♐	237°48′	237°35′	237°21′	237°07′	236°53′	236°38′	236°23′
1	238 51	238 38	238 24	238 10	237 57	237 42	237 28
2	239 53	239 41	239 28	239 14	239 01	238 47	238 33
3	240 56	240 44	240 31	240 18	240 05	239 52	239 38
4	241 59	241 47	241 35	241 22	241 10	240 57	240 44
5	243 03	242 51	242 39	242 27	242 15	242 02	241 50
6	244 06	243 55	243 43	243 32	243 20	243 08	242 56
7	245 09	244 59	244 47	244 37	244 25	244 13	244 02
8	246 13	246 03	245 52	245 42	245 30	245 19	245 08
9	247 17	247 07	246 57	246 47	246 36	246 25	246 14
10	248 21	248 11	248 02	247 52	247 42	247 31	247 21
11	249 25	249 16	249 07	248 57	248 48	248 38	248 28
12	250 29	250 21	250 12	250 03	249 54	249 45	249 35
13	251 34	251 26	251 17	251 09	251 00	250 51	250 42
14	252 38	252 31	252 22	252 15	252 06	251 58	251 49
15	253 43	253 36	253 28	253 21	253 13	253 05	252 57
16	254 47	254 41	254 33	254 27	254 19	254 12	254 04
17	255 52	255 46	255 39	255 33	255 26	255 19	255 12
18	256 57	256 51	256 45	256 39	256 33	256 27	256 20
19	258 02	257 56	257 51	257 45	257 40	257 34	257 28
20	259 07	259 02	258 57	258 52	258 47	258 41	258 36
21	260 12	260 08	260 03	259 59	259 54	259 49	259 44
22	261 17	261 13	261 09	261 05	261 01	260 56	260 52
23	262 22	262 18	262 15	262 11	262 08	262 04	262 00
24	263 28	263 24	263 21	263 18	263 15	263 12	263 09
25	264 33	264 30	264 27	264 25	264 22	264 20	264 17
26	265 38	265 36	265 33	265 32	265 29	265 28	265 26
27	266 44	266 42	266 40	266 39	266 37	266 36	266 34
28	267 49	267 48	267 46	267 46	267 44	267 44	267 43
29	268 55	268 54	268 53	268 53	268 52	268 52	268 52
♑	270 00	270 00	270 00	270 00	270 00	270 00	270 00
1	271 05	271 06	271 07	271 07	271 08	271 08	271 09
2	272 11	272 12	272 14	272 14	272 16	272 16	272 18
3	273 16	273 18	273 20	273 21	273 23	273 24	273 26
4	274 22	274 24	274 26	274 28	274 31	274 32	274 34
5	275 27	275 30	275 33	275 35	275 38	275 40	275 43
6	276 32	276 36	276 39	276 42	276 45	276 48	276 51
7	277 38	277 41	277 45	277 50	277 52	277 56	278 00
8	278 43	278 47	278 51	278 55	278 59	279 04	279 08
9	279 48	279 52	279 57	280 01	280 06	280 11	280 16

Southern Latitudes

	0	1	2	3	4	5	6
10	280°53′	280°58′	281°03′	281°08′	281°13′	281°19′	281°24′
11	281 58	282 04	282 09	282 15	282 20	282 26	282 32
12	283 03	283 09	283 15	283 21	283 27	283 33	283 40
13	284 08	284 14	284 21	284 27	284 34	284 41	284 48
14	285 13	285 19	285 27	285 33	285 41	285 48	285 56
15	286 17	286 24	286 32	286 39	286 47	286 55	287 03
16	287 22	287 29	287 38	287 45	287 54	288 02	288 11
17	288 26	288 34	288 43	288 51	289 00	289 09	289 18
18	289 31	289 39	289 48	289 57	290 06	290 15	290 25
19	290 35	290 44	290 53	291 03	291 12	291 22	291 32
20	291 39	291 49	291 58	292 08	292 18	292 29	292 39
21	292 43	292 53	293 03	293 13	293 24	293 35	293 46
22	293 47	293 57	294 08	294 18	294 30	294 41	294 52
23	294 51	295 01	295 13	295 23	295 35	295 47	295 58
24	295 54	296 05	296 17	296 28	296 40	296 53	297 04
25	296 57	297 09	297 21	297 33	297 45	297 58	298 10
26	298 01	298 13	298 25	298 38	298 50	299 03	299 16
27	299 04	299 16	299 29	299 41	299 55	300 08	300 22
28	300 07	300 19	300 33	300 46	300 59	301 13	301 27
29	301 09	301 22	301 36	301 50	302 03	302 18	302 32
♒	302 12	302 25	302 39	302 53	303 07	303 22	303 37
1	303 14	303 28	303 42	303 57	304 11	304 26	304 42
2	304 16	304 31	304 45	305 00	305 15	305 30	305 46
3	305 18	305 33	305 48	306 03	306 18	306 34	306 50
4	306 20	306 36	306 51	307 06	307 22	307 38	307 54
5	307 22	307 38	307 54	308 09	308 25	308 42	308 58
6	308 24	308 40	308 56	309 12	309 28	309 44	310 02
7	309 25	309 42	309 58	310 14	310 31	310 48	311 05
8	310 26	310 43	311 00	311 16	311 38	311 51	312 08
9	311 27	311 44	312 01	312 18	312 35	312 53	313 11
10	312 28	312 45	313 02	313 20	313 37	313 55	314 14
11	313 28	313 46	314 03	314 21	314 39	314 57	315 16
12	314 29	314 46	315 04	315 22	315 40	315 59	316 18
13	315 29	315 47	316 05	316 23	316 41	317 00	317 20
14	316 29	316 47	317 06	317 24	317 42	318 01	318 21
15	317 29	317 47	318 06	318 24	318 43	319 02	319 22
16	318 29	318 47	319 06	319 25	319 44	320 03	320 24
17	319 28	319 47	320 06	320 25	320 45	321 04	321 25
18	320 27	320 46	321 06	321 25	321 45	322 05	322 26
19	321 27	321 46	322 06	322 25	322 45	323 06	323 27

Southern Latitudes

	0	1	2	3	4	5	6
20	322°26′	322°45′	323°05′	323°25′	323°45′	324°06′	324°27′
21	323 25	323 44	324 04	324 24	324 45	325 06	325 27
22	324 23	324 43	325 03	325 24	325 45	326 06	326 27
23	325 22	325 42	326 02	326 23	326 44	327 05	327 27
24	326 20	326 40	327 01	327 22	327 43	328 04	328 26
25	327 18	327 39	328 00	328 21	328 42	329 03	329 25
26	328 16	328 37	328 58	329 19	329 41	330 02	330 24
27	329 14	329 35	329 56	330 17	330 39	331 01	331 23
28	330 11	330 33	330 54	331 15	331 37	331 59	332 22
29	331 09	331 30	331 52	332 13	332 35	332 57	333 20
♓	332 06	332 28	332 49	333 11	333 33	333 55	334 18
1	333 04	333 25	333 47	334 09	334 31	334 53	335 16
2	334 01	334 22	334 44	335 06	335 29	335 51	336 14
3	334 58	335 19	335 41	336 03	336 26	336 49	337 12
4	335 55	336 16	336 39	337 01	337 24	337 47	338 10
5	336 51	337 13	337 36	337 58	338 21	338 44	339 08
6	337 48	338 10	338 33	338 55	339 18	339 41	340 05
7	338 44	339 07	339 30	339 52	340 15	340 38	341 02
8	339 40	340 04	340 27	340 49	341 12	341 35	351 59
9	340 37	341 00	341 23	341 46	342 09	342 32	342 56
10	341 33	341 56	342 19	342 42	343 06	343 29	343 53
11	342 29	342 52	343 15	343 38	344 02	344 25	344 49
12	343 25	343 48	344 11	344 34	344 58	345 21	345 45
13	344 20	344 44	345 07	345 30	345 54	346 18	346 42
14	345 16	345 40	346 03	346 26	346 50	347 14	347 38
15	346 12	346 35	346 59	347 22	347 46	348 10	348 34
16	347 07	347 31	347 55	348 18	348 42	349 06	349 30
17	348 03	348 27	348 51	349 14	349 38	350 02	350 26
18	348 58	349 22	349 46	350 09	350 33	350 57	351 21
19	349 54	350 18	350 42	351 05	351 29	351 53	352 17
20	350 49	351 13	351 37	352 01	352 25	352 49	353 13
21	351 44	352 08	352 32	352 56	353 20	353 44	354 08
22	352 39	353 03	353 27	353 51	354 15	354 39	355 03
23	353 35	353 58	354 22	354 46	355 10	355 34	355 58
24	354 30	354 53	355 17	355 41	356 05	356 29	356 53
25	355 25	355 48	356 12	356 36	357 00	357 24	357 48
26	356 20	356 43	357 07	357 31	357 55	358 19	358 43
27	357 15	357 38	358 02	358 26	358 50	359 14	359 38
28	358 10	358 33	358 57	359 21	359 45	360 09	360 33
29	359 05	359 28	359 52	360 16	360 40	361 04	361 28

Parallels:
Their Hidden Meaning

Dedication

To John McCormick, who masks his great erudition under a wickedly and delightfully witty exterior, and who is a true and generous-hearted friend. His incisive mind has dispelled much of the mists that befog so much of astrology.

Preface

There are three major ways in which planets in a horoscope are related to each other. This is vitally important since such relationships are the major source of the meaning of such a chart. They are related by aspects, including those minor aspects now termed harmonics, that are widely used by nearly all astrologers. Over the past sixty years, and mainly due to the genius of Alfred Witte, it has been increasingly recognized that planetary pictures, based on midpoints and hard aspects to them, are also an essential form of relationship. During previous centuries the Arabic Parts, based on the same principle, were also employed by many astrologers. The third mode of relationship is not new and yet is not nearly as much used as it ought to be in modern times. I refer to parallels of declination.

Fairly frequently a chart is dominated by some major configuration, and at times by more than one. Failure to recognize such a configuration results in failure to interpret that chart correctly. The major configuration may be of three types. A grand cross, grand trine or similar transversal and aspectual combination is a well-known type that is widely recognized. A second type is a major planetary picture, so that if one knows nothing about midpoints one may completely miss the boat with certain horoscopes where there is no apparent dominant combination in longitude and declination. The third type is based on a powerful configuration in declination. I shall cite cases where a failure to examine the parallels and contraparallels would have resulted in a failure to find the main meaning of that horoscope. Currently the most neglected one of the three types is the last, since sophisticated modern astrologers do recognize planetary pictures.

But the importance of parallels is by no means limited to the reading of radical charts. They are important in both the theory of transits and in progressions and directions. Powerful parallels or contraparallels that explain the inexplicable may occur due to slow-moving outer major planets. I have studied such transits in declination for thirty years and found them to be essential. The area where the role of declination is least understood is in progressions and directions. There is some recognition of parallels in secondary and other forms (minor and tertiary) of progression, but none at all in the realm of directions. Nor am I referring to rapt parallels. Just as one may direct bodies by solar, Ascendant and vertical arc in longitude, so may one also move them via those three arcs in declination. It ought also to be noted that during recent years Reinhold Ebertin and Roger Hutcheon have found that transiting midpoints in declination are quite effective.

In Dr. Dean's *Recent Advances in Natal Astrology* he cites about 100 sources on opinions as to the validity of parallels in the natal chart. Seventy percent either had no opinion or no interpretation. Twenty percent considered them to be unimportant or inoperative. Only ten percent considered them important. He notes that in timing via transits, progressions and directions, they are more generally thought to be important by such astrologers as Brahy, Carter, DeLuce, Ebertin, Lilly, and Ptolemy. I maintain that if they are dynamically vital then they ought to be equally so statistically, i.e. in any radical horoscope. In the last part of this book I explain the method of directing bodies via declination arcs.

Most astrologers are agreed that the most potent aspects are the conjunctions and oppositions. In many instances, but not in all, planets that are in conjunction are also in parallel. Just as frequently bodies in opposition are in contraparallel. This may well account for the extra wight given to conjunctions and oppositions. While parallel is due to the same, or nearly the same, declination of two bodies, both being north or both being south, a contraparallel finds them the same distance in declination from the equator, or nearly the same, one north and the other south.

There is a difference of opinion about contraparallels with some astrologers not finding them different from parallels (Carter, Davison, Hutcheon, and Sepharial). Other astrologers share our views that they do differ (T.P. Davis, Mayo, and Watters). When I say "our," I refer to my wife and her thirty years of experience, and my research collaborator Eleanor Hesseltine. Our views about the differences between parallels (Z) and contraparallels (X) are also based on thousands of cases of transits, declination arc directions, and secondary progressions, which we surmise not to be the case for the most part for those who have the other viewpoint.

I believe it is essential to cite the views of those astrologers whose reputations are such that we must respect them, however we might differ with them. Thus, Carl Payne Tobey rejects parallels completely and has a superb reputation as a research astrologer. In his later years he became convinced that all that was not ecliptical was invalid, causing him to reject the Midheaven, too! I believe that in this case he allowed a theory to affect his judgment. I feel that many of the disagreements that do exist about the validity of parallels, and contraparallels being different, are due in most cases to the failure to test this valuable branch of astrology. Frankly I find this to be really shocking. It is the purpose of this book to fill in this glaring gap. The only other book on the subject is by the late esteemed L. Furze-Morrish of Australia. L. Furze-Morrish was not sure whether contraparallels differed from parallels.

This book is not a "cookbook," where every possible combination is interpreted. While such books are very popular they have the demerit of oversimplification. If Mars square Saturn is to be interpreted, there are the following possible modifying factors: 1) what signs are involved; 2) what houses are involved; 3) are any other bodies making strong and major aspects to Mars or Saturn or to both of them; 4) how does the square integrate into the whole pattern of the chart, or fail to do so, etc. I shall illustrate my points from actual cases and often will not give the whole chart in order to protect the identity of the individual.

After giving a few cases that illustrate how crucial declination can be in some horoscopes, I will describe the three kinds of parallels. This will lead on naturally into the knotty issue of orbs, which is almost totally misunderstood. For the orbs are not fixed, but operate on a sliding scale. Tables will be given to simplify the application of this. I will cite some cases where two bodies are in both a trine and a contraparallel in order to show how this ought to be interpreted. The matter of transits, progressions, and directions will then follow.

These are my main contentions: Parallels are of major importance in horoscopy. Contraparallels are different in nature from parallels. Some charts cannot be interpreted in their main thrust if declination is omitted. Declination is just as vital dynamically (transits, progressions, etc.) as statistically.

Note: Almost forty years ago Carl Payne Tobey did a statistical study of stock prices and planetary values for a Wall Street firm. One of the meaningful factors was that stock prices rose when Mars had a higher declination than Jupiter and/or Saturn. Carl has apparently forgotten this statistically significant result, but I have always been so impressed by his research that I have not!

Some astrologers have suggested that bodies in very high declination have special significance; that may be so but has not been proven. I do surmise that bodies in very low declination are weaker than other values. The Sun at twenty-seven degrees Pisces is conjunct its own place at two degrees Aries, but is also contraparallel it. So, low declinations are of limited strength.

Recommended books are *Planetary Pictures in Declination* by Roger Hutcheon and *Parallels of Declination* by L. Furze-Morrish.

1

Parallels: The Key

The natal horoscope of Walt Disney is an excellent example of the importance of declinations. Figure 1 shows it without declinations and with Campanus houses. He was born at 12:30 a.m. Central Standard Time, Chicago, Illinois, 87W37, 41N42 (geocentric, which is used throughout this book) on December 5, 1901.

Pluto was not discovered until about twenty-eight years later; so, if it is omitted, the sole body above the horizon is Neptune in the tenth house, which is descriptive of what he was known for, i.e. fantasy via film. Actually, the other universal body of the collective unconscious, Pluto, is also elevated since it is in the ninth house and opposite the Sun. He had a tremendous and worldwide impact on hundreds of millions of people. Can it be said that this pattern is sufficiently unique to account for this? I should say not!

The lunar eclipse one year before his birth on December 4 was in opposition to both his Sun and Uranus within a three degree limiting orb. And a little over four days after his birth, there was a cazimi alignment of Uranus with the Sun, a kind of an eclipse so that his Uranus is exceptionally powerful in this chart. As Witte noted, the cardinal points relate people to the world at large, which was especially true of Disney as his Neptune is at 0 Cancer 33. Yet many others were born with this, too.

The bodies in his chart from the Sun to Venus, except for Mars, are a stellium in declination as they are all parallel to each other. And that elevated Neptune is contraparallel to all of them, which creates a Fanhandle in declination with all the great potential of the stellium pouring out through that Neptune. Their declinations are: Neptune, +22°15′; Sun, -22°18′; Saturn, -22°26′; Jupiter, -22°48′; Venus, -22°49′; and Uranus, -22°51′. Mars at -24°15′ is not a part of that stellium in declination. It is, however, widely opposed to Neptune in longitude so may be thought of as part of this extraordinary configuration. And the close square of Mars to the Moon is vital in integrating the Moon into the pattern. Only Mercury is completely outside the whole as Pluto does oppose both the Sun and Uranus in longitude. I defy anyone to have forecasted Disney's uniqueness and impact on the world if this remarkable configuration in declination were overlooked. Of course, he also had Mercury/Venus (midpoint at 28 Sagittarius 34) = Sun/Jupiter (midpoint at 28 Sagittarius 57), which was a fortunate planetary picture for him.

Figure 2 is the chart of a man whose career was his main interest. Yet it has only four aspects to the Midheaven, the point of career, and none of them is a major aspect. Pluto is nine minutes from a sesquiquadrate to his Midheaven, Venus is semisquare the Midheaven, Neptune is 1°48′ from a quincunx to the Midheaven, and Mercury is quintile (72°) the Midheaven. This is hardly enough to account for the crucial importance to him of his career interests in the investment field and as chairman of the board of directors of a small railroad. It also is true that his Mercury is only eleven minutes from quintile his Midheaven. His Midheaven has a declination of -18°44′.

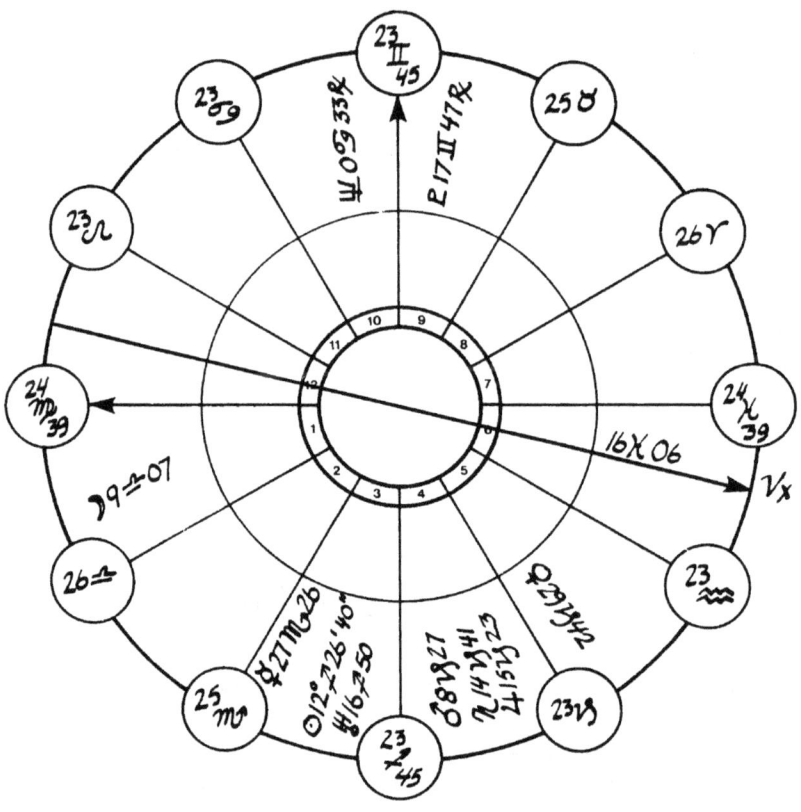

Figure 1
Walt Disney
December 5, 1901, 12:30 AM CST, Chicago, Illinois
Campanus Houses

The relevant bodies, which are parallel the Midheaven, are: Sun, -17°14′; Saturn, -17°39′; Moon, -18°31′; and Mercury, -19°38′. Therefore, he has both lights in parallel to his Midheaven plus Mercury and Saturn. According to the system of orbs I will describe later, the Sun-Saturn-Moon-Midheaven are all parallel each other with Mercury parallel the Moon and Midheaven only. This, too, is a kind of stellium.

Saturn is in the tenth house of career, indicative of the heavy responsibilities he carried in business. The Moon at the cusp of his eighth house refers to the many investors whose money he dealt with. The Sun and Mercury are late in the sixth house. He rendered a service to investors. One expression a sixth house Sun can take is that some subordinates (sixth house) of the native are men who have authority (Sun); in this case, the president of the railroad, who was under him. Actually the Moon and Mercury are also in contraparallel to the Ascendant at 28 Taurus 10, and Mercury opposes it in longitude, thus making them both quite important. As the Moon governs the sign Cancer in his second

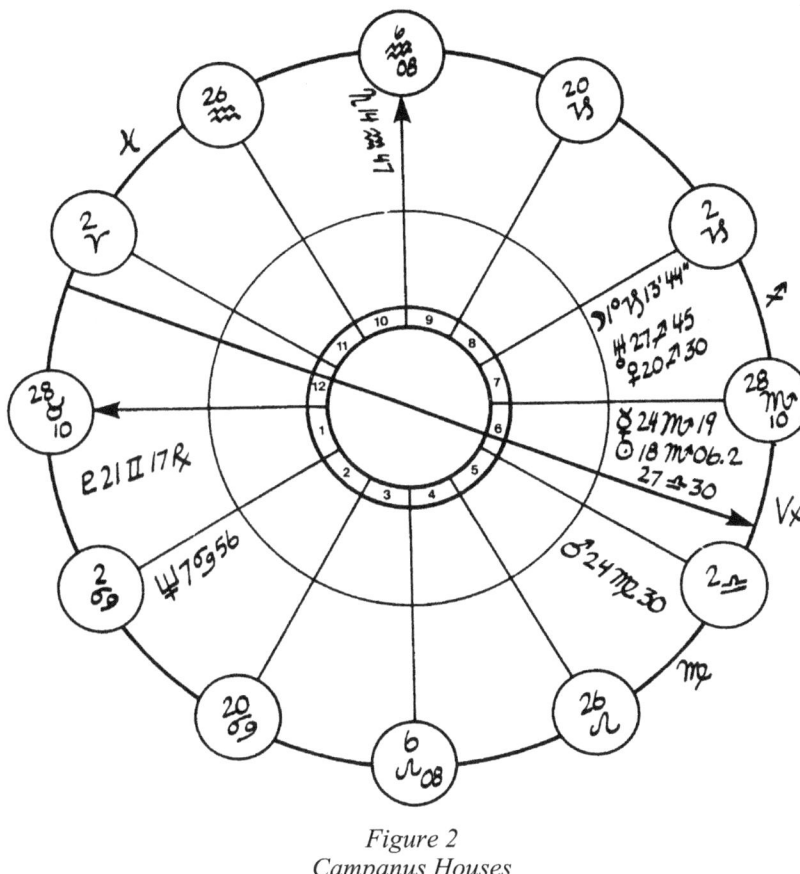

Figure 2
Campanus Houses

house and is at the cusp of his eighth house, finances, including the assets of others, were of major importance in his life. And the closeness of the Moon to zero degrees Capricorn was another augury of its vital place in his life in dealing with his investor-clients.

Figure 3 is the horoscope of a man. The major configuration in this chart is the opposition of the conjunction of Jupiter and Pluto in Cancer to Saturn in Capricorn with a square to Uranus in Aries making a T-cross. It is also true that this is a planetary picture: Saturn/Uranus = Pluto/Jupiter since the midpoint of Saturn and Uranus is 5 Pisces 24 in sesquiquadrate to the midpoint of Pluto and Jupiter at 20 Cancer 15 within nine minutes. Thus, this is a very powerful combination.

However, in order to have a potent effect on anyone born in that period it must be linked with one or more of the lights and angles. There is no major linkage of his three angles to his chart except for the Mars conjunct Neptune trine to the Midheaven, although the angles correlate to the cardinals. His eleventh house Moon in Aquarius has a beautiful trine to his Gemini Sun in the third house. And he has had many long-lasting friendships with women. The Saturn to Pluto-Jupiter opposition is partially resolved due to the trine to the Saturn end from the second house conjunction in Taurus of the Venus-Mercury conjunction which also sextiles Pluto and Jupiter. If parallels are not used, the Sun-Moon trine has little relationship to the rest of the chart, although the Moon is semisquare the Ascendant and Midheaven within about four degrees. This is a lesser aspect, although it fits with the importance to him of friendships in relating to the world at large—cardinals and angles. His employment was for some time in a service capacity—Mars conjunct Neptune, co-rulers of the Ascendant, trine the Midheaven from the sixth house. He also has done a great deal of writing—Gemini Sun in the third.

Suffice it to say that the Sun is parallel both Pluto and Jupiter, that Saturn is parallel the Moon, and that Sun-Pluto-Jupiter are contraparallel Moon-Saturn. Thus there are four parallels and six

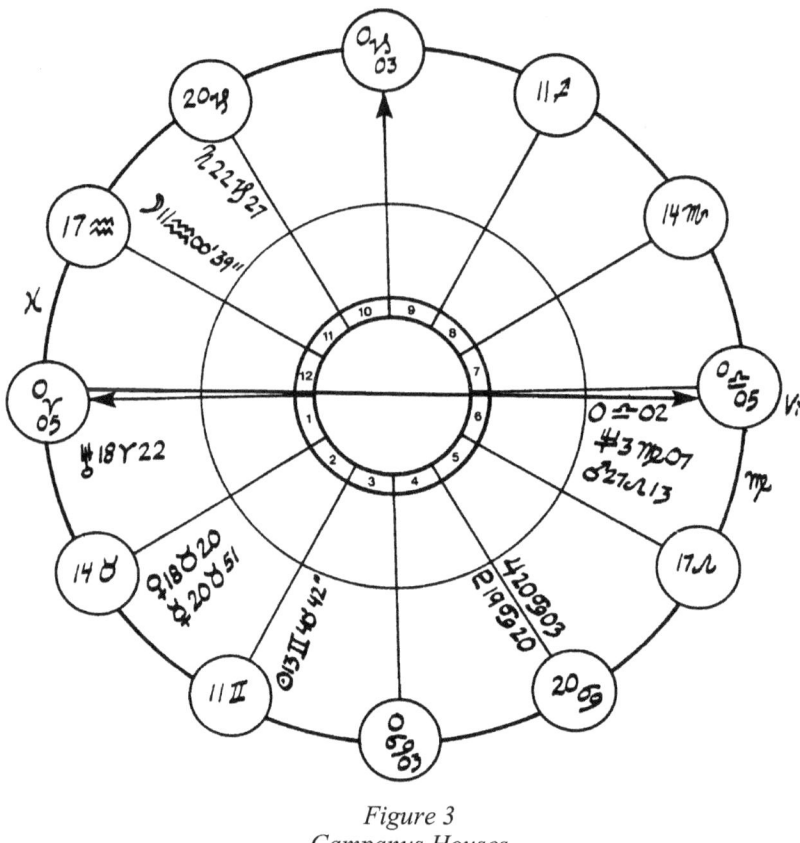

Figure 3
Campanus Houses

contraparallels versus only one conjunction, two oppositions, and one trine. His older and athletic brother (Sun in the third house) was the apple of his mother's eye (Pluto parallel Sun with Pluto being the main planet of the mother and of psychological ties). The sibling rivalry had a traumatic effect on him. The Pluto-Sun was also indicative of a stronger attachment to his mother than to his father (Saturn contraparallel Sun).

Saturn-Moon conjunctions and parallels, among other things, signify in a man's chart, his search for a strong woman—especially true here due to their eleventh house placement. This also is linked with friendships with older women. Indeed, the opposition and contraparallel of Pluto-Jupiter to Saturn is at the cusp of his fifth and eleventh houses (Campanus) which gives that powerful combination a strong emotional meaning. In addition, Saturn and Pluto are the main planets of security (father-mother images and archetypes). Strong configurations of these two planets with the lights always underscore security and the need for more of it.

Underlying the Moon trine Sun is the contraparallel, so that in closer relationships with women there have been problems not at all indicated by the trine. This is one excellent example of the hidden meanings of parallels. Saturn is dominant through being the most elevated body, in its own sign and at its South Node. Pluto is at its North Node so that the Saturn-Pluto opposition has an unusually fated character.

It would be a basic misinterpretation of this horoscope to omit its parallels and contraparallels. I know the native well enough to be sure of this. In Disney's chart the main effects of declination were interplanetary. In the second one the main effects were on the Midheaven. In this case the main effects are on the lights so that the three cases illustrate the various ways in which the effects of declination can be dominant in a horoscope.

2

Types of Parallels

There is more than one type of parallel and contraparallel of declination. There are three kinds which are illustrated in Diagram A. The straight line at the bottom represents the plane of the Earth's equator. The curved line is the ecliptic, cutting the equator at the left at zero degrees Aries and the right at zero degrees Libra. The angle between the two lines is about 23°27'. Therefore, the perpendicular line from the middle of the curved line (zero degrees Cancer) to the equator has a value of +23°27' declination because at zero degrees Cancer the ecliptic (and Sun) has its maximum declination north of the equator. Any line drawn parallel to the equator is then a parallel of declination.

The letter P stands for some planet which is slightly north of the ecliptic, say 1°14', as was the case with Mars on October 1, 1949 at the birth of Mao's China. Its longitude was about 15 Leo 00 and its declination was +17°31'. The obliquity of the ecliptic was then about 23°26'. It decreases about one minute every two years. Any body, B, having the same, or nearly the same, declination as Mars would then be bodily parallel to Mars—actually a B parallel. We have postulated a body, B, at an ecliptic position J as the graph shows. This is the best known and the most potent of the three types of parallel. B need not have exactly the same declination as P; we shall examine this question of orbs very soon. Note that the parallel of declination at +17°31' not only has P and B on it, but also cuts the ecliptic at the points F and G. They are the ecliptic equivalents to this declination. Were the Sun, Midheaven, Ascendant, or Vertex (none of which have celestial latitude) at either of these two points—F is at 10 Leo 51 and G is at 19 Taurus 09—they would be in exact parallel to P. How then are the positions of these ecliptic equivalent of +17°31' found? When the Sun had that declination in that year (1949) it had these two values. Note that the sum of 19°09' and 10°51' equals 30°; it always does. Therefore, by finding one of them it is easy to find the other one, i.e. 30° - 19°09'N = 10°51'. In addition, memorize this:

Aries is parallel Virgo and contraprallel Pisces.
Taurus is parallel Leo and contraparallel Aquarius.
Gemini is parallel Cancer and contraparallel Capricorn.

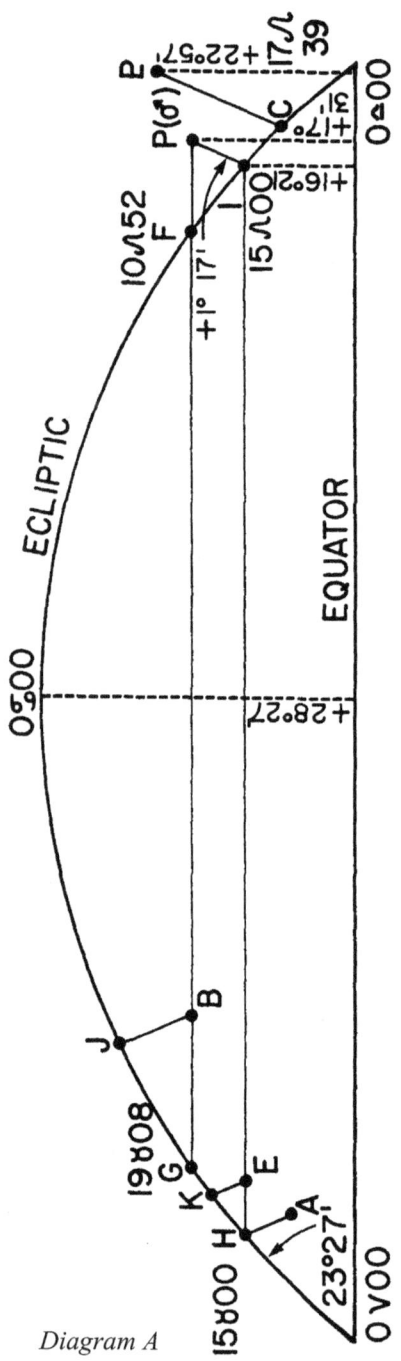

Diagram A

Cancer is parallel Gemini and contraparallel Sagittarius.
Leo is parallel Taurus and contraparallel Scorpio.
Virgo is parallel Aries and contraparallel Libra.

Therefore, as the 19°09' is in Taurus the 10°51' must be in Leo. Finding these ecliptic equivalents is the key to the orbs of parallels.

Planets act not only through their bodily place but also via their ecliptic intercepts. All that needs to be done is to drop a perpendicular line from P to the ecliptic at I to find the intercept. To a large extent, astrologers use these intercepts rather than the body of the planet or Moon. A dotted line is drawn through I, a second parallel of declination, which in this case is the declination of the planet's ecliptic intercept I and not its bodily declination. What, then, is the declination of 15 Leo 00? One finds the declination of the Sun (in 1949) when it is at 15 Leo 00 from Table II. It has a declination of -16°21'. It not only intersects the ecliptic at I, but this second parallel of declination also intersects it at H as noted on Diagram A. What is then said is that H and I are in exact parallel.

In addition, a planet bodily at A, whose ecliptic intercept is at H, is in antiscion parallel (an A parallel) to P. This is more indirect and less powerful. This second type of parallel has been known to astrologers since at least the time of Ptolemy. It is also based on the symmetry principle which is at the base of midpoint theory. H and I are equidistant from zero degrees Cancer—in this case just 45° on either side of it. A body at 15 Taurus 00 is antiscion P; a body at 15 Scorpio 00 is what I term contrascion P.

On October 1, 1949 when Mars was at 15 Leo 00, Venus was at 19 Scorpio 39 and thus within the maximum orb of plus or minus five degrees which is allowable for an antiscion or a contrascion. Venus' declination was -19°07' so that its ecliptic equivalents were at 25 Scorpio 23 and 4 Aquarius 37. But 4 Aquarius 37 is too far from an opposition to Mars' ecliptic equivalent of 10 Leo 51 to fall within a bodily contraparallel if an orb of five degrees is used.

Note what has been done. The ecliptic equivalents of both Venus and Mars have been found and in so doing their declinations have been converted into longitudinal equivalents so that their orb can be measured from an opposition in the conventional manner. This is how declination orbs are measured, for they are not fixed but are variable in value. Venus is contrascion Mars but is not contraparallel (B type) it, the contrascion being not as strong. They happen, in addition, to be in square (orb of 4°39′) so that this is a far more powerful square than it seems to be.

A body at C would be conjunct P. In this example, Pluto at 17 Leo 39 is at C, only 2°39′ from a conjunction to Mars. However, it has a high declination of +22°57′ so that it is not in any kind of parallel to Mars. Only their respective ecliptic intercepts are in conjunction. This makes this conjunction less strong than one that combines both a parallel and a conjunction. Finally, a planet can be imagined at E on the HI parallel of declination line, its EI being at K, which would then be in a third kind of parallel to P. This is termed an ecliptic or E parallel. In an E parallel, the second body is bodily parallel to the ecliptic intercept of P. In an A parallel, the second body has its EI in parallel to the EI of P—the most indirect of the three. In a B parallel, both bodies are in parallel and ecliptic intercepts do not enter into the matter. We find that all three work. It can be argued that there must be two kinds of conjunction: Where the conjunction is between the EIs only and where in addition to the conjunction of the EIs the bodies are in parallel. The second of the two ought to be considerably stronger than the other conjunction or any of the parallels. In this very strong case an orb of greater than five degrees may be permissible.

What is behind what I have been saying? It is the whole issue of the third dimension of space. Aspects measured only along the ecliptic are two dimensional and disregard the third dimension. The use of declination is one way of seeking to correct for the usual omission of the third dimension. Why should declination be used instead of celestial latitude? This is an excellent question. When the importance between a New Moon and a solar eclipse is distinguished, giving the latter much more potency, it includes consideration of latitude. At a solar eclipse the difference between the celestial latitude of the Moon and of the Sun is quite limited in contrast to a New Moon. How then can the use of parallels of declination be justified. If one considers that an outer planet hardly changes its declination at all during one day then it can be said that due to the Earth's diurnal rotation the planet moves along a fixed parallel of declination and in so doing comes into a kind of conjunction with any other body having that same, or nearly the same, declination. That is the recognized theoretical basis for parallels. It is only valid since they also stand up under the test of practice.

3

Orbs of Parallels

Let me clarify the sliding scale orbs of declination. The Sun when at zero degrees Aries has no declination as it is then crossing the equator. When its longitude is five degrees further along at five degrees Aries, its declination is about two degrees north so that the usual one degree orb for declination is far too narrow for low declinations. When at zero degrees Cancer it can be assumed the Sun is 23°26′ north. Then what is its declination five degrees further along at five degrees Cancer? It is 23°21′ north or less than six minutes difference in declination as contrasted with two degrees in low declination. This is a clear example of how the declination orbs change and why the ecliptic equivalent method of turning declination values into the ecliptic values of conventional aspects is employed.

The furthest distance the Sun (and Midheaven, Ascendant, or Vertex) can be above or below the equator is about +23°27′. When, for instance, the Sun is reaching zero degrees Capricorn at the beginning of winter in the northern hemisphere, the Sun hardly moves at all from day to day in declination. This is why zero degrees Capricorn and zero degrees Cancer are termed the solstices (sol–Sun, stice–standing still). It is obvious that the ecliptic equivalent technique will not work "above the turn," the turn being 23°27′ north or south. Therefore, if a body has a declination greater than this value the ecliptic equivalent method cannot be used. The Sun's semi-diameter is 0°16′ so that 23°27′ + 16′ = 23°43′, which extends the Sun's declination orb somewhat. Since the Midheaven, Ascendant, and Vertex are created by the intersection of the Sun's path with the three local planes (meridian for Midheaven, horizon for Ascendant, and prime vertical for Vertex), they may also be given an orb of an extra sixteen minutes. As the Moon's semi-diameter is from fifteen to sixteen minutes, any planet with sixteen minutes of the Moon's declination when the Moon is above 23°27′ may be considered to be in parallel with the Moon. In all other cases the orb may have to be cut to only one minute of declination.

Many astrologers will prefer to use those orbs of declination whose ecliptic equivalent is equal to five degrees or less. Up to about twenty degrees of declination plus or minus five degrees of longitude is equivalent to nearly plus or minus two degrees of declination in low declinations, decreasing to plus or minus about one degree of declination. It is only over 20°30′ of declination that the declination orbs commence to become very small. Those who are conservative may prefer to use ecliptic equivalents of plus or minus three degrees instead of five degrees orbs. This policy gives the following results:

Declination	Declination Orb +/-
1°12′	1°11:30′
5°36′	1°10′
10°00′	1°05′
14°24′	0°58′
18°48′	0°45′
23°12′	0°10:30′

Ecliptic equivalent is plus or minus three degrees in all instances. Up until fairly high declinations the declination orbs are not greatly different from the traditional one degree.

There are three tables in the back of this book. Table I gives the declination (north) for every ten minutes of arc from 0° to 20°; every five minutes of arc from 20° to 23°; every one minute of arc from 23° to 23°26′; and from 23°26′ to 23°26′, forty-five minutes by one-quarter second increments. For each value of declination given, there are the two longitudes or ecliptic equivalents that have this same declination when the Sun is there. They are given to the nearest one minute.

Between the rows are differences in longitude to aid interpolation. From 0° to 20° the longitude differences are for every one minute of declination; from 20° to 23° of declination they are for every five minutes of declination; from 23° to 23°26′ of declination they are for every one minute of declination. Values of declination more exact than to the nearest minute of arc are essential for slow motions in declination and in high declination.

The table is for northern declinations so that the longitudes in the two columns are for the first half of the zodiac. To use Table I for southern declinations, add 180° or six signs to the longitude values. Table III enables one to correct for changes in the obliquity of the ecliptic, and gives the corrections to the longitudes of Table I for every decade before or after 1950 and for all declinations above twelve degrees, north or south, as they are negligible below thirteen degrees.

Table II is also very useful. From zero degrees Aries to zero degrees Gemini it gives the north declinations to the nearest tenth of a minute of arc for every half degree of longitude. It does the same for Libra and Scorpio—the twin column to the right gives the declinations from the end of Virgo to zero degrees Leo, and from the end of Pisces to zero degree Aquarius. From zero degrees Gemini to zero degrees Cancer and zero degrees Sagittarius to zero degrees Capricorn, the declinations are given for even whole degrees of longitude. Thus, for the longitude of any Midheaven, Ascendant, or Vertex, one can easily find the declination from Table II.

Suppose one wants to find the ecliptic equivalents of two bodies which may be in contraparallel. One of them is +22°03′ and the other is -22°34′. The date is in 1910. At +22°00′ in Table I the ecliptic equivalent is 10 Gemini 18:18 and at 22N05 it is 10 Gemini 53:4. The change is 3.51′ for every half minute. As 23°03′ is three minutes more than twenty-two degrees, this is six times one-half minute.

Then 6 x 3.51' = 21.1' which is added to the value at 22° to result in 10 Gemini 39:4. For great accuracy this can be corrected from Table III. By interpolation between 22° and 23° the error in longitude for a decade is 57' at 22°03' and 76' at 22°34'. For the four decades (1950-1910) this becomes -2.3' at 22°03', and -3.0' at 22°34' (minus as 1910 is earlier than 1950). This gives 10 Gemini 37:2 at +22°03' and also 19 Cancer 22:8. In like manner the corrected value at -22°34' is 14 Sagittarius 21:1 and 15 Capricorn 38:9. The two bodies in their ecliptic equivalents are then within five degrees of an opposition, and the values are very accurate.

4

How Parallels Modify A Chart

A woman who is a professional nurse had her chart rectified by me. Her Midheaven is at 26 Taurus 20 and has a declination of +19°21′. Her Neptune at 9 Leo 19 is in her twelfth house with a declination of +17°50′. Its ecliptic equivalents (from Table I) are 9 Leo 38 and 20 Taurus 22. I use an orb of more than five degrees for aspects that involve the lights or angles so that this is a parallel to the Midheaven. Since she works in hospitals (twelfth house) there should be something not only in her twelfth house but also linking it to the Midheaven or point of career. Without this parallel this would not have been the case. This is a simple and typical example of the vital importance of parallels.

The rectified Midheaven of a man is 27 Capricorn 54 with a declination of -20°35′. It is trine his Sun in the first house at 0 Gemini 18:32. This certainly sounds excellent for success in his career and in dealing with those in authority (Sun and Midheaven). The Sun's declination is +20°13′. On the basis of both the antiscion and ecliptic equivalent principle, the Sun is parallel to 29 Cancer 41:30 and therefore is contraparallel to his Midheaven. This has been a good test of the efficacy of contraparallels and on the issue of whether they are different from parallels. He is a very intelligent and capable man who is just now in his late forties coming into his own. Venus at 1 Taurus 32 is square the Midheaven; the Moon at 28 Cancer 34 is opposite it. Saturn at 23 Capricorn 00 is conjunct it from the ninth house side. The first two bodies are benefics, and the third is essentially dignified in its own sign.

There is a well-known myth that Saturn conjunct the Midheaven brings a terrible fall from a high position as was the case with Napoleon. But one can cite the case of Marc Edmund Jones, who has Saturn and the Moon conjunct his Leo Midheaven (the native is similar but his Moon opposes the Midheaven). I have grown very tired of waiting for Marc to have his terrible fall! As he said of this configuration, if you mind your p's and q's, it is no problem. Possibly it might delay success but also would make it last longer.

Certainly under Saturn one must work hard as the native has. He has had difficulties with men in authority from time to time (Sun and Midheaven in contraparallel). This has been the major factor delaying the success that is now coming to him and that he is certain to experience. He has acquired a lot of education, but his doctorate was recent. This fits with Saturn in and ruling Capricorn in his ninth house. The Sun is so benefic—more so even than Jupiter—that to have both lights to his angles is an augury of success and of some impact on the world (angles show such impact whether or not there is merit). The Moon opposite the Midheaven fits with his past work in public relations even though it is an opposition aspect. The saying *per aspera ad astra* (through difficulties to the stars) really fits this extraordinary man.

In Chapter 1, the third case cited was of a man with the Sun and Moon in both a trine and contraparallel. A woman is a similar case in that her Moon in the sixth house at 9 Leo 24 is in close trine to her ninth house Sun at 9 Sagittarius 17. Hers is a fire trine, the man's being in air; hers is in the sixth and ninth houses, his being in the eleventh and third. So they are by no means identical.

Her Moon is at +22°40′ declination in contraparallel to the Sun at -21°51′. The ecliptic equivalents of the Moon's declination are, from Table I, 14 Cancer 20 and 15 Gemini 40, which is only a little more than five degrees from a longitudinal opposition to the Sun. In aspects between the lights, or lights to angles, one certainly may use a seven and a half degree maximum orb but this is a matter for the discretion and judgment of the astrologer. Her Midheaven is at 17 Sagittarius 06 so she also has a contraparallel of the Moon to the Midheaven which fits with her public work. Actually the Moon is also a little less than eight degrees from a trine to her Midheaven, wide and weak but having some significance. Her work is quite important, involves many people and she has some authority—Sun is widely conjunct her Midheaven with an orb just under eight degrees. As both the Sun and Moon are aspecting the Midheaven, such wide orbs have some weight. The Midheaven is at -22°49′ declination.

Her Moon is not only in the sixth house but also rules the first and the Cancer part of it. One might expect excellent relationships with subordinates, but actually she has trouble with them. This can be attributed to the contraparallel, which also shows difficulties with the opposite sex (Sun-Moon) that would not be anticipated from such a close trine. One more factor must be considered. Her natal Saturn is at 20 Sagittarius 09 conjunct her Midheaven, and is one reason she works with the aged. Since its declination is -21°53′, its ecliptic equivalents are 9 Sagittarius 03 and 20 Capricorn 57. Therefore, Saturn, while not conjunct her Sun, is closely parallel it. Although the aspect is wide due to translation of light, it may be said that Saturn is also contraparallel her Moon, a further index to the challenges posed to her by those under her authority.

Aspects of lights to the angles are always benefic, although if they are hard aspects or contraparallels they bring problems. David Susskind's chart has the Midheaven at 18 Virgo 50. He was born December 19, 1920 in New York City. Jupiter is at 18 Virgo 32 conjunct the Midheaven, as is Saturn at 24 Virgo 34. The Midheaven's declination is +4°25′, Jupiter's is +5°37′, and Saturn's is +4°04′. His Moon at 6 Aries 48 in his fourth house has no apparent relationship to the Midheaven, but has a declination of +4°53′ whose ecliptic equivalents are 12 Aries 22 and 17 Virgo 28, which puts it into a parallel with his Midheaven. Success before the public is best if both Jupiter and the Moon favor the Midheaven of a horoscope. His talk show has been on television longer than any other, and he has for years been a most successful producer.

His wife's chart is also interesting. The Midheaven at 23 Cancer 44 is +21°22′ declination with the

Sun at 24 Aries 07 squaring it; Saturn at 23 Capricorn 02 with a declination of -21°14' is opposite it; the Moon at 21 Pisces 23 trines it; and the Ascendant at 17 Libra 56 has a declination of -7°02'. Both lights aspect the Midheaven even though one of them squares it, so she has been quite successful in her television career in Canada, where she was born.

Her first success occurred before she met and married David. Note that the Saturn opposition to the Midheaven has not prevented success; actually she is a very hard worker and has much character as well as being a beautiful woman. Much of her success has been in personal (Ascendant) interviewing. The Moon at a declination of -5°17' is parallel the Ascendant (personal contacts with the public) with ecliptic equivalents of 16 Pisces 30 and 13 Libra 30. The sixth house Moon (her work) is conjunct and parallel Venus at 16 Pisces 52 at the end of the fifth house. Its declination at -6°15' puts it even closer to a parallel to the Ascendant, as well as ruling it.

In Chapter 6 the case of a woman with Pluto contraparallel the Midheaven and Ascendant will be discussed. A similar case is that of a man with the Midheaven at 25 Scorpio 48 and -19°13' declination; Ascendant at 3 Aquarius 42 with a declination of -19°19'; Pluto at 9 Cancer 14 in the sixth house with a declination of +20°14' and ecliptic equivalents of 29 Cancer 40 and 0 Gemini 40, both being within five degrees of the contraparallel to the angles. Mercury is at 25 Gemini 24 retrograde with a declination of +19°22' and is contraparallel to both the angles. It is closely quincunx the Midheaven and Pluto is sesquiquadrate the Midheaven within 1°34'.

During the war when he was far away from the United States (Pluto ruling the ninth house Scorpio) he lost one lung (Pluto in the sixth house). Mercury in and ruling Gemini (lungs) is near the end of the fifth house with the cusp of the sixth Campanus house at 29 Gemini 00. The combination of Pluto and Mercury has affected him personally (Ascendant) and his career (Midheaven) in a mainly sixth house way. The Sun at 27 Gemini 59 nearly in the sixth house is an additional indication of the vital issue of health matters in his life.

The last case is that of a man with a Midheaven of 29 Aquarius 54 and an Ascendant of 24 Gemini 08. Using Campanus, the second house cusp is 23 Cancer 00 and the third house cusp is 12 Leo 00. He had a stellium in Cancer:

Mercury	4 ♋ 39	+19°54:5'	1 ♌ 10	28 ♉ 50
Moon	11 ♋ 36	+25°40'	Antiscion	18 ♊ 24
Pluto	16 ♋ 52	+21°36'	22 ♋ 20	7 ♊ 40
Sun	23 ♋ 30:5	+21°24'	Same	6 ♊ 39:5
Venus	28 ♋ 48	+21°41'	21 ♋ 47	8 ♊ 13
Saturn	13 ♐ 17	-20°49'	3 ♐ 08 Antiscion	26 ♑ 52 16 ♑ 43

Saturn is bodily contraparallel Mercury-Pluto-Sun-Venus and is contrascion the Moon. As in the case of Walt Disney, this is a Fanhandle in declination. The bodies not actually in the second house—Mercury, Moon, Pluto—are so positioned as to have some effect on it except for Mercury; indeed, the Moon rules the sign on its Campanus cusp.

This man was of superior intelligence and yet could not make the amount of money consonant with his clear capabilities, i.e. due to a severe psychological block. Much of this was due to his early environment. His father had been put in an institution as his sole reaction to everything was rage. The contraparallels of Saturn to that second house stellium and the rulership by Saturn of the eighth house went far to describe this situation.

The powerful involvement of Saturn and Pluto with his lights accented his driving need for security; he unconsciously felt he must be taken care of by someone—Pluto is the planet, negatively, of dependency and need. His major problem was this and not the fact that he was gay.

The trine of Mercury to his Midheaven gave him excellent intellectual and communication skills. He was a good teacher (Cancer). I feel sure that without those contraparallels of Saturn it would not have been possible to see a major challenge in his life from this chart. Actually he had some unusual abilities, but they had little chance to be realized in life due to his severe psychological hangups.

It may be argued, as T. Patrick Davis, Hutcheon, and others have done, that declination is somewhat less overt than longitudinal aspects. It certainly is not less powerful if one takes the trouble to check it extensively as some astrologers have done and all astrologers ought to do.

5

Transits in Declination

Some years ago a lady who had experienced a serious nervous breakdown consulted me. The reasons for it were obscure. In her twenties she had taken a job on the west coast as an assistant to the director of a successful television talk show. When she was promoted, her reaction was to have the breakdown and flee back to her family on the east coast. It was so serious she gained forty pounds and was given shock treatments. The basic pattern of her chart is the cradle.

A cradle is composed of an opposition linked by sextiles and trines. In her case the first house Sun in Aquarius opposes the seventh house Pluto in Leo. Above the horizon the Sun sextiled planet B and trined planet C while B was in trine to Pluto and C was sextile it. With so many soft aspects, one can gain much help and as a result can become rather dependent and remain relatively immature, thus the symbol of the cradle. If there is a fifth body making a sextile to the fourth one, the cradle becomes a cradle with hood; it is only one sextile short of the rare grand hexagon. Too many so-called harmonious aspects are by no means an unmixed blessing. Under them one either takes the easy way, as criminals often do, or simply never tries very hard to do anything.

The lady is the baby of her family and a bit spoiled. On the other hand, they expect a good deal of her as she has plenty of ability. She is personable and attractive. In November 1976, Pluto by transit reached the sesquiquadrate of her Sun, thus energizing the natal opposition. But this was not enough. The natal Moon is in Cancer so its antiscion was about fourteen degrees Gemini. In December 1976, transiting Neptune reached the contrascion of her Moon. Therefore, she was besieged by the two psychological planets. It was in December that she experienced the nervous breakdown.

When she came to see me, the two transits were not quite over; she was better, although not yet out of the woods. I felt she had been too dependent on the help of others (cradle) and that she needed more confidence in herself, which is what I concentrated on during the interview. It was only due to her use of astrology that she had been able to bring herself to leave her home for the first time. I feel sure that with the ending of the two transits she emerged once more as a functioning and productive human being.

Astrologers at times have grave responsibilities and should act in accordance with such. When confronted with those who need major psychological help, the astrologer should refer the client to trained therapists.

It is astrological tradition that the two malefics are Mars and Saturn. I consider their place has been taken now by Neptune and Pluto, the problem planets. Of course, they are not bad at all; indeed, no planet is really malefic. It is simply that some are more of a problem and present more difficulties in handling their energies effectively and constructively.

It is a major task to handle aspects of stress by Neptune and Pluto simultaneously and at the same time keep one's balance. Their meaning is intangible and mainly psychological. There is no reason, however, that they must remain problem planets for a long period.

Another woman has a 24 Scorpio 55 Midheaven with a -19°02′ declination; Ascendant at 1 Aquarius 45 with a +19°47′ declination; Sun at 6 Aquarius 16 with a -18°42′ declination; Moon at 0 Scorpio 09 with a -16°25′ declination (thus square the Ascendant and Sun); Neptune at 1 Leo 09 retrograde with a +19°37′ declination (opposite Sun and Ascendant and square the Moon); Pluto at 1 Cancer 39 retrograde with a +18°15' declination (trine the Moon); and Uranus at 15 Aquarius 09 with a -16°55′ declination.

These are the parallel and contraparallel aspects: Uranus parallel Moon, Sun parallel Midheaven, Neptune contraparallel Midheaven, Pluto contraparallel Midheaven, and Mars contraparallel Moon. Mars is at 25 Leo 10 retrograde and has a declination of +17°21′N. Its ecliptic equivalents are 15 Scorpio 16 and 14 Aquarius 44. Pluto's ecliptic equivalents are 8 Leo 05 and 21 Taurus 55. There are five parallels and twelve contraparallels, or seventeen in all. If those shown by conjunction and opposition are omitted, there are fourteen aspects not shown in longitude. Pluto has seven parallels and contraparallels, Mars has six, Neptune has four, and Uranus has three. Two of the three angles are involved, and both lights. The native is an unusual woman who is highly sensitive (Neptune-Pluto) and independent (Uranus parallel Moon).

The first significant transit was in longitude: Neptune square Sun and natal opposition from December 1958 to a station only five and a half minutes from the last square to the Sun on July 18, 1960. That is the month she filed for divorce—man (Sun) and emotional stress (hard aspects of Neptune). She had first consulted a psychiatrist in the summer of 1959. In August 1960, she voluntarily committed herself to an institution for the purpose of emotional and psychological therapy, but had real difficulty in getting out of it.

The sixth house natal bodies are Pluto and Saturn at 11 Cancer 14 retrograde. Throughout 1962, Saturn by transit was parallel her Ascendant, Sun, and Midheaven, but as it also was conjunct her Ascendant and Sun in longitude during that time, this is not so striking. It is the slower and more powerful Pluto transits that mainly account for her troubles. It was contraparallel her Ascendant from late October 1961 until the end of June 1964. She didn't manage to hold a steady job until May 1964. The transiting contraparallels of Pluto to her Midheaven from October 1963 until late March 1966 were really a help to her since Pluto is natally in biquintile (144°) to her Midheaven. The final break with her doctor and the ending of living on pills occurred in September 1964. It was in that month that Pluto made its first contraparallel to her Sun, setting off the natal contraparallel. The breaking of a tie with a man is characteristic of Pluto squares, oppositions, or contraparallels to the Sun. Transiting

Neptune first reached a parallel to the Moon, which activated the natal square, late in December 1964, the month in which she quit her job.

It is unnecessary to continue with these strong outer planet parallels and contraparallels, for it should be evident that they are as potent as conjunctions, oppositions, and square in longitude. Major transits of Neptune and Pluto to her lights and angles did not end until mid-1975. Yet from all this she has become more constructively responsive to the high and subtle energies that these two planets can bring if one is attuned to hem. Neptune really requires one to decentralize the ego; Pluto, planet of research, enables one to penetrate the secrets of nature and to transmute sexual energies for creativity. Aspects to Mercury-Venus-Mars, which are certainly significant, could be mentioned but they are not as important as the ones cited.

The next case exemplifies the transits of Uranus and Pluto. This is the chart of a woman born August 26, 1926, 3:31:48 p.m., Greenwich Mean Time, 58N15, 8E48. The Midheaven is at 8 Scorpio 15, the Ascendant at 22 Sagittarius 33, and the Vertex at 14 Leo 02. The Sun is at 2 Virgo 33 in the huge Campanus seventh house but affects the eighth house, with a cusp of 16 Virgo 46. The Sun's declination is $+10°32'$, making it parallel to 27 Aries 32. The Moon at 16 Aries 47 is in the second house, but affects the next one whose cusp is 25 Aries 33. The Moon has a low declination of $+1°32'$, whose ecliptic equivalents are 3 Aries 52 and 26 Virgo 08.

First to be examined are the parallels by the transits of Uranus to the Moon. Natally, Uranus is at 28 Pisces 26 with a declination of $+1°21'$ and thus contraparallel to the Moon. Uranus' ecliptic equivalents are 28 Pisces 26 and 1 Libra 34. Both Uranus, natally square the Ascendant, and the Moon are in the second house. They are the two main bodies of change and travel. Therefore, when Uranus was parallel the Moon, financial instability, which in turn might have to do with local travel (Moon affecting the third house), could be expected. The transit has extra importance since the two bodies are in a natal aspect.

The first exact contact was on November 10, 1967, the second on February 28, 1968, and the third on August 23, 1968. During that nine and a half months she was concerned about getting a new car, experiencing difficulties with her husband about this due to irregular finances. It was also in the fall of 1967 that she commenced to study astrology at an elementary level (third house) with a woman (Moon, ruling much of the seventh house) who is quite Uranian. In addition, the native later worked on and off for the Uranian woman, resulting in erratic income.

The more recent transits of Pluto in parallel to her Sun have been even more potent. Pluto natally is at 15 Cancer 26 with a declination of $+21°04'$. It was semisquare the Sun. Both Pluto and the Sun are in the seventh house natally. When Pluto was parallel the Sun (1976 to 1978), it was in the eighth house over which the Sun has some influence. So, important financial developments with men (Sun) which would be somewhat problematic (semisquare) could be anticipated. In addition, Pluto is always vital psychologically in a subtle way. In early December 1975 Pluto was stationary in declination, and thus extra strong at $+1°51'$. Its ecliptic equivalent is 1 Virgo 46, which is fifty-two minutes from the Sun. Thus it could be said the transit series started then if an orb of one degree is used. The first exact parallel was on October 5, 1976, the second on February 15, 1977, the third on August 16, 1977, and the final one in late May 1978 when Pluto was stationary in declination in exact parallel to the Sun.

She was separated from her husband, but due to a joint financial interest in their home, she was still tied (Pluto) to him (an outward, visible sign of an inner and subtle psychological reality). At the end of May 1978 he relinquished his last financial interest (eighth house) in the home, which signified the end of their relationship. Often under a long, slow Pluto transit there is a deep and gradual transformation in the psychology of a relationship which is not realized until the very end of the transit series, as was the case here. In January 1977 her son and daughter-in-law moved into her home, which was alright at first but soon became otherwise—second exact parallel occurred a month later.

On the third one in August there was severe difficulty due to the lack of sanity (negative Pluto) of her daughter-in-law. She has not seen them since and it looks as though the other man in her life, her son (Sun) has also changed his tie with her. In the case of the son, there were also financial factors (eighth house) in the situation. Clearly this was a major pair of developments in her life not shown by any other transit.

There is a remaining important consideration. Suppose Saturn crosses back and forth over one's Ascendant for nine months. Does this mean this is the length of its transit series? The answer is not necessarily, because it may have started as a parallel to the Ascendant before it was conjunct it or it may continue to be parallel to it after the conjunction has ended. Often the conjunction and parallel series overlap. It is quite important to take this into consideration because it is possible, for example, to tell someone that the depressive and restrictive influence of Saturn will be over in April when instead it will continue for another six months. In addition, any transit series is most potent when the parallels and conjunctions overlap (or oppositions and contraparallels), and in the latter part of the series more than in the initial part unless the series starts with a stationary position.

6

Parallels by Progression

Day-for-a-year or secondary (major) progressions are well-known to most astrologers. They are almost always limited, however, to aspects in longitude. They can be equally significant in declination. This is especially true of the three outermost planets and Saturn. Obviously the secondary progression of such bodies is slow. When in high declination they can be extraordinarily slow and thus affect the native's life for many years, or even for the entire life, in a dominant manner.

An example is a woman who has Pluto elevated in the tenth house conjunct the Midheaven in Cancer and in natal contraparallel to both the Moon in Aquarius in the fifth house of children and to the Sun conjunct Saturn in Sagittarius late in the second house. Indeed, Pluto governs the first or Scorpio part of that financial second house. Saturn rules the Capricorn fourth house of home and property. The Sun-Saturn-Moon are in parallel and in contraparallel to Pluto. Below are the sign and house positions and the ecliptic equivalents of part of her horoscope.

Body	House	Sign	Ecliptic Equivalents		Declination
Saturn	2	9 ♐ 49	1 ♐ 08:9	28 ♑ 51:1	-20°23:7
Moon	5	15 ♒ 11	28 ♑ 25:1	1 ♐ 34:54	-20°29:2
Pluto	10	16 ♋ 49	23 ♋ 54:7	6 ♊ 05:18	+21°19:9
Sun	2	7 ♐ 06	7 ♐ 06:5	22 ♑ 53:30	-21°30:3
MC	10	10 ♋ 18		19 ♊ 42	+23°01:2
ASC	1	8 ♎ 46		21 ♓ 14	-3°32′
Jupiter	6	23 ♓ 48	20 ♓ 31:1	9 ♎ 28:9	-3°45:5
Venus	1	20 ♎ 42	15 ♎ 34:5	14 ♓ 25:5	-6°08′

The parallels and contraparallels of the two malefics, the authority and security bodies Saturn and Pluto, to her lights have created major security problems for her. They are offset by the parallels of the two benefics, Venus and Jupiter, to her Libra Ascendant, which Venus rules. She has a charming personality and is an attractive woman. She is divorced. Her former husband is prominent in his field. She has a number of children (Moon in the fifth house) whose relationship to her is vital to her sense of security—Moon parallel Saturn and contraparallel Pluto. She has owned real estate, which is another part of her security—Saturn ruling the fourth house from the second house and being a general indicator of real estate, too.

Pluto by secondary progression in 1978 reached the contraparallel to the Sun. As Pluto governs the second house and the Sun is in the latter part of that house, to be expected, among other things, were severe economic difficulties, also affecting her property (Saturn) and children (Moon). After having enjoyed a good income, she has in the past few years been deprived of nearly all of it. Due to certain problems affecting her via her former husband, she has been financially threatened by the authorities with the loss of all income and her home and land. She has been robbed by relatives and strangers—Pluto on the negative side is devious, dishonest, and secretive. A prominent man who is close to her has been experiencing major economic setbacks and has been publicly slandered—the Sun ruling her eleventh house. There are no sufficiently strong adverse factors via transit, direction, etc. These tragic developments can be accounted for only by Pluto's powerful contraparallel.

Failure to use the natal parallels and contraparallels would result in a major misinterpretation of the chart. In addition to the inability to account for the foregoing traumatic events whose extent has only been touched on briefly, her basic chart is dominated by parallels. Secondary progressions are more effective and last longer when applying than when separating. This is why she has been under Pluto's dark shadow for a number of years, and why I surmise she will come out into the sunlight after this year, assuming that she is all in one piece! There are few things in astrology comparable in power to the slow secondary progressions, whether direct or converse. Oddly enough, there is more recognition of these progressed parallels than there is of the radical ones.

One reason for the title of this book—*Parallels: Their Hidden Meanings*— is the hidden nature of parallels, since they are quite unapparent in the usual flat two-dimensional chart. Therefore, their meanings are hidden since they do not appear at all in most horoscopes.

Figure 4 is the chart of a woman. Natally there are contraparallels to both the Midheaven and the Ascendant from Pluto in the sixth house. Pluto governs Scorpio on the cusp of the ninth and tenth houses. Although she has done a great deal of writing all her life (Sun with Mars in the third house), she has not yet had her work published (ninth house rules publishing, among other things).

Since Pluto has much to do with the mother, it is notable that she lost her mother at age twenty through death. Later, religion (also ninth house) became quite important in her life as the central axis around which it revolves. Note, too, the close contraparallel of the seventh house Neptune in Leo at $+18°34'$ to her Midheaven at $-18°30'$. Its meaning has been made clear due to the very slow exact contraparallel by it to the Midheaven by secondary progression in 1943-44. At that time, and during much of the prior four years (she was first married in 1940), she was confused, unhappy, and in conflict over her marriage. Neptune is also opposite the Ascendant. This case is an example of the power of a slow secondary Neptune.

Regressions or converse secondaries are just as important. For them, one uses the converse adjusted calculation date. Thus, if the adjusted calculation date is three months after birth, the converse adjusted calculation date is three months before it.

An example is the chart of a man born December 15, 1922 at 5:49 p.m., Eastern Standard Time, 10:49 p.m. Greenwich Mean Time. Each month equals two hours by progression and each four min-

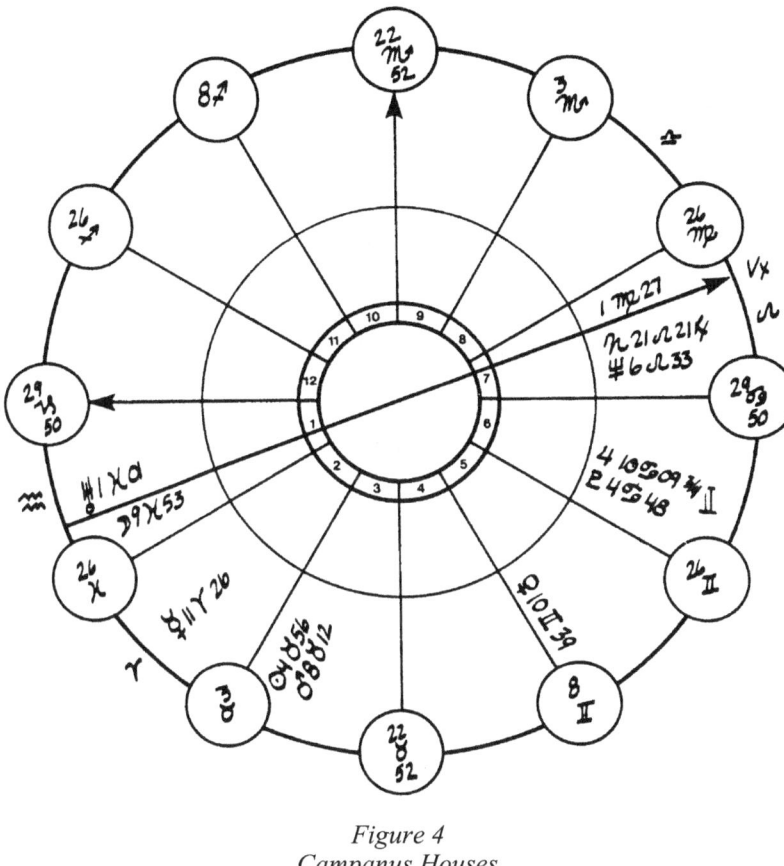

Figure 4
Campanus Houses

utes of time is a day by secondary progression. Thus the 10:49 p.m. equals 22 hours, 49 minutes after the previous midnight (used for the adjusted calculation date and the converse adjusted calculation date). This by progression equals eleven months and twelve days. When using the adjusted calculation date, subtract; do the opposite for the converse adjusted calculation date. His converse adjusted calculation date is October 27, 1923, and is equivalent to midnight Greenwich Mean Time at the start of his birthday. The Midheaven is at 21 Pisces 25 and has a declination of -3°24′. Natal Saturn is at 18 Libra 23 and has a declination of -5°02′, which is increasing so that by converse motion it is decreasing in the direction of a parallel to the Midheaven.

By converse secondary progression it reached there in the early spring of 1969. At that time he was having major career difficulties. Since it rules the seventh house, the troubles also involved his wife. It is not necessary to give the entire chart and in this way his identity is protected. This case is an example of a slow secondary regression. The four outermost planets are vital not only because of their slowness but also because in each case the progressed aspect is the exact completion of a natal aspect within orb of the aspect.

My conception chart is an example of the secondary progression and regression of Uranus. My conception ©) epoch occurred on January 14, 1911 at 75W08, 39N54 (geocentric) and my birth (B) on October 9, 1911. Below are the values of the Midheaven-Uranus-Sun, which from the ninth house opposed the conjunction of the Moon and Neptune in the third house. Only the square of Saturn at twenty-nine degrees Aries has helped me keep one foot on the ground in my thinking; the C chart defines the Jungian thinking function.

Factor	Longitude	Latitude	Decl.	Ecl. Equiv.	Decl. of Intercept
MC	26 0 10	0:00	-20°55:5	Same	Same
Uranus	25 0 09	-0:29	-21°35:4	11 0 13:4	-21°06:9
Sun	23 0 26:23	0:00	-21°24:8	Same	Same
Moon	20 4 32:54	+4:29:5	+26°17:5	None	21:52:7
Neptune	20 4 05R	-0:39	22:35:4	15 4 09.9	21:56:9

The Greenwich Mean Time of the chart was 5:21 p.m. so that the adjusted calculation date was April 20, 1910, and the converse adjusted calculation date for regressions was October 8, 1911. In June 1927, by regression, Uranus parallel Sun occurred. I was supposed to go on an around-the-world cruise during which I would study the last year of high school—all ninth house where Sun and Uranus are. This came up in 1927 for the fall 1928 trip, but I didn't go, which was unexpected and a shock to me. I never forgot it! By progression, Neptune contraparallel the Sun took place in March 1937, while in September of that year Uranus by regression was at the declination of the Moon's ecliptic intercept. This period was emotionally confusing (Neptune) and I was separated (Uranus) from an important woman (Moon). This period was also an important turning point in my thinking, which ever since has been focused mainly on astrology.

The progressed parallels and contraparallels of other planets are significant, too, of course, especially if they are near or at a station in declination. For the slower a planet moves, the more potent it is in its effects.

7

Declination Arc Directions

Diagram B depicts the celestial sphere looked at from the east toward the west. Of main interest is the right spherical triangle MRS. M is at the Midheaven (zero degrees Aries is placed there), S is at the Sun on the ecliptic, and R is at the right ascension place of the Sun on the equator. M to R is the right ascension, M to S is the Sun's longitude and its solar arc, and S to R is the declination arc that the Sun is above the equator. This triangle is the key to all modes of direction.

As the Sun moves from the Midheaven and zero degrees Aries to S, it defines the (true) solar arc (in celestial longitude). Its true solar arc in right ascension is defined by the distance in right ascension from M to R, this being the basis of all valid primary directions.

What then of the solar declination arc, RS? It may be used to direct all bodies and the Midheaven. Suppose this arc is ten degrees. Then, if the Moon were moving away from the equator radically—increasing in declination whether southward or northward—this declination arc would be added to the natal or radical value so as to direct it further away. Doing so might bring it to a parallel or contraparallel of one or more planets. The arc's length is not affected by errors in the time of birth, making it extremely valuable in timing.

If the body passes beyond 23°27' north or south, it has overshot the turn. Suppose it moves to 24°37'. This is 1°10' beyond the turn, so that it must be brought back from there by that amount, i.e. 23°27' - 1°10' = 22°17'. As a result, it is 22°17' and is now decreasing in declination. All bodies are given the motion of the Sun in declination and since the Sun turns at 23°17' (as of 1917; the turn will be at 23°26:5 in 1982), all bodies directed by solar, Ascendant, or vertical declination arc must also turn there. All one has to do is measure the amount of the overshoot and bring it back by that amount.

One can put a lower case "I" after the radical declination to show that it is increasing. Similarly, if it is decreasing at birth, one can place a lower case "d" after the declination. It is important to know in which direction it is moving. Suppose Mars is 6°22' north (decreasing) and that the solar declination or other declination arc is 13°47'. It will only require 6°22' to reach the equator so that the rest of the arc will be on the other side of the equator; Mars will then be increasing in declination, i.e. 13°47' -

6°22' = 7°25' as the distance it has moved southward. It is then written as -7°23'i. These solar declination arcs vary in speed from twenty-four minutes a year, when the Sun has a low declination, to nearly zero minutes when the Sun has a high declination, so that they are more variable than is the case with solar arc in longitude or in right ascension.

If the chart has been rectified or if the time is probably accurate, one may also use the Ascendant and vertical declination arcs. They are most stable when the Ascendant or Vertex is moving slowly—in the northern hemisphere from Cancer to Sagittarius. How does one find them? By finding the declination of the radical Ascendant and Vertex by using Table II. Then add the solar arc in longitude to the Midheaven and with this progressed Midheaven find the new (progressed) Ascendant and Vertex, using the terrestrial latitude of the radical or natal place of the chart. This gives the progressed Ascendant and Vertex positions. One then finds their declinations from Table II. Then the distance form the natal to the progressed Ascendant measured in declination is the Ascendant declination arc.

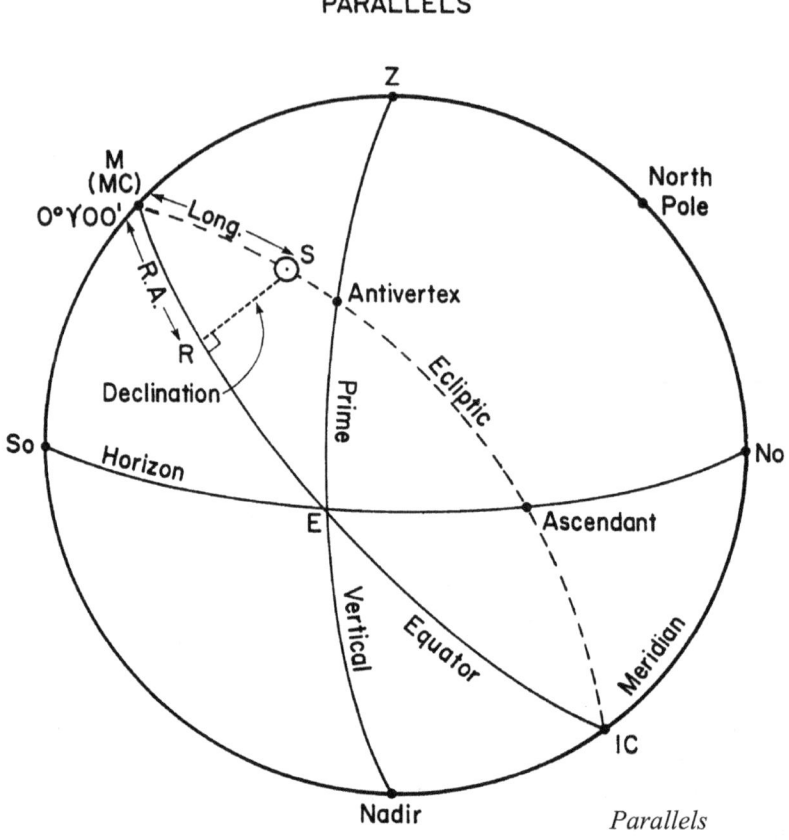

Parallels

The Midheaven of an example from a rectified horoscope is 7 Aquarius 04 and the latitude is +51°15' (geocentric). To find the Vertex use the IC (7 Leo 04) as thought it were the Midheaven and use the co-latitude (90° minus the latitude) which is -38°45' as though it were the latitude. The resultant "Ascendant" is the Vertex and is at 1 Scorpio 44. Its declination is -12°05'i. The solar arc for the event was +23°56', which added to the natal Midheaven, gives 1 Pisces 00 as the progressed Midheaven and an IC of 1 Virgo 00. At the co-latitude of -38°45', it gives a progressed Vertex of 20 Scorpio 38, whose declination is -17°52:5i.

As the difference between the declination of the progressed Vertex and the natal declination is +5°47', this is the vertical declination arc. (The + in front of any arc means that it is direct; converse arcs are preceded by a - sign.) The man's Sun is at 24 Scorpio 36 in his sixth house and rules the sign

Leo in the fourth house. The Sun's natal declination is -18°55:75i; added to the vertical declination arc, the result is -24°43′. The turn that year was at 23°36:9 so the overshoot was 1°16:35. Subtract this from the turn, as it is an overshoot, to obtain -22°10:55. For this natal Midheaven the Ascendant is at 11 Gemini 31:8, whose declination is +22°10:45i.

Thus the Sun, the most powerful benefic, came to a contraparallel of his Ascendant as he uprooted himself (Sun rules the fourth house) and moved to another land. Yet in the long term this proved to be beneficial as the Sun is the greatest benefic. I cite this as an example of how to calculate and use a vertical declination arc. There are fewer aspects by declination than by longitude but they can be very important.

The next example is to determine when his Saturn came to a parallel of his Midheaven by solar declination arc. His Midheaven declination is -18°30:75′d. Saturn at 8 Capricorn 50 in his eighth house is at -22°44:3d. As it is decreasing, it may be moved to a parallel of the Midheaven, the arc required being +4°13:55. This arc is added to the Sun's declination: -18°55:75i + 4°13:55 = -23°09:3i. Using the adjusted calculation date of March, it is found that the direction occurred in mid-January 1957. Saturn governs the ninth house of higher education. At the time he had to settle for a lower degree than he wanted for career success (Midheaven). This was major since the Sun in that part of space (Sagittarius and in that high declination) was moving only four minutes a year. Moved by the Ascendant declination arc, his Ascendant was contraparallel Saturn in July 1965 (they are natally contraparallel). What the Ascendant had done was to move from Gemini up to the turn at zero degrees Cancer and back down to the contraparallel of his Saturn. This was personally frustrating, but the loss of a position resulted in a new job three months later.

It also is possible to use converse solar, Ascendant, and vertical arc directions. There is some evidence that converse directions (I term them conversions) and converse progressions (I call them regressions) may be more fated than the direct ones.

There is one other thing that can be done with the solar declination arc. It can be used to move the Midheaven. Starting at zero degrees Aries or zero degrees Libra, the solar arcs in longitude, right ascension, and declination all give the same progressed or regressed Midheaven. If it is started anywhere else, these three modes of solar arc direction give three different Midheavens, all of which are valid. An example follows.

My natal Moon is at 11 Taurus 26 and has a declination of +16°10:8i. My Midheaven is at 27 Pisces 09 and is -1°08′d. I am not old enough to have had the Midheaven reach bodily parallel of the Moon. From Table II find the declination of the Moon's ecliptic intercept, i.e. the declination of the Sun when it is at the Moon's position in Taurus. This declination is +15°16′ so that from the MC's declination to it there is +16°24:2 (15°16:2 + 1°08′). The Sun at 15 Libra 43 natally has a declination of -6°11:5i so the solar declination arc is added to this and gives -22°35:7i.

My adjusted calculation date is August 14, 1911. Therefore, using that adjusted calculation date my Sun had this value in the latter part of September 1970. This was an ecliptic parallel of the Midheaven to the Moon. In that month I took an office in New York City. I was receiving considerable publicity as I was lecturing at the center of a huge floral zodiac six days a week.

My Moon in the eleventh house rules my Ascendant at 16 Cancer 14. Some problems occurred as the Midheaven and Moon are natally semisquare. Both the lecturing job and the office fifty miles from my home meant a great deal of travel for me (Moon and Uranus are the two main bodies of travel). The rate of the solar declination arc was seven minutes a year. Since the Moon's semi-diameter is more than fifteen minutes, one could argue that some effects of this could be experienced for some months before and after the direction. I commenced my lecturing in May 1970 and continued it until the end of October. I co-sponsored a large international convention at New York University in January 1970 (natal Moon in the eleventh house).

The foregoing examples should be sufficient to illustrate how to work out declination arc directions. All values have been calculated more accurately than usual in order to show the accuracy of their timing. Since the angles and lights are the most potent factors in any chart, I have concentrated on them.

The credit for the discovery of solar and Ascendant declination arc belongs to Edgar R. Wagner and Eleanor Hesseltine, one of the great unrecognized astrologers. These methods were tested by the Roy C. Firebrace, who was especially impressed by the declination arcs.

Once one has determined the preconceptual epochs of the Sun and Moon, twenty-two and sixteen months before birth, one can only time and determine the postnatal epochs of the Sun and Moon by using one of these three modes of declination arc (direct or converse) as they are not timed by longitude or right ascension.

8

Parallels in Synastry

In the first chapter of this book I did not include the application of declinations and parallels to chart comparison (synastry). Many astrologers may not realize it, but standard synastry is under a cloud.

A few years ago the accomplished Thomas Shanks did a statistical study of 1,000 married couples based on data from Michel Gauquelin. He won the Gold Medal of the Cambridge Circle for this excellent computerized piece of work. He studied virtually every possible cross-aspect between the natal horoscopes, somewhat over 160 of them. Only one was significant at the five percent level—Moon conjunct Ascendant—and one was borderline—Sun to the Ascendant.

However, two criticisms could have been made. The number of cross-aspects was not counted. In my three decades as a consultant astrologer I have found that a relationship must have a number of such aspects if it is to be important. Second, parallels and contraparallels between charts were not included in the study. In my experience they are quite vital (Shanks' study did reveal that a number of aspects in the composite chart were statistically significant.)

Many years ago Nicholas DeVore, creator of the *Encyclopedia of Astrology*, told me that he considered that only conjunctions and oppositions between charts were significant. Alexandra Mark made a statistical study of cross-aspects of Venus-Mars and Sun-Moon using nearly as many cases as the Shanks study. She found that trines were not significant statistically. Thus that study confirmed DeVore's views. My wife Vivia has suggested that squares must also be included as indicative, not of compatibility issues, but rather of the interfering effects of external conditions. A man and woman may be quite compatible, but due to the distance apart at which they live, other obligations that one or both have, and other factors, there may be serious impediments to their relationship.

Now if the only really important cross-aspects are conjunctions, oppositions, and squares, then parallels and contraparallels, due to their relationships to conjunctions and oppositions respectively, may also be valuable in assessing the relationship potential between two people. Let us, therefore, consider the role of parallels and contraparallels, including antiscia and contrasicia, and ecliptic parallels and contraparallels.

Figures 5 and 6 are the natal charts of Marilyn Monroe and Arthur Miller, to whom she was married and later divorced. She was born June 1, 1926 in Los Angeles, California at 9:26 a.m., Pacific Standard Time, as rectified by Ronald Davison of England. The longitude was 118W15 and the geocentric latitude was 33N52.

Arthur Miller, one of the leading playwrights, was born October 17, 1915 in New York, New York at an unknown time so I have erected a solar chart for him based on noon positions for New York. As a result, it is only the Moon whose declination is quite uncertain (by about plus or minus two and a half degrees). Longitudinal orbs of three degrees will be used (all orbs are being read in longitude via the ecliptic equivalent).

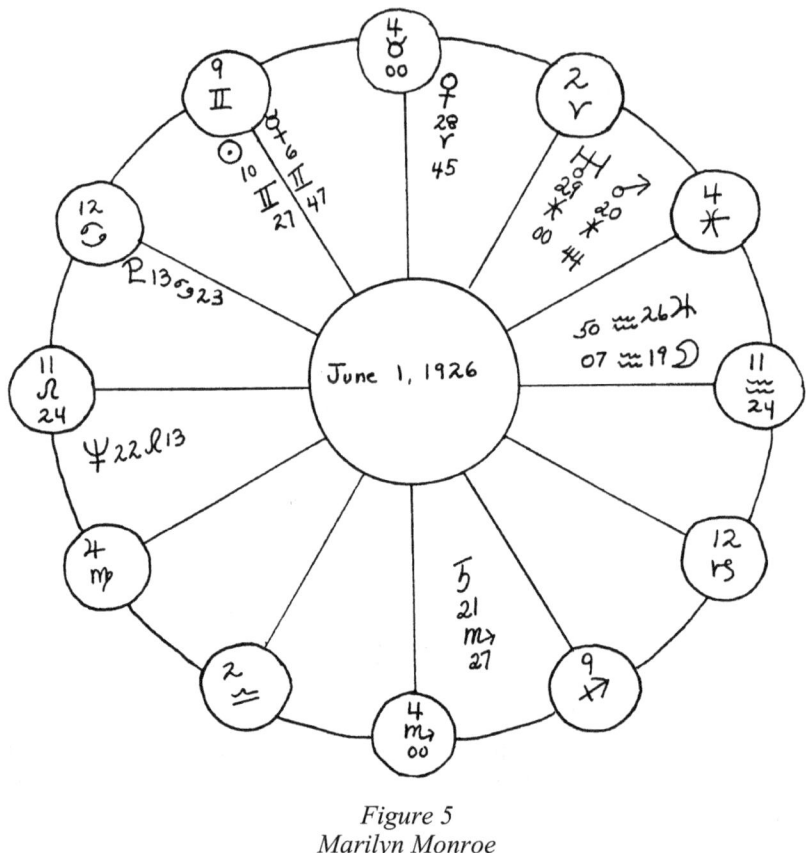

Figure 5
Marilyn Monroe

The cross-aspects in longitude, the conventional ones, are mainly to her Midheaven at 4 Taurus 00. His Mercury-Venus conjunction in early Scorpio is opposite that Midheaven, and his early Leo Neptune is square it. There were stresses between them over her career. His Jupiter is conjunct her Mars, a generous combination. And his Saturn was barely (2°59′) conjunct her Pluto, indicative of insecurity factors. Thus, there are five such conventional cross-aspects, whereas there are no less than twelve by declination, only one of which is a repetition of a longitudinal aspect.

The longitude and the antiscia positions are given in Table I. From this it can be learned whether there are any antiscia or contrascia between the charts of Monroe and Miller.

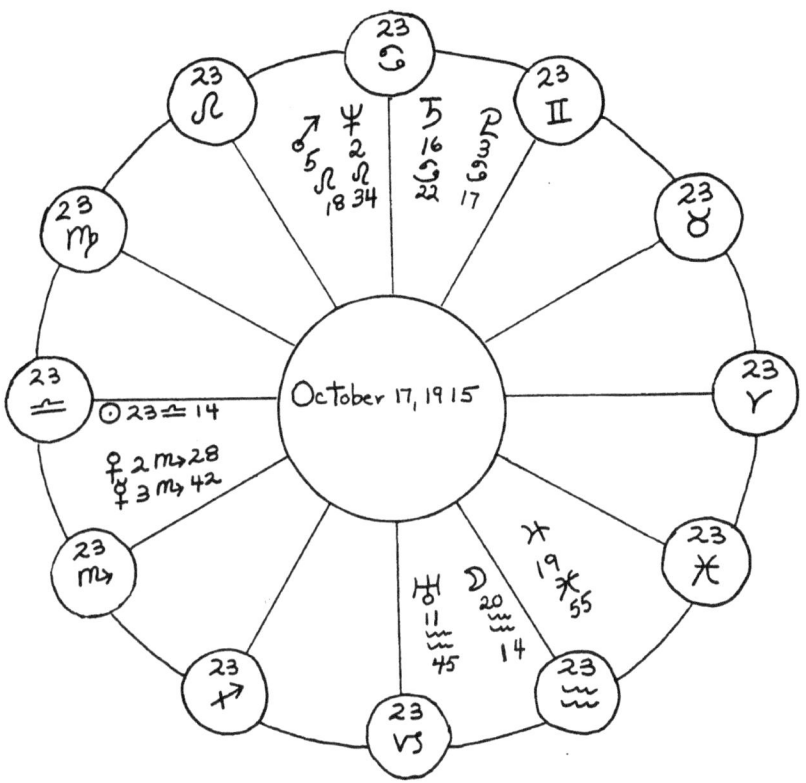

Figure 6
Arthur Miller

Marilyn Monroe		**Arthur Miller**		
Longitude	**Antiscia**		**Longitude**	**Antiscia**
4 ♉ 00	26 ♌ 00	MC		?
11 ♌ 24	18 ♉ 36	ASC		?
22 ♐ 31	7 ♑ 29	Vertex		?
10 ♊ 27	19 ♋ 33	Sun	23 ♎ 14	6 ♓ 46
19 ♒ 7	10 ♏ 53	Moon	20 ♒ 14?	9 ♏ 10?
6 ♊ 47	23 ♋ 13	Mercury	3 ♏ 42	26 ♒ 18
28 ♈ 45	1 ♍ 15	Venus	2 ♏ 28	27 ♒ 32
20 ♓ 44	9 ♎ 16	Mars	5 ♌ 18	24 ♉ 42
26 ♒ 50	3 ♏ 10	Jupiter	19 ♓ 55	10 ♎ 05
21 ♏ 27	8 ♒ 33	Saturn	16 ♋ 22	13 ♊ 38
29 ♓ 00	1 ♎ 00	Uranus	11 ♒ 45	18 ♏ 15
22 ♌ 13	7 ♉ 47	Neptune	2 ♌ 34	27 ♉ 26
13 ♋ 23	16 3 37	Pluto	3 ♋ 17	26 ♊ 43

The sole antiscion (parallel) is that of her Jupiter to his Mercury—both underlined. The orb is a fairly close 0°32′. She had a cheering effect on his mental outlook. The ecliptic parallels, and the ecliptic equivalents they are based on are from Table II.

Marilyn Monroe			**Arthur Miller**			
Decl. S	Planet	Ecl. Eq. S	Ecl. Eq. S	Planet		Decl. S
-23:14	Vertex·	7 ♑ 29	22 ♐ 31			
+22:01	Sun	19 ♋ 33	10 ♒ 27	20 ♋ 23	8 ♊ 37	Saturn	+21:53
+21:40	Mercury	21 ♋ 53	8 3 07			
+21:13	Pluto	24 ♋ 28	5 3 32			
				29 ♋ 59	0 ♊ 01	Mars	+20:09
				3 ♌ 54	26 ♉ 00	Neptune	+19:18
				8 ♌ 21	21 ♉ 39	Pluto	+18:11
				9 ♒ 18	20 ♏ 42	Uranus	-17:56
+17:42	Moon	10 ♒ 10	19 ♏ 5			
+17:20	ASC	11 ♌ 24	18 ♉ 36			
-15:50	Saturn	16 ♒ 42	13 ♏ 18			
			18 ♒ 56	11 ♏ 04	Mercury	-15:09
+14:29	Neptune	21 ♌ 03	8 ♉ 57			
			?21 ♒ 38	?8 ♏ 22	Moon	?-14:18
-13:21	Jupiter	24 ♒ 32	5 ♏ 28			
+12:51	MC	26 ♌ 00	4 ♉ 00			
				29 ♒ 13	0 ♏ 27	Venus	-11:38
+9:01	Venus	6 ♍ 51	23 ♈ 09	6 ♓ 48	23 ♎ 12	Sun	-9:01
-5:40	Mars	15 ♓ 38	14 ♎ 22			
				16 ♓ 17	13 ♎ 43	Jupiter	-5:25
-1:05	Uranus	27 ♓ 17	2 ♎ 43			

Note that his Saturn is ecliptic-parallel her Sun by 3°22′—a bit wide, but it is a light. This is a binding aspect, and he may have tried to discipline her. The other aspect is an ecliptic contraparallel of his Uranus to her Ascendant (orb of only 0°21′), which is why they eventually separated. This is also a regular ("bodily") contraparallel with an orb of 2°06′, indicating its strength as a result of the duplication. The only other duplication is the parallel of his Jupiter to her Mars (orb 0°39′), which is also a conjunction in longitude.

Arthur Miller has Uranus contraparallel Pluto, which meshes with her Moon contraparallel her Leo Ascendant. As a result, his Pluto is parallel her Ascendant and is contraparallel her Moon. This is a very potent psychological influence, basically separative in nature. Marilyn sought intellectual stimulus via her husband and his friends. This is shown, as are the difficulties, by the double Mercury-Saturn contacts: his Mercury parallel her Saturn, 2°14′, and her Mercury parallels his Saturn (orb of 1°30′). While this does add mental depth, it spells out communication problems. And his Mercury is contraparallel her Neptune (orb of 2°07′) which showed that he really didn't understand her at all well! Yet there was genuine love since there is a very close contraparallel of her Venus to his Libra Sun—two minutes in declination and only five minutes in the longitudinal equivalent. The considerable number of aspects between their charts shows the importance to both of them of their relationship. This is not as clearly shown by aspects in longitude only.

Actually this technique must still be tested to be sure that it is not merely a chance phenomenon. Using orbs of plus or minus three degrees, we find the normal expectancy is for six cross-aspects via longitude (conjunctions, oppositions, and squares) three for antiscia and contrascia, three for ecliptic parallels and contraparallels, and three for bodily parallels and contraparallels, or nine via declination plus six via longitude for a total of fifteen.

In the case just reviewed there are fourteen (omitting his angles), which is above normal expectancy. Now, narrow the orbs to plus or minus one degree for longitudes and for the ecliptic equivalents. Then there ought to be two via longitude and three via the various modes of declination, or a total of five. This is better, since there are seven. And for the sake of consistency, angles are excluded since they are not available for Miller. The seven are: Jupiter conjunct Mars, Mercury antiscion Jupiter, Uranus ecliptic-contraparallel Ascendant, Uranus parallel Moon, Jupiter parallel Mars, and Sun contraparallel Venus. The deviation above chance is solely due to the bodily parallels and the contraparallels, of which there are three versus a normal one.

Of course, the issue is not solely one of the frequency of aspects. For if they are only random phenomena, then their nature will not fit the relationship between the two people. Conceivably, a merely normal number of aspects may be highly significant if they very accurately fit the nature of the relationship. This is one cogent reason why a crude statistical assessment of astrological factors may be inadequate as a measure of judgment.

It may be argued that the ability to predict is a valid test. If a competent astrologer is presented with a merely normal number of interchart aspects which, however, give an accurate picture of the relationship, he or she will be able to describe that relationship quite accurately. And this would be quite impossible if those interchart factors were actually only of a random character. This must be one reason why some capable astrologers who do not happen to have a scientific orientation have serenely disregarded the whole issue of statistics. Astrology is unique in that it endeavors to deal with qualitative as well as quantitative factors.

Table I

Decl.	Ecliptic Equiv. S		Decl.	Ecliptic Equiv. S	
0:00	0 AR 00.0 2.51	00 LI 00.0	3:30	8 AR 49.6 2.54	21 VI 10.4
0:10	0 AR 25.1 2.51	29 VI 34.9	3:40	9 AR 15 2.54	20 VI 45
0:20	0 AR 50.3 2.51	29 VI 9.7	3:50	9 AR 40.4 2.55	20 VI 19.6
0:30	1 AR 15.4 2.51	28 VI 44.6	4:00	10 AR 5.8 2.55	19 VI 54.2
0:40	1 AR 40.5 2.51	28 VI 19.5	4:10	10 AR 31.3 2.55	19 VI 28.7
0:50	2 AR 5.7 2.52	27 VI 54.3	4:20	10 AR 56.8 2.55	19 VI 3.2
1:00	2 AR 30.8 2.52	27 VI 29.2	4:30	11 AR 22.4 2.56	18 VI 37.6
1:10	2 AR 56 2.52	27 VI 4	4:40	11 AR 47.9 2.56	18 VI 12.1
1:20	3 AR 21.2 2.52	265 VI 38.8	4:50	12 AR 13.6 2.56	17 VI 46.4
1:30	3 AR 46.3 2.52	26 VI 13.7	5:00	12 AR 39.2 2.57	17 VI 20.8
1:40	4 AR 11.5 2.52	25 VI 48.5	5:10	13 AR 4.9 2.57	16 VI 55.1
1:50	4 AR 36.7 2.52	25 VI 23.3	5:20	13 AR 30.6 2.58	16 VI 29.4
2:00	5 AR 1.9 2.52	24 VI 58.1	5:30	13 AR 56.3 2.58	16 VI 3.7
2:10	5 AR 27.1 2.52	24 VI 32.9	5:40	14 AR 22.1 2.58	15 VI 37.9
2:20	5 AR 52.4 2.53	24 VI 7.6	5:50	14 AR 48 2.59	15 VI 12
2:30	6 AR 17.6 2.53	23 VI 42.4	6:00	15 AR 13.9 2.59	14 VI 46.1
2:40	6 AR 42.9 2.53	23 VI 17.1	6:10	15 AR 39.8 2.6	14 VI 20.2
2:50	7 AR 8.2 2.53	22 VI 51.8	6:20	16 AR 5.8 2.6	13 VI 54.2
3:00	7 AR 33.5 2.53	22 VI 26.5	6:30	16 AR 31.8 2.61	13 VI 28.2
3:10	7 AR 58.8 2.54	22 VI 1.2	6:40	16 AR 57.9 2.61	13 VI 2.1
3:20	8 AR 24.2 2.54	21 VI 35.8	6:50	17 AR 24 2.62	12 VI 36

Decl.	Ecliptic Equiv.	S	Decl.	Ecliptic Equiv.	S
7:00	17 AR 50.2	12 VI 9.8	10:30	27 AR 15.5	2 VI 44.5
	2.62			2.79	
7:10	18 AR 16.4	11 VI 43.6	10:40	27 AR 43.4	2 VI 16.6
	2.63			2.8	
7:20	18 AR 42.7	11 VI 17.3	10:50	28 AR 11.3	1 VI 48.7
	2.63			2.81	
7:30	19 AR 9	10 VI 51	11:00	28 AR 39.4	1 VI 20.6
	2.64			2.82	
7:40	19 AR 35.4	10 VI 24.6	11:10	29 AR 7.6	0 VI 52.4
	2.65			2.83	
7:50	20 AR 1.9	9 VI 58.1	11:20	29 AR 35.9	0 VI 24.1
	2.65			2.84	
8:00	20 AR 28.5	9 VI 31.5	11:30	0 TA 4.3	29 LE 55.7
	2.66			2.85	
8:10	20 AR 55.1	9 VI 4.9	11:40	0 TA 32.8	29 LE 27.2
	2.67			2.86	
8:20	21 AR 21.7	8 VI 38.3	11:50	1 TA 1.4	28 LE 58.6
	2.67			2.88	
8:30	21 AR 48.5	8 VI 11.5	12:00	1 TA 30.2	28 LE 29.8
	2.68			2.89	
8:40	22 AR 15.3	7 VI 44.7	12:10	1 TA 59.1	28 LE .9
	2.69			2.9	
8:50	22 AR 42.1	7 VI 17.9	12:20	2 TA 28.1	27 LE 31.9
	2.7			2.92	
9:00	23 AR 9.1	6 VI 50.9	12:30	2 TA 57.3	27 LE 2.7
	2.7			2.93	
9:10	23 AR 36.1	6 VI 23.9	12:40	3 TA 26.6	26 LE 33.4
	2.71			2.95	
9:20	24 AR 3.3	5 VI 56.7	12:50	3 TA 56.1	26 LE 3.9
	2.72			2.96	
9:30	24 AR 30.5	5 VI 29.5	13:00	4 TA 25.7	25 LE 34.3
	2.73			2.98	
9:40	24 AR 57.8	5 VI 2.2	13:10	4 TA 55.5	25 LE 4.5
	2.74			2.99	
9:50	25 AR 25.1	4 VI 34.9	13:20	5 TA 25.4	24 LE 34.6
	2.75			3.01	
10:00	25 AR 52.6	4 VI 7.4	13:30	5 TA 55.5	24 LE 4.5
	2.76			3.03	
10:10	26 AR 20.1	3 VI 39.9	13:40	6 TA 25.7	23 LE 34.3
	2.77			3.04	
10:20	26 AR 47.8	3 VI 12.2	13:50	6 TA 56.2	23 LE 3.8
	2.77			3.06	

Decl.	Ecliptic Equiv. S		Decl.	Ecliptic Equiv. S	
14:00	7 TA 26.8	22 LE 33.2	17:30	19 TA 5.6	10 LE 54.4
	3.08			3.68	
14:10	7 TA 57.6	22 LE 2.4	17:40	19 TA 42.4	10 LE 17.6
	3.1			3.73	
14:20	8 TA 28.6	21 LE 31.4	17:50	20 TA 19.6	9 LE 40.4
	3.12			3.77	
14:30	8 TA 59.8	21 LE .2	18:00	20 TA 57.3	9 LE 2.7
	3.14			3.82	
14:40	9 TA 31.2	20 LE 28.8	18:10	21 TA 35.5	8 LE 24.5
	3.16			3.87	
14:50	10 TA 2.9	19 LE 57.1	18:20	22 TA 14.2	7 LE 45.8
	3.19			3.92	
15:00	10 TA 34.7	19 LE 25.3	18:30	22 TA 53.4	7 LE 6.6
	3.21			3.98	
15:10	11 TA 6.8	18 LE 53.2	18:40	23 TA 33.2	6 LE 26.8
	3.23			4.04	
15:20	11 TA 39.1	18 LE 20.9	18:50	24 TA 13.6	5 LE 46.4
	3.26			4.1	
15:30	12 TA 11.7	17 LE 48.3	19:00	24 TA 54.6	5 LE 5.4
	3.28			4.17	
15:40	12 TA 44.5	17 LE 15.5	19:10	25 TA 36.3	4 LE 23.7
	3.31			4.24	
15:50	13 TA 17.6	16 LE 42.4	19:20	26 TA 18.7	3 LE 41.3
	3.34			4.31	
16:00	13 TA 51	16 LE 9	19:30	27 TA 1.8	2 LE 58.2
	3.36			4.39	
16:10	14 TA 24.6	15 LE 35.4	19:40	27 TA 45.8	2 LE 14.2
	3.39			4.48	
16:20	14 TA 58.5	15 LE 1.5	19:50	28 TA 30.6	1 LE 29.4
	3.43			4.57	
16:30	15 TA 32.8	14 LE 27.2	20:00	29 TA 16.3	0 LE 43.7
	3.46			2.32	
16:40	16 TA 7.4	13 LE 52.6	20:05	29 TA 39.6	0 LE 0.4
	3.49			2.35	
16:50	16 TA 42.3	13 LE 17.7	20:10	0 GE 3.1	29 CA 56.9
	3.53			2.38	
17:00	17 TA 17.5	12 LE 42.5	20:15	0 GE 26.8	29 CA 33.2
	3.56			2.4	
17:10	17 TA 53.1	12 LE 6.9	20:20	0 GE 50.9	29 CA 9.1
	3.6			2.43	
17:20	18 TA 29.2	11 LE 30.8	20:25	1 GE 15.2	28 CA 24.8
	3.64			2.46	

Decl.	Ecliptic Equiv. S		Decl.	Ecliptic Equiv. S	
20:30	1 GE 39.9 2.5	28 CA 20.1	22:15	12 GE 6.8 3.85	17 CA 53.2
20:35	2 GE 4.8 2.53	27 CA 55.2	22:20	12 GE 45.3 3.99	17 CA 14.7
20:40	2 GE 30.1 2.56	27 CA 29.9	22:25	13 GE 25.2 4.15	16 CA 34.8
20:45	2 GE 55.7 2.6	27 CA 4.3	22:30	14 GE 6.8 4.34	15 CA 53.2
20:50	3 GE 21.8 2.64	26 CA 38.2	22:35	14 GE 50.1 4.55	15 CA 9.9
20:55	3 GE 48.1 2.68	26 CA 11.9	22:40	15 GE 35.6 4.79	14 CA 24.4
21:00	4 GE 14.9 2.72	25 CA 45.1	22:45	16 GE 23.5 5.08	13 CA 36.5
21:05	4 GE 42.2 2.77	25 CA 17.8	22:50	17 GE 14.3 5.43	12 CA 45.7
21:10	5 GE 9.8 2.81	24 CA 50.2	22:55	18 GE 8.6 5.87	11 CA 51.4
21:15	5 GE 38 2.86	24 CA 22	23:00	19 GE 7.3 1.24	10 CA 52.7
21:20	6 GE 6.6 2.92	23 CA 53.4	23:01	19 GE 19.7 1.26	10 CA 40.3
21:25	6 GE 35.8 2.97	23 CA 24.2	23:02	19 GE 32.3 1.29	10 CA 27.7
21:30	7 GE 5.5 3.03	22 CA 54.5	23:03	19 GE 45.1 1.31	10 CA 14.9
21:35	7 GE 35.9 3.1	22 CA 24.1	23:04	19 GE 58.3 1.34	10 CA 1.7
21:40	8 GE 6.9 3.17	21 CA 53.1	23:05	20 GE 11.7 1.37	9 CA 48.3
21:45	8 GE 38.6 3.24	21 CA 21.4	23:06	20 GE 25.4 1.41	9 CA 34.6
21:50	9 GE 11 3.32	20 CA 49	23:07	20 GE 39.5 1.44	9 CA 20.5
21:55	9 GE 44.2 3.41	20 CA 15.8	23:08	20 GE 53.9 1.48	9 CA 6.1
22:00	10 GE 18.3 3.51	19 CA 41.7	23:09	21 GE 8.7 1.52	8 CA 51.3
22:05	10 GE 53.4 3.61	19 CA 6.6	23:10	21 GE 24 1.57	8 CA 36
22:10	11 GE 29.5 3.73	18 CA 30.5	23:11	21 GE 39.7 1.62	8 CA 20.3

Decl.	Ecliptic Equiv.	S
23:12	21 GE 55.8	8 CA 4.2
	1.67	
23:13	22 GE 12.6	7 CA 47.4
	1.74	
23:14	22 GE 30	7 CA 30
	1.81	
23:15	22 GE 48	7 CA 12
	1.88	
23:16	23 GE 6.8	6 CA 53.2
	1.97	
23:17	23 GE 26.6	6 CA 33.4
	2.08	
23:18	23 GE 47.3	6 CA 12.7
	2.2	
23:19	24 GE 9.3	5 CA 50.7
	2.34	
23:20	24 GE 32.7	5 CA 27.3
	2.52	
23:21	24 GE 58	5 CA 2
	2.76	
23:22	25 GE 25.5	4 CA 34.5
	3.06	
23:23	25 GE 56.2	4 CA 3.8
	3.51	
23:24	26 GE 31.3	3 CA 28.7
	4.23	
23:25	27 GE 13.5	2 CA 46.5
	5.76	
23:26	28 GE 11.1	1 CA 48.9
	2.01	
23:26	28 GE 31.2	1 CA 28.8
	2.62	
23:26	28 GE 57.4	1 CA 2.6
	6.26	
23:26	00 CA 00	00 CA 00

Table II

Long. S	Decl. S	Long. S	Long. S	Decl. S	Long. S
0 AR 30	+0:11.9 .4'	29 VI 30	11 AR 00	+4:21.2 .39'	19 VI 00
1 AR 00	+0:23.9 .4'	29 VI 00	11 AR 30	+4:33 .39'	18 VI 30
1 AR 30	+0:35.8 .4'	28 VI 30	12 AR 00	+4:44.7 .39'	18 VI 00
2 AR 00	+0:47.7 .4'	28 VI 00	12 AR 30	+4:56.4 .39'	17 VI 30
2 AR 30	+0:59.7 .4'	27 VI 30	13 AR 00	+5:08.1 .39'	17 VI 00
3 AR 00	+1:11.6 .4'	27 VI 00	13 AR 30	+5:19.8 .39'	16 VI 30
3 AR 30	+1:23.5 .4'	26 VI 30	14 AR 00	+5:31.4 .39'	16 VI 00
4 AR 00	+1:35.4 .4'	26 VI 00	14 AR 30	+5:43 .39'	15 VI 30
4 AR 30	+1:47.3 .4'	25 VI 30	15 AR 00	+5:54.6 .39'	15 VI 00
5 AR 00	+1:59.2 .4'	25 VI 00	15 AR 30	+6:06.2 .39	14 VI 30
5 AR 30	+2:11.1 .4'	24 VI 30	16 AR 00	+6:17.8 .38	14 VI 00
6 AR 00	+2:23 .4'	24 VI 00	16 AR 30	+6:29.3 .38'	13 VI 30
6 AR 30	+2:34.9 .4'	23 VI 30	17 AR 00	+6:40.8 .38'	13 VI 00
7 AR 00	+2:46.8 .4'	23 VI 00	17 AR 30	+6:52.3 .38'	12 VI 30
7 AR 30	+2:58.6 .39'	22 VI 30	18 AR 00	+7:03.8 .38'	12 VI 00
8 AR 00	+3:10.5 .39'	22 VI 00	18 AR 30	+7:15.2 .38'	11 VI 30
8 AR 30	+3:22.3 .39'	21 VI 30	19 AR 00	+7:26.6 .38'	11 VI 00
9 AR 00	+3:34.1 .39'	21 VI 00	19 AR 30	+7:37.9 .38'	10 VI 30
9 AR 30	+3:45.9 .39'	20 VI 30	20 AR 00	+7:49.3 .38'	10 VI 00
10 AR 00	+3:57.7 .39'	20 VI 00	20 AR 30	+8:0.6 .38'	9 VI 30
10 AR 30	+4:09.5 .39'	19 VI 30	21 AR 00	+8:11.9 .37	9 VI 00

Long. S	Decl. S	Long. S	Long. S	Decl. S	Long. S
21 AR 30	+8:23.1 .37'	8 VI 30	2 TA 00	+12:10.3 .35'	28 LE 00
22 AR 00	+8:34.3 .37'	8 VI 00	2 TA 30	+12:20.6 .34'	27 LE 30
22 AR 30	+8:45.5 .37'	7 VI 30	3 TA 00	+12:30.9 .34'	27 LE 00
23 AR 00	+8:56.6 .37'	7 VI 00	3 TA 30	+12:41.2 .34'	26 LE 30
23 AR 30	+9:07.7 .37'	6 VI 30	4 TA 00	+12:51.3 .34'	26 LE 00
24 AR 00	+9:18.8 .37'	6 VI 00	4 TA 30	+13:01.5 .34'	25 LE 30
24 AR 30	+9:29.8 .37'	5 VI 30	5 TA 00	+13:11.5 .33'	25 LE 00
25 AR 00	+9:40.8 .37'	5 VI 00	5 TA 30	+13:21.5 .33'	24 LE 30
25 AR 30	+9:51.8 .36'	4 VI 30	6 TA 00	+13:31.5 .33'	24 LE 00
26 AR 00	+10:02.7 .36'	4 VI 00	6 TA 30	+13:41.4 .33'	23 LE 30
26 AR 30	+10:13.6 .36'	3 VI 30	7 TA 00	+13:51.2 .33'	23 LE 00
27 AR 00	+10:24.4 .36'	3 VI 00	7 TA 30	+14:01 .32'	22 LE 30
27 AR 30	+10:35.2 .36'	2 VI 30	8 TA 00	+14:10.8 .32'	22 LE 00
28 AR 00	+10:45.9 .36'	2 VI 00	8 TA 30	+14:20.4 .32'	21 LE 30
28 AR 30	+10:56.7 .36'	1 VI 30	9 TA 00	+14:30.1 .32'	21 LE 00
29 AR 00	+11:07.3 .35'	1 VI 00	9 TA 30	+14:39.6 .32'	20 LE 30
29 AR 30	+11:17.9 .35'	0 VI 30	10 TA 00	+14:49.1 .31'	20 LE 00
0 TA 00	+11:28.5 .35'	0 VI 00	10 TA 30	+14:58.5 .31'	19 LE 30
0 TA 30	+11:39 .35'	29 LE 30	11 TA 00	+15:07.9 .31'	19 LE 00
1 TA 00	+11:49.5 .35'	29 LE 00	11 TA 30	+15:17.2 .31'	18 LE 30
1 TA 30	+11:59.9' .35'	28 LE 30	12 TA 00	+15:26.4 .31'	18 LE 00

Parallels: Their Hidden Meaning

Long. S	Decl. S	Long. S	Long. S	Decl. S	Long. S
12 TA 30	+15:35.6 .3'	17 LE 30	23 TA 00	+18:31.7 .25'	7 LE 00
13 TA 00	+15:44.7 .3'	17 LE 00	23 TA 30	+18:39.2 .25'	6 LE 30
13 TA 30	+15:53.7 .3'	16 LE 30	24 TA 00	+18:46.6 .25'	6 LE 00
14 TA 00	+16:02.7 .3'	16 LE 00	24 TA 30	+18:54 .24'	5 LE 30
14 TA 30	+16:11.6 .29'	15 LE 30	25 TA 00	+19:01.3 .24'	5 LE 00
15 TA 00	+16:20.4 .29'	15 LE 00	25 TA 30	19:08.5 .24'	4 LE 30
15 TA 30	+16:29.2 .29'	14 LE 30	26 TA 00	+19:15.6 .23'	4 LE 00
16 TA 00	+16:37.9 .29'	14 LE 00	26 TA 30	19:22.6 .23'	3 LE 30
16 TA 30	+16:46.5 .28'	13 LE 30	27 TA 00	+19:29.6 .23'	3 LE 00
17 TA 00	+16:55 .28'	13 LE 00	27 TA 30	+19:36.4 .23'	2 LE 30
17 TA 30	+17:03.5 .28'	12 LE 30	28 TA 00	+19:43.2 .22'	2 LE 00
18 TA 00	+17:11.9 .28'	12 LE 00	28 TA 30	+19:49.9 .22'	1 LE 30
18 TA 30	+17:20.2 .27'	11 LE 30	29 TA 00	+19:56.5 .22'	1 LE 00
19 TA 00	+17:28.5 .27'	11 LE 00	29 TA 30	+20:02.9 .21'	1 LE 30
19 TA 30	+17:36.7 .27'	10 LE 30	0 GE 00	+20:09.4 .21'	0 LE 00
20 TA 00	+17:44.7 .27'	10 LE 00	1 GE 00	+20:21.9 .2'	29 CA 00
20 TA 30	+17:52.8 .26'	9 LE 30	2 GE 00	+20:34 .2'	28 CA 00
21 TA 00	+18:0.7 .26'	9 LE 00	3 GE 00	+20:45.8 .19'	27 CA 00
21 TA 30	+18:08.6 .26'	8 LE 30	4 GE 00	+20:57.2 .18'	26 CA 00
22 TA 00	+18:16.3 .26'	8 LE 00	5 GE 00	+21:08.2 .18'	25 CA 00
22 TA 30	+18:24 .25'	7 LE 30	6 GE 00	+21:18.9 .17'	24 CA 00

Long. S	Decl. S	Long. S	Long. S	Decl. S	Long. S
7 GE 00	+21:29.1 .16'	23 CA 00	28 GE 00	+23:25.8 .01'	2 CA 00
8 GE 00	+21:38.9 .16'	22 CA 00	29 GE 00	+23:26.5 0'	1 CA 00
9 GE 00	+21:48.3 .15'	21 CA 00	0 CA 00	+23:26.7 0'	0 CA 00
10 GE 00	+21:57.3 .14'	20 CA 00	0 LI 30	-0:11.9 .4'	29 PI 30
11 GE 00	+22:05.9 .14'	19 CA 00	1 LI 00	-0:23.9 .4'	29 PI 00
12 GE 00	+22:14.1 .13'	18 CA 00	1 LI 30	-0:35.8 .4'	28 PI 30
13 GE 00	+22:21.9 .12'	17 CA 00	2 LI 00	-0:47.7 .4	28 PI 00
14 GE 00	+22:29.2 .12'	16 CA 00	2 LI 30	-0:59.7 .4'	27 PI 30
15 GE 00	+22:36.1 .11'	15 CA 00	3 LI 00	-1:11.6 .4'	27 PI 00
16 GE 00	+22:42.6 .1'	14 CA 00	3 LI 30	-1:23.5 .4'	26 PI 30
17 GE 00	+22:48.6 .09'	13 CA 00	4 LI 00	-1:35.4 .4'	26 PI 00
18 GE 00	+22:54.2 .09'	12 CA 00	4 LI 30	-1:47.3 .4'	25 PI 30
19 GE 00	+22:59.4 .08	11 CA 00	5 LI 00	-1:59.2 .4'	25 PI 00
20 GE 00	+23:04.1 .07'	10 CA 00	5 LI 30	-2:11.1 .4'	24 PI 30
21 GE 00	23:08.4 .06'	9 CA 00	6 LI 00	-2:23 .4'	24 PI 00
22 GE 00	+23:12.3 .06'	8 CA 00	6 LI 30	-2:34.9 .4'	23 PI 30
23 GE 00	+23:15.6 .05'	7 CA 00	7 LI 00	-2:46.8 .4'	23 PI 00
24 GE 00	+23:18.6 .04'	6 CA 00	7 LI 30	-2:58.6 .39'	22 PI 30
25 GE 00	+23:21.1 .03'	5 CA 00	8 LI 00	-3:10.5 .39'	22 PI 00
26 GE 00	+23:23.1 .03'	4 CA 00	8 LI 30	-3:22.3 .39'	21 PI 30
27 GE 00	+23:24.7 .02'	3 CA 00	9 LI 00	-3:34.1 .39'	21 PI 00

Long. S	Decl. S	Long. S	Long. S	Decl. S	Long. S
9 LI 30	-3:45.9 .39'	20 PI 30	20 LI 00	-7:49.3 .38'	10 PI 00
10 LI 00	-3:57.7 .39'	20 PI 00	20 LI 30	-8:00.6 .38'	9 PI 30
10 LI 30	-4:09.5 .39'	19 PI 30	21 LI 00	-8:11.9 .37'	9 PI 00
11 LI 00	-4:21.2 .39'	19 PI 00	21 LI 30	-8:23.1 .37'	8 PI 30
11 LI 30	-4:33 .39'	18 PI 30	22 LI 00	-8:34.3 .37'	8 PI 00
12 LI 00	-4:44.7 .39'	18 PI 00	22 LI 30	-8:45.5 .37'	7 PI 30
12 LI 30	-4:56.4 .39'	17 PI 30	23 LI 00	-8:56.6 .37'	7 PI 00
13 LI 00	-5:08.1 .39'	17 PI 00	23 LI 30	-9:07.7 .37'	6 PI 30
13 LI 30	-5:19.8 .39'	16 PI 30	24 LI 00	-9:18.8 .37'	6 PI 00
14 LI 00	-5:31.4 .39'	16 PI 00	24 LI 30	-9:29.8 .37'	5 PI 30
14 LI 30	-5:43 .39'	15 PI 30	25 LI 00	-9:40.8 .37'	5 PI 00
15 LI 00	-5:54.6 .39'	15 PI 00	25 LI 30	-9:51.8 .36'	4 PI 30
15 LI 30	-6:06.2 .39'	14 PI 30	26 LI 00	-10:02.7 .36'	4 PI 00
16 LI 00	-6:17.8 .38'	14 PI 00	26 LI 30	-10:13.6 .36'	3 PI 30
16 LI 30	-6:29.3 .38'	13 PI 30	27 LI 00	-10:24.4 .36'	3 PI 00
17 LI 00	-6:40.8 .38'	13 PI 00	27 LI 30	-10:35.2 .36'	2 PI 30
17 LI 30	-6:52.3 .38'	12 PI 30	28 LI 00	-10:45.9 .36'	2 PI 00
18 LI 00	-7:03.8 .38'	12 PI 00	28 LI 30	-10:56.7 .36'	1 PI 30
18 LI 30	-7:15.2 .38'	11 PI 30	29 LI 00	-11:07.3 .35'	1 PI 00
19 LI 00	-7:26.6 .38'	11 PI 00	29 LI 30	-11:17.9 .35'	0 PI 30
19 LI 30	-7:37.9 .38'	10 PI 30	0 SC 00	-11:28.5 .35'	0 PI 00

Long. S	Decl. S	Long. S	Long. S	Decl. S	Long. S
0 SC 30	-11:39.35'	29 AQ 30	11 SC 00	-15:07.9 .31'	19 AQ 00
1 SC 00	-11:49.5 .35'	29 AQ 00	11 SC 30	-15:17.2 .31'	18 AQ 30
1 SC 30	-11:59.9 .35'	28 AQ 30	12 SC 00	-15:26.4 .31'	18 AQ 00
2 SC 00	-12:10.3 .34'	28 AQ 00	12 SC 30	-15:35.6 .3'	17 AQ 30
2 SC 30	-12:20.6 .34'	27 AQ 30	13 SC 00	-15:44.7 .3'	17 AQ 00
3 SC 00	-12:30.9 .34'	27 AQ 00	13 SC 30	-15:53.7 .3'	16 AQ 30
3 SC 30	-12:41.2 .34'	26 AQ 30	14 SC 00	-16:02.7 .3'	16 AQ 00
4 SC 00	-12:51.3 .34'	26 AQ 00	14 SC 30	-16:11.6 .29'	15 AQ 30
4 SC 30	-13:01.5 .34'	25 AQ 30	15 SC 00	-16:20.4 .29'	15 AQ 00
5 SC 00	-13:11.5 .33'	25 AQ 00	15 SC 30	-16:29.2 .29'	14 AQ 30
5 SC 30	-13:21.5 .33'	24 AQ 30	16 SC 00	-16:37.9 .29'	14 AQ 00
6 SC 00	-13:31.5 .33'	24 AQ 00	16 SC 30	-16:46.5 .28'	13 AQ 30
6 SC 30	-13:41.4 .33'	23 AQ 30	17 SC 00	-16:55 .28'	13 AQ 00
7 SC 00	-13:51.2 .33'	23 AQ 00	17 SC 30	-17:03.5 .28'	12 AQ 30
7 SC 30	-14:01 .32'	22 AQ 30	18 SC 00	-17:11.9 .28'	12 AQ 00
8 SC 00	-14:10.8 .32'	22 AQ 00	18 SC 30	-17:20.2 .27'	11 AQ 30
8 SC 30	-14:20.4 .32'	21 AQ 30	19 SC 00	-17:28.5 .27'	11 AQ 00
9 SC 00	-14:30.1 .32'	21 AQ 00	19 SC 30	-17:36.7 .27'	10 AQ 30
9 SC 30	-14:39.6 .32'	20 AQ 30	20 SC 00	-17:44.7 .27'	10 AQ 00
10 SC 00	-14:49.1 .31'	20 AQ 00	20 SC 30	-17:52.8 .26'	9 AQ 30
10 SC 30	-14:58.5 .31'	19 AQ 30	21 SC 00	-18:00.7 .26'	9 AQ 00

Long. S	Decl. S	Long. S	Long. S	Decl. S	Long. S
21 SC 30	-18:08.6 .26'	8 AQ 30	4 SA 00	-20:57.2 .18'	26 CP 00
22 SC 00	-18:16.3 .26'	8 AQ 00	5 SA 00	-21:08.2 .18	25 CP 00
22 SC 30	-18:24 .25'	7 AQ 30	6 SA 00	-21:18.9 .17'	24 CP 00
23 SC 00	-18:31.7 .25'	7 AQ 00	7 SA 00	-21:29.1 .16'	23 CP 00
23 SC 30	-18:39.2 .25'	6 AQ 30	8 SA 00	-21:38.9 .16'	22 CP 00
24 SC 00	-18:46.6 .25'	6 AQ 00	9 SA 00	-21:48.3 .15'	21 CP 00
24 SC 30	-18:54 .24'	5 AQ 30	10 SA 00	-21:57.3 .14'	20 CP 00
25 SC 00	-19:01.3 .24'	5 AQ 00	11 SA 00	-22:05.9 .14'	19 CP 00
25 SC 30	-19:08.5 .24'	4 AQ 30	12 SA 00	-22:14.1 .13'	18 CP 00
26 SC 00	-19:15.6 .23'	4 AQ 00	13 SA 00	-22:21.9 .12'	17 CP 00
26 SC 30	-19:22.6 .23'	3 AQ 30	14 SA 00	-22:29.2 .12'	16 CP 00
27 SC 00	-19:29.6 .23'	3 AQ 00	15 SA 00	-22:36.1 .11'	15 CP 00
27 SC 30	-19:36.4 .23'	2 AQ 30	16 SA 00	-22:42.6 .10'	14 CP 00
28 SC 00	-19:43.2 .22'	2 AQ 00	17 SA 00	-22:48.6 .09'	13 CP 00
28 SC 30	-19:49.9 .22'	1 AQ 30	18 SA 00	-22:54.2 .09'	12 CP 00
29 SC 00	-19:56.5 .22'	1 AQ 00	19 SA 00	-22:59.4 .08'	11 CP 00
29 SC 30	-20:02.9 .21'	0 AQ 30	20 SA 00	-23:04.1 .07'	10 CP 00
0 SA 00	-20:09.4 .21'	0 AQ 00	21 SA 00	-23:08.4 .06'	9 CP 00
1 SA 00	-20:21.9 .20'	29 CP 00	22 SA 00	-23:12.3 .06'	8 CP 00
2 SA 00	-20:34 .20'	28 CP 00	23 SA 00	-23:15.6 .05'	7 CP 00
3 SA 00	-20:45.8 .19'	27 CP 00	24 SA 00	-23:18.6 .04'	6 CP 00

Long. S	Decl. S	Long. S
25 SA 00	-23:21.1 .03'	5 CP 00
26 SA 00	-23:23.1 .03'	4 CP 00
27 SA 00	-23:24.7 .02'	3 CP 00
28 SA 00	-23:25.8 .01'	2 CP 00
29 SA 00	-23:26.5 0'	1 CP 00
0 CP 00	-23:26.7	0 CP 00

Table III

Declinations North or South	Longitudes Error per Decade
13°	0.12'
14°	0.14'
15°	0.15'
16°	0.175'
17°	0.19'
18°	0.22'
19°	0.25'
20°	0.30'
21°	0.37'
22°	0.50'
23°	0.96'
23°03'	1.00'
23°06'	1.07'
23°09'	1.16'
23°12'	1.27'
23°15'	1.42'
23°18'	1.655'
23°19'	1.76'
23°20'	1.89'
23°21'	2.05'
23°22'	2.26'
23°23'	2.545'
23°24'	2.98'
23°25'	3.754'
23°26'	5.835'
23°26'30"	10.80'

Use the following spans of years for values of the obliquity at the turn:

23°27′15″—1870-1901
23°27′—1902-1933
23°26′45″—1934-1965
23°26′30″—1966-1997

Years are inclusive.

The values in Table I are for 1950. Consider, for example, someone born in 1930 or 20 years before the Table I values and that the declination was +19°00′. At +19°00′, the ecliptic equivalent is 24 Taurus 24.6. Table III shows that the error for 10 years is 0.25′ at 19° north or south, so that for 20 years it will be twice as much or 0.5′. Since 1930 is earlier than 1950, this must be subtracted from the position of Gemini. The correct placement is 24 Gemini 24.1 to the nearest 0.1′ of arc. If the year is 1980, and the declination -23°06′, the error for 10 years at that declination is 1.07′ and for 30 years after 1950 is +3.2′ which is added to 20 Sagittarius 25.4 to give 20°28.6′. If the declination is less than 13° north or south, any error is small.

The Technique
of Rectification

Introduction

　　This book has been properly dedicated to Miss Eleanor Hesseltine to whom we owe so much about the technique of rectification. We should say that all that experience plus the use of orbs, which at maximum range from five minutes before the event to fifteen minutes after it, has conclusively demonstrated the fallacy of both: one degree orbs and such measures as one degree a year or the mean motion of Naibod or 59′08″ a year. We use only the true solar arc and the Ascendant and vertical arcs derived from it in both longitude and declination, and direct and converse.

　　And it is more than appropriate to give deep thanks to my wife Vivia, without whom these publications would not have been printed. Her book, *Aspects to Horoscope Angles*, is just as essential as this one in learning how to rectify an inaccurate birth time. For there is little in the literature on the meaning of planetary aspects to the Ascendant, Midheaven and Vertex. In her book, too, will be found a crucial new discovery she made about such aspects, based on a careful examination of the charts she or I or both of us have rectified.

　　It is impossible to emphasize too much the importance of careful and rigorous examination of the placement of the Ascendant and of the planets in the houses before one uses any arcs of direction. One can find an Ascendant and house orientation that is quite plausible but also wrong. That is to say that one can often find an incorrect placing of the angles for which one can find several convincing reasons to justify such a placement. I used the word rigorous. One really must try hard to be rigorous and consistent in one's interpretations if one is to avoid self-deception. When it comes to directions, I have used a simple arbitrary test, i.e. at least eight major directions, to or by the angles, must ``fit'' not only as to time, but also as to correct meaning before one may consider that the angles are probably right. I suggest that some similar minimum number of factors must fit not only as to directions and events, but also as to their radical static pattern of relationships of houses and angles to lights and planets.

　　I will admit that no one house system is generally agreed upon to be right, but unlike Reinhold Ebertin who ducks this thorny issue by simply not using houses, I use them, but regard intermediate house divisions as not sharp, but rather that one house shades into the next one except at the angles. Charles Carter gave one unit to signs, two units to houses, and two units to aspects. Thus it would seem more important to understand house positions than those in the signs. Does Mr. X have his natal Mars in his second house? Does the chart fit the typical life pattern of circumstances and conditions that the various bodies in the various houses would require? Probably no one astrologer fully understands the answers to all such questions. One astrologer may be very sharp about the house position of Saturn, another astrologer may be excellent at the Moon in the houses, etc. So, use your specialty.

　　In relating bodies to each other, use should always be made of both declinations and midpoints since vital relationships will be missed if one fails to use them. When one has studied a chart with care one can often find one or more pivotal areas, factors, or axes arising out of the complex of relationships. Then the house positions of such foci should prove to be quite significant. In rectifying any horoscopes the astrologer is fitting the signs to the houses, especially the signs to the angles; and the lights and planets to the houses, too. Thus, more attention should be given than usual to the sign on the Midheaven. I believe with Edward Johndro, and found that Marc Edmund Jones assented, that the signs divide into two sections more significantly than into three (the traditional decanates). This discrimination can be most helpful in considering the positioning of the Midheaven and Ascendant in any preliminary rough placement.

One can use the focal factors defined by Jones also. Thus the house position of the singleton in a bucket pattern is critical, or the house position of the leading planet in a bowl or locomotive pattern. There are many, many considerations and the competent astrologer will examine most of them carefully before making a placement of the angles prior to directional testing. It would be well indeed to have a checklist of all such factors that one may feel one understands so that, until it becomes automatic, one systematically checks off these various factors. Most astrologers are too Neptunian and, to be less polite about it, sloppy and careless. This is why more system, rigor, and thoroughness and less psychism, fuzziness, etc. would benefit most of us. At least that is the conclusion I have reached after forty-three years of study and twenty-five years of rectification. There is nothing that will teach you more basic astrology than practicing rectification as much as you can.

Charles A. Jayne
December 4, 1974

The Tools

The solar arc is the distance in longitude from the natal Sun to the Sun progressed by the well-known secondary or day-for-year method. It is extremely simple and easy to determine and is added to everything in the chart except the Ascendant or Vertex. If one has an accurately rectified chart, one can also use the Ascendant and vertical arcs. One adds the solar arc to the natal, or radical, Midheaven. The resultant Midheaven is the progressed Midheaven. Then one finds the Ascendant that corresponds in a tables of houses to this new Midheaven (using the geocentric latitude and not the geographic for finding an Ascendant or Vertex). This new Ascendant is then the progressed Ascendant. This method for finding the progressed Midheaven and Ascendant is used by the Church of Light and by Mr. Davison, president of the Astrological Lodge in England. The arc from the natal or radical Ascendant to the progressed Ascendant is then the Ascendant arc. If in the tables of houses when the Midheaven moves sixty minutes the Ascendant moves, say forty-five minutes, but the Sun is actually moving only fifty-eight minutes a year, then the annual rate of the Ascendant arc will obviously be 45/60 x 58′ or only 43.5′ a year. One uses a similar procedure for finding the annual rate of the vertical arc.

One finds the Vertex, the third angle of a chart, by using the IC as though it were a Midheaven in a tables of houses and the co-latitude (which equals ninety degrees less the geocentric latitude) as though it were the latitude in a tables of houses. The resulting "Ascendant" is actually the Vertex, which is always due west in the chart. The arc from the natal Vertex to the progressed Vertex is the vertical arc. These are the three longitude arcs that we use.

To find the declination arcs, proceed as follows. First find the declinations of the three angles. The declination of the Sun when conjunct the Midheaven gives the declination of the Midheaven, the declination of the Sun conjunct the Ascendant or Vertex gives their declinations—a simple matter of interpolation in any ephemeris. The solar declination arc is the distance that the Sun has moved in declination by secondary progression (or by solar arc as they are the same). If it is at 19°00′ (+ for north and - for south) radically and moves to +23°27′ (4°27′) and then turns (as it always does at this value of the declination) and moves to 19°00′ again (but now with a decreasing declination, whereas radically it was an increasing declination), then it has moved an additional 4°27′ + 4°27′). If it starts at -5°00′, it has crossed the equator, there the declination is 0°00′ and so it has moved 5°00′ + 5°00′; or 10°00′ of solar declination arc in all, if it then moves to +5°00′. Mark in the chart whether the declination is radically increasing or decreasing.

Having found the declinations of both the radical and progressed Ascendants, the difference between the two will be the Ascendant declination arc, the same being true in the finding of the vertical declination arc, provided one takes account of going to the turn and turning back, as described above. To find the annual rate of the solar declination arc is easy; one merely looks in the ephemeris to find its daily motion when in the part of the zodiac that the secondary progressed Sun may be. For the annual rates of the Ascendant and vertical declination arcs, one first finds the daily (annual) motion of the Sun when it is in the part of the zodiac that the progressed Ascendant (or Vertex) is. Then if the Ascendant arc is 43.5′ per year and the Sun's motion in that part of the zodiac should be fifty-eight minutes in longitude and, say sixteen minutes in declination (per day or year by direction), then the equation is: the annual rate of the Ascendant (or vertical) declination arc—(43.5/58.0 x 16′ or is just 12′ a year—and dividing by twelve, is just one minute per month.

One follows exactly the same procedure in finding all the converse arcs, only take the distance that the Sun has moved by converse secondary progression. If a planet is above the turn, its declination is increasing or decreasing radically, it is caused always to decrease when it is directed by any of these three declination arcs. In addition, no body directed by them may be moved above the turn since all is based on the motion of the Sun itself in declination.

1

The Technique of Rectification

The best test of astrological competence that I know of is the ability to rectify charts, but I daresay that nearly all astrologers, except a very small handful, would fail if this were made the criterion for their permission to practice professionally. Why should rectification be given such an overall value? To rectify a chart one must have a good knowledge of all the main phases of astrology: the meaning of the signs, houses, planets, aspects, the ability to interpret, to see the chart as a whole and to pick out the focal features, the ability to cast the chart correctly, the ability to interpret the chart dynamically (a rare ability) as well as statically. I do not know of any single activity an astrologer can engage in that does more to teach astrology than the endeavor to rectify horoscopes.

A serious criticism may be made of most astrologers, i.e. they are far abler to interpret a chart statically (three-dimensions) than dynamically (four-dimensions). Much rectification develops the latter, thus greatly aiding the ability to interpret transits, progressions, and directions in trying to forecast future conditions. I can think of no more necessary discipline and skill for a young astrologer who aspires to be a good professional than to practice, practice, practice the rectification of charts.

I find, from much experience, that few astrologers are sufficiently objective about their own charts or of those close to them to rectify them accurately or dependably. This should be constantly kept in mind. If you are going to work on your own chart, work with at least one other compatible and competent astrologer. This is what Miss Hesseltine, Dr. Wagner, and I found and we almost always worked in pairs and at times all three of us worked together.

My wife is a very competent astrologer and an excellent rectifier and interpreter, and yet she and I took an incredibly long time to rectify her chart. Indeed, we twice had the right Ascendant only to abandon it before finally coming back to it again. Her chart has clicked off major and minor events like clockwork for years so that we know it is correct. We were not sufficiently objective about her chart as we had too strong an emotional relationship to do good work on it. This proved to be a most valuable object lesson to both of us. Most of the remarks made by astrologers I have known about their own charts seem to me to be singularly unimpressive compared with other work of theirs I know about which is always of a much higher order.

There is a belief that many astrologers hold that the finding of the lunar or conception epoch and its chart will automatically enable one to rectify one's horoscope. This is, I am afraid, a fool's paradise. And I say this with much assurance since our experience with this lunar or conception chart has been so extensive. As Johndro originally found, after a study of 200 cases, the Moon at conception is within orb of a conjunction or opposition to the birth Ascendant but usually not exactly in aspect to it. The same is true of the relationship of the birth Ascendant to the conception Moon.

Since Johndro, his late partner W. Kenneth Brown, Miss Hesseltine, and myself have worked on at least 500 conception charts, I think we can speak with some authority in this matter. In any case, the experience of a number of capable astrologers (Carter, Hone, Fagan, etc.) has been that there is not an exact interchange between the Moons and Ascendants of the birth and conception epochs. So they don't help in rectification.

I suppose one could rectify a chart by means of transits alone, but it would be an amazingly tedious task at best, and we don't recommend it; although, the capable Captain Schwickert has done so with some success.

Secondary progressions (major, day for year) are nearly standard among the majority of astrologers and certainly should be employed, but it is best not to limit oneself to them. Our group, after extensive experience, rejects the one degree a year method favored by many and also the measure of Naibod—59′08″ a year—favored by many more astrologers. We also reject as minor or invalid all the symbolic directions that have been brought forward.

We find that the usual primaries and sidereal time directions are also invalid, although Captain Schwickert, Countess Wassike and others have done strongly indicative work on directions on the equator that should be studied further. Brown and Johndro used directions on the prime vertical and horizon—based on the true motion of the Sun—with great success and we assume that they are probably valid, though cumbersome, and thus less easy to work with than the solar arc directions of Dr. Wagner and the late Alfred Witte.

We have done some work with the minor progressions made famous by the Church of Light (one lunar revolution equals one year of life) and Troinski's tertiary progressions (one day equals one lunar revolution), but they are certainly too fast for the bodies within the orbit of Jupiter so that in their way they are just as limited as the secondary progressions, though useful adjuncts. I shall mainly use solar and Ascendant arc directions (and vertical arc, too).

As a practicing astrologer I have found that many given times of birth are inaccurate, which is a major reason for the necessity for rectification. I am not at all convinced that the astrological time of birth, i.e. the time that works, is also the time of the first breath, the emergence of the head, the cutting of the umbilical cord, or of any of the various physiological indicia of birth.

I think the tendency has been to overemphasize the importance of the physiological and to underestimate the importance of the psychological, which I take also to be the astrological, in determining the moment of birth. I do not say that the discrepancy need be or usually is a large one, but I suspect that there is one. If six doctors who observed a birth with accurate watches testified that birth occurred at 6:19 a.m., but the rectification of the chart by several competent astrologers showed that birth occurred at 6:22:30 a.m., and if this was confirmed by current events accurately and consistently clicked off for many years, then I would accept the astrological time for all astrological purposes, and not the medical time of birth.

My own birth time was given as 10:53 p.m. Eastern Standard Time (i.e. given to the exact minute—usually an indication of an accurate time), but the rectified time, which has worked for a decade on all aspects to and by the angles of my chart, turned out to be 10:39:30 p.m. Eastern Standard Time—a discrepancy of thirteen and a half minutes. In taking aspects by Ascendant arc to the Midheaven, this discrepancy would translate itself into an error of about a year in timing.

Thus, given times, conception charts and other supposed aids to accuracy of a birth time are not as much of a help as astrologers would like to believe. After all, there is that human tendency to hope to get the answers easily or through some neat little system.

An additional note of caution should be sounded in these preliminary remarks. Many astrologers of the older generation use orbs of plus or minus one degree in progressions and directions. Frankly, this is shocking to me since it is much too large. Indeed, the use of such orbs could explain why it has been so hard for so many otherwise competent astrologers to discriminate between $1°, 59:08'$ a year, and the true solar arc (whose rate varies from a little over $57'$ to a little over $1°01'$ a year).

Using much narrower orbs, our group found that only the true solar arc (distance over which the Sun has moved in the secondary progression) is valid. Generally speaking, orbs should not exceed five minutes before the aspect is exact and fifteen minutes after it is exact (a span of four months), though the majority of the event should lie within a month—i.e. from a week before the exact aspect to about three weeks after it. There are some exceptions to this.

In the case of Saturn, events never have been observed to occur before the aspect is exact and almost always to lag after it is exact, which should be kept in mind. The same is true of the Sun, although not as markedly so. Aspects of secondary Mars can lead the exact aspect (occur before it) by a fairly large interval, and I know of no one who knows why this should be so.

The planets whose influence most consistently leads the time of the exact aspect is future-oriented Neptune. By far the most accurate and exact timer of the known planets is Uranus. It virtually never deviates by more than plus or minus two minutes between aspect and event and is usually near zero. This makes Uranus of the utmost value and importance in the final very exact setting of the angles and in running tests on their accuracy. A secondary Moon, much more minor in its effects than usually realized since so rapid is its motion, is also accurate, but the faster the motion the more accurate and more minor.

Most of the work done until recently by our group employed classical methods, i.e. the Ptolemaic aspects. We did not use midpoints or the planetary pictures of Witte. In more recent years our work has changed and we have been using these other ways of relating planets. This actually makes my task of description and demonstration easier. On the other hand, the Witte methods of rectification appears to me to be very effective and at one time Reinhold Ebertin wrote me mentioning the merits of Witte's *Regelwerks* (rules of planetary pictures) in rectification. Therefore, those who are interested in this crucially important technique, the rectification of a chart, should not overlook the discoveries and methods of the Hamburg School (Uranian System).

One of the most important tasks preliminary to rectification is the taking of a case history of the client, because rectifying the chart requires accurate dating in the person's life of many major events. Taking down a full case history is a valuable and even necessary procedure in any case. The astrologer should also be a psychologist whose main task is to understand the client and his or her social, family, and psychological conditioning. In order to do this, a good case history is as essential to an astrologer as to a doctor or a psychoanalyst.

Therefore, one needs to develop skill in interrogation because some people present a real problem when it comes to remembering the dating of even many of the most major events in their past lives. They are beset with all kinds of psychologically protective memory blocks. And one has also to be careful of overly facile memories, which may be inaccurate as to dates and thus seriously misleading to the astrologer. The clients may, therefore, have to do some research on their own lives.

What types of events are particularly useful in rectification? The so-called adverse events are best: deaths, accidents, illnesses, operations, loss of position, loss of money, loss of property, and all the slings and arrows of outrageous fortune. Furthermore, difficult or stressful occurrences for those close to the person can be as important as those happening directly to the person. Thus, if one's mother has a hysterectomy (usually an affliction to or by Pluto or to an angle or body in Scorpio), this should show in the chart just as, if the person is a woman, her own hysterectomy should show.

Of course, not all such events will be useful in rectification because in rectification one is almost exclusively concerned with aspects to or by the angles, the Midheaven, and Ascendant (the Vertex is not usually used in rectification). And only some of the events of life occur on aspects to or by the angles. However, major aspects to or by the angles correlate to major events as a rule and that is why it is best to concentrate on major events when rectifying; in addition, they are most often remembered.

Deaths of parents, if such deaths have occurred, have traditionally been among the best events for rectification. Usually the death of the father involves a Saturn affliction and even more often the death of the mother involves a Pluto affliction (in the 2,000 charts rectified by our group, eighty percent of the deaths of mothers occurred under Pluto afflictions).

There has been a tendency to consider that the Midheaven and Ascendant are widely different from each other and that the events connected with them are usually in different categories. But this is an exaggeration, for while they are not the same, one can have an illness or operation on a square to the Midheaven from a body directed from a radical position in the sixth house nearly as often as due to an opposition to the Ascendant from such a radical body.

There are, of course, differences. Career affairs, parents, prestige, and generally less personal matters are more often connected with aspects to or by the Midheaven than the Ascendant, the latter being more personal in general. The formation or breakup of a marriage is more likely, for instance, to take place on aspects to or by the Ascendant than to or by the Midheaven, but not exclusively so; people do both marry and separate on aspects to or by the Midheaven.

In the usual meaning of the term, squares, oppositions, or contraparallels to or by either angle time adverse events, the trines and sextiles time favorable or desired occurrences. The conjunction and the parallel are neutral aspects. Whether a conjunction or parallel to or by the Midheaven or Ascendant will be adverse or favorable then depends on the generally benefic or malefic nature of the body that makes that aspect. As a rule, the Sun, Moon, Mercury, Venus, and Jupiter are benefic; Mars, Saturn,

Neptune, and Pluto are malefic; Uranus can act either way. While the Sun conjunct the Midheaven is always favorable by itself, its conjunction to the Ascendant can be quite adverse in its effects. Furthermore, any body that is at the Descendant is not conjunct the cusp of the seventh house, but acts as though in opposition to the Ascendant. The same is true for a body at the Nadir—it is not conjunct the cusp of the fourth house, but acts as though in opposition to the Midheaven. This is quite important.

The sex or polarity of a planet is quite important to the interpretation of its effects. The following bodies tend to be masculine or to refer, in events and life situations, to men: Sun, Mars, Jupiter (but not markedly so; could be a woman), and Saturn. The following bodies are usually feminine: Moon, Venus, Neptune, and Pluto (though the latter may refer to a man in a woman's chart where the relationship is sexual or potentially so). Mercury is neutral, can be either sex: Uranus is bisexual and can be either sex. In the case of the very young or the very old, these distinctions may not apply, i.e. Saturn can mean a very old woman, the Moon may refer to a very young boy.

In addition, the essential nature of a body (as, for instance, whether it be masculine or feminine, favorable or adverse) may be modified by being in close powerful aspect to one or more bodies. For example, consider a person with Venus in the second house in close opposition to Saturn in the eighth house. The progressed Ascendant comes to a conjunction of Venus and a man dies. While Venus is basically feminine, it is here colored through its close opposition to masculine Saturn. In addition, while death is of the eighth house and a second house Venus would, therefore, normally not indicate death (unless it ruled the sign in the eighth house), its close aspects to the eighth house Saturn make all the difference.

Since deaths are so vital in rectification, it is important to review the rules that cover them. Adverse aspects to bodies in the eighth house, or that rule the sign there, or where, as here, the body is in close adverse aspect to a body in the eighth house, may mean death. A body radically in the eighth house, progressed to a conjunction of the Midheaven (if the body is, as in this case, a malefic) or to a square of the Ascendant may indicate death, or a square of the progressed Midheaven to a body in the eighth house or an opposition of the progressed Ascendant to one in that house may bring the death of another person.

The planets most often connected with death are Saturn and Pluto. Indeed, I term them "roving delegates" since even if they are in no way connected with the eighth house, afflictions of them can mean death, especially afflictions of the angles or lights (Sun or Moon).

This first chapter is devoted solely to various preliminary considerations. There are quite a number of them which are relevant and important. A special one, for instance, relates to the age of the person whose chart is being corrected. It is quite difficult to rectify the chart of a child because there have been, comparatively, so few major events, while the reverse is generally true in the case of elders.

But there is an additional consideration. Many aspects have a somewhat different meaning in the chart of a child as contrasted with the activation of the same aspects by direction in the horoscope of an adult. An aspect that shows the onset of a passionate love affair for an adult can hardly have this meaning for a two-year-old boy. Therefore, many aspects in the charts of very young children have been found to refer to events in the parents' lives and others who may be very close to said children. Such things should be obvious, but it is easy to neglect them.

This is not the place to discuss the special problems in the rectification of unknown birth times, but the most important single preliminary consideration is a careful study of the overall pattern of the chart in relation to the house structure. One can spend a great deal of time almost uselessly in the calculation of arcs in connection with events if the time of birth is markedly erroneous. One has first, therefore, to determine whether the overall pattern as it appears for the given time of birth is such as to describe the main features of the life and character. I shall discuss a certain case since it is such a good example.

The positions of the planets in the chart are given to the nearest degree only since I am not now concerned with exact arcs of direction and specific events, but rather with the overall fit, or lack of it, of the whole pattern with the form of the life and the general character of the native.

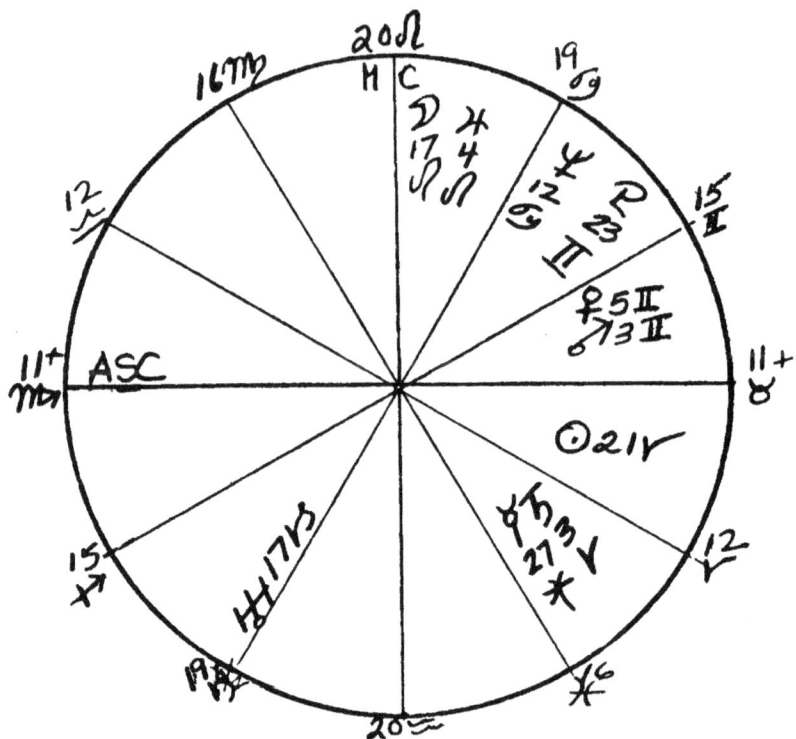

Horoscope of an auditor erected for given time

There were a series of things about this chart that did not fit with the man's life and character even though it was set up for the given time of birth. He had been quite athletic when young, had almost made the U.S. Olympic Team, and at one time had decided to be an instructor in sports and physical education. But he shifted to accounting and auditing as his main life work and when I met him he had been an auditor for the U.S. Army for many years with a fair degree of success. He had never been married, though he was about 47 years old when I interviewed him professionally. While he had been fairly successful, he actually had never done overly well financially.

A man with a Scorpio Ascendant, with a conjunction of Venus and Mars in the seventh house, in sextile to Jupiter on one side and to Saturn on the other would hardly be single, especially since Venus was so well aspected in his seventh house and was the ruler of the sign on its cusp. This certainly did not fit.

His Midheaven in Leo hardly fit with the type of career he had, particularly when one considers the planets ruling his finances. Jupiter in the ninth house rules the Sagittarius second house and was not only trine Saturn, but also sextile Venus and Mars. This, one would think, would bring considerable financial success, and with Sun in the sixth house trine the Midheaven, his career should have been a marked success. (It was found, when the Midheaven had been shifted, that directions of his Sun to this trine to the Midheaven did mark his best periods and major promotions.)

I concluded, therefore, that he must have been born about two hours later, resulting in the shifting of each house roughly one sign later. The Midheaven in Virgo fit the auditing and bookkeeping career. Mercury, which rules the Midheaven, was conjunct Saturn, which rules Capricorn on the second house cusp and thus his income (a Mercury-Saturn conjunction seems very descriptive of this exacting type of work).

The advance of the Ascendant into early Sagittarius placed it in opposition to Venus conjunct Mars—an affliction—and Pluto in the seventh house squared the Midheaven; all seventh house bodies were afflicted (Pluto also squared Mercury, ruler of the Gemini seventh house), which is why he had never married. The Ascendant in Sagittarius fit, too, with the love of sports and outdoor activities.

The Moon in the ninth house fit with the considerable amount of travel he had done, especially through his army service. His well-aspected Jupiter in the eighth house I have found to indicate financial success with other people's money—in this case as an auditor. With Uranus in the second house opposite the eighth house Neptune, his own finances had presented a problem to him, especially as his Sun in square to this opposition formed the handle of the T-cross. The strongly angular Mars in the rectified chart is typical of those who are athletic or physically very active.

Having placed the angles approximately where I thought they really belonged, I then proceeded to endeavor to rectify the chart from events and exact directional arcs. I was within a degree or so, the chart proved to be easy to rectify, and a considerable number of events agreed in a convincing manner with the directions.

Had I been satisfied to start with the given time, I might have spent days, even weeks, in a fruitless endeavor to find a Midheaven in Leo and an Ascendant in Scorpio that would work. By doing what I did, I saved myself much time and effort and was able to correct the chart successfully.

In this case, where the error was about two hours, the error was a really serious one, affecting the reading of the whole radical pattern and its static interpretation (needless to say, no accurate timing would really be possible with a chart this much in error). Therefore, a primary rule to follow before you use any arcs of direction is: Are the planets in the right houses in terms of the life and character?

Of course, those who are extra skillful in detecting Ascendants might have surmised from this approach alone that his Ascendant could not have been in Scorpio, should have been in Sagittarius. The study of the Ascendant and its importance goes without saying as a vital preliminary consideration. Many astrologers, however, seem to fail to realize that planets in close aspect (especially square or opposition) to the Ascendant can have a strong modifying effect on it, though they usually do recognize the importance of conjunctions to it.

2

Rectification Process

Let me repeat what appear to me to be the essential factors for successful rectification: general astrological competence, correct methods and tools in rectification, much experience in the technique of rectification, and sufficient and accurate data. Without general astrological competence, successful rectification is virtually impossible; one should not even have to speak of this. But there are a number of astrologers who meet this qualification who I am sure are unable to rectify charts with any degree of fairly consistent success. The next requisite is the right tools (methods of direction) and techniques. Without this, even much effort and experience can only produce poor results. This is one of the two main reasons why so few astrologers can rectify charts. And then there is the actual time, effort, and experience in the art of rectification. Without this general competence and the right methods, success is not possible. The secondary progressions plus the solar Ascendant and vertical arc directions are some of the best tools with which to work. Finally, if a client supplies insufficient or inaccurate data, that alone can make any accurate rectification of the moment of birth impossible.

Actually, it is preferable, though not essential, that a person whose chart is being rectified be interviewed at length. There are good reasons for this. In the beginning, one seeks to pass from the main stressful events of life to the chart, i.e. to find planetary combinations and, in particular, aspects to or by the angles that correlate with these events. But once one has a tentative rectification, it is then best to pass from the chart to the events, i.e. to find out from the person whether at the time of a certain aspect between an angle and a planet or light a certain type event occurred.

In order to follow this latter procedure it is much better to have the individual where he or she can be questioned. Otherwise, it is necessary to have a full list of the events of the life. One often cannot obtain the dates of even major events to the day, but usually the month and year are sufficient, especially if the individual can say it happened late or early in the month. To have the year alone of an important event in the life is almost useless, though if one is given the season of the year and the year this can be somewhat helpful.

Let us look at the case of a woman who was born September 19, 1916 in San Francisco, 122W26,

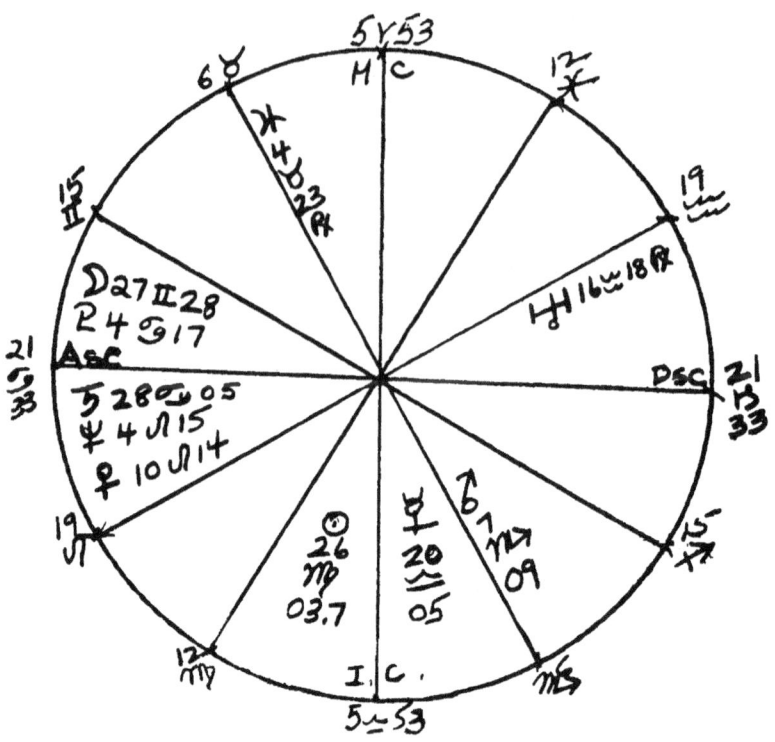

37N36. The given time of birth was 1:36 a.m., Pacific Standard Time, but on rectification it was found that birth had actually occurred almost exactly one hour earlier, i.e. at 12:40 a.m. The given time gave an Ascendant in early Leo and a Midheaven in the latter part of Aries. Nothing about the lady seemed to fit with a Leo Ascendant as she was shy and overly sensitive. In addition, her career as a commercial artist was not sufficiently strongly indicated, although by the technique of Marc Edmund Jones, Venus is the vocational indicator since it is the first one of the four bodies (Mercury, Venus, Mars, and the Moon) to rise ahead of the Sun. But there was still another consideration that seemed very important in this chart.

As many readers may know, Jones found that overall horoscope patterns fall into seven broad types, a classification that has become quite famous. One of these is the bucket pattern in which all the bodies except one are on one side of the zodiac, while the remaining single planet is on the other side of the zodiac. Here we note that in the order of the signs all the bodies lie between Jupiter in early Taurus and Mars opposite it in early Scorpio, except for Uranus, a singleton body at mid-Aquarius; thereby it becomes the handle of the bucket. Indeed, it receives special and strong emphasis just because it is alone. It seemed to me, therefore, that major aspects by or to Uranus from the angles of the chart would have to have unusual importance in her life, and such was not the case for any time close to the given time.

Note that Uranus is near the end of the seventh house and rules Aquarius in the first part of the eighth house, thus being a primary indicator of deaths. In this connection, too, it should be noted that Uranus is widely opposite the midpoint of the Sun and Moon at 11 Leo 46 and that Venus is conjunct this midpoint of Sun and Moon, a planetary picture of considerable potency. Therefore, deaths can also be shown by directions of the close square of the two lights.

Her brother died on February 7, 1926, her mother on May 1, 1941, her father on May 7, 1936, and her fiance of poliomyelitis on September 12, 1949, a month before he was due to come to the United States from England to marry her. Since Uranus is a primary significator of death in this chart, and since it rules the latter part of her seventh house of marriage, it seemed quite possible that an adverse aspect of it might show the sudden death of the fiancé. The solar arc for the fiance's death was 32°32′ (the arc over which the Sun has moved by secondary progression). A Midheaven of 8 Taurus 25 at the geocentric latitude of birth gives an Ascendant of 16 Leo 18 opposite the natal Uranus. Then if we subtract 32°32′ from that Midheaven, this would give a natal Midheaven of 5 Aries 53 if the progressed Ascendant opposed Uranus when her fiancé died. This then became a tentative rectification of the chart.

The question was if this were correct, would other major directions fit with other major events in her life? The solar arc for the death of the brother was 9°11′ so that he died between the time the Moon squared the Midheaven and the third house Sun (brother) opposed it. Indeed, if this arc is added to the Moon/Sun midpoint, it reached 20 Leo 57, which is only four minutes from a sesquiquadrate to the Midheaven.

The solar arc for the mother's death is 24°13′. Now the tentative Midheaven gives a radical Ascendant of 21 Cancer 33 so that when the solar arc for the mother's death is added to her natal Moon, it reaches 21 Cancer 41, only eight minutes past the conjunction to this Ascendant. This was not favorable in this case due to the powerful radical square to the Sun. Indeed, when there is a fairly close aspect between two bodies, such as this quarter Moon square, events often occur between the time that the first one and second one aspect a given factor.

In this case the Sun squared the Ascendant in late May 1942 and, after her mother's death, she acquired her first job and moved to another city in March and April of that year. In other words, these developments occurred just before the aspect to the Ascendant and the Sun aspect. Note that the Sun and the Ascendant are in a radical sextile which does much to resolve the stress of the progressed square.

If the Ascendant-Uranus opposition was so potent, it may be asked what transpired when the progressed Ascendant was contraparallel natal Uranus? Uranus at birth was at 16°39′ south declination. Where is the Sun in longitude in Leo when it has the opposite declination of +16°39′? It would be at 13 Leo 56 so that when the Ascendant reached that point it would be contraparallel Uranus.

How is it decided when this occurs? Place the Ascendant at 13 Leo 56 and determine where the Midheaven must be. Then the arc from the natal Midheaven at 5 Aries 53 to the progressed Midheaven gives the solar arc for an Ascendant arc opposition of the Ascendant or Uranus in declination. Then add this solar arc to the natal Sun and find how long it takes the Sun to reach there. In this case, it requires nearly thirty years—August 1946.

I asked the woman what had happened at that time as it should have involved her relationship with her fiancé and been separative. It turned out she had gone to England on April 13, 1946 to see her fiancé and had returned at the end of July 1946, this being the separation from him. Note that, as is so often the case, she traveled under this Uranus aspect. In 1949 his death prevented his trip to the United States. I found that she had Uranus trine the Ascendant by solar arc in early June 1952 and that on June 18 that year she again went to England to visit her fiance's parents. There was again a trip involving the same situation, but as it was a pleasant one, it occurred on a trine. I concluded the chart was correctly rectified.

The natal trine of her Venus to her Midheaven was also indicative of her career as a commercial artist since the closest aspects to the Midheaven are the best single, though not the sole, indices of a person's career potential. Note that her Pluto is in the twelfth house in radical square to her Midheaven. When Pluto reached the trine of that Midheaven by solar arc in October 1948, she experienced underhanded (Pluto) difficulties in her job and left it to become a freelance worker on November 22 that year. From the beginning of May 1957—Midheaven square Uranus—she experienced much stress and difficulty in her work (Midheaven) and in that interval once more went abroad to England (Uranus—travel). In August, right after her return under secondary Mars trine Midheaven, her career situation started to straighten out and to get considerably better.

Since the sign in the fifth house is Scorpio, a love affair might be expected when Pluto reached the Ascendant. It reached there by Ascendant arc (the distance from the natal to the progressed Ascendant, the latter being given by the position of the Midheaven progressed by solar arc) in November 1939. She had met her first male friend on September 24, 1939. It is usually the case that an aspect to the Ascendant by the Sun in a woman's chart signifies a man. Whether this was the case in the spring of 1942 when the solar arc Sun squared the Ascendant is not known. But when this aspect repeated by the slower, and therefore more potent, Ascendant arc in August 1950, there was an important man in her life. Due to the square, she had differences with the man, but the natal sextile brought a partial resolution.

The question of the father's death remains. He died in a railroad accident in Japan. Accidents usually involve Mars, Saturn, or Uranus, or a combination of two of them. Since Saturn so often indicates the father, look to it first; but its aspects by the various arcs do not account for this event. The solar arc was 19°17′; the Ascendant arc was 14°33′; the vertical arc was 13°53′ (the distance from the natal to the progressed Vertex).

If one takes the arc moved over by the Sun in declination in the secondary progression, this is the solar declination arc which can also be used for directing radical bodies. It was 7°38′ at her father's death. The natal declination of her Mars is 14°12′ and it is increasing in declination natally. The declination of her natal Ascendant is +21°43′.

Since Mars' declination is increasing, add the 7°38′ to the natal declination of Mars, obtaining 21°50′ at the time of the death, and thus placing it seven minutes in declination past the contraparallel to the Ascendant (or about three months before his death, when the aspect was exact). Mars is radically opposition the midpoint of Uranus and Neptune (rulers of the eighth house) and square the midpoint of Moon and Sun. In some house systems it would be natally in the fourth house (father). Thus, the major events in her life appear to fit well with these major directions to and by her angles (Midheaven and Ascendant).

In closing, let me point out that while it is always advisable to look for a position of the angles close to the given time, it is even more important that the planetary patterns, Ascendant and house positions fit with the character, temperament and, dynamically, with the major events of the life. In this case the singleton Uranus gave us an immediate clue to the sudden death of the fiancé, while her bearing and temperament were such that a Leo Ascendant was impossible. Therefore, it is strongly suggested that the reader do some careful study of the chart and of the person (latter includes personal history) before resorting to arcs of direction.

3

Additional Examples

Five cases will be cited in this chapter as additional examples of rectification. The first one was a woman born on October 13, 1928, 73W39, 40N27 at a given time of 5:00 a.m. Eastern Standard Time. Her chart is given in Figure 1.

Having her first house, Sun, Moon, and Ascendant all in Libra gave her a strong personality projection. Mars conjunct the Midheaven and square her Ascendant from the end of the ninth house increased her aggressiveness. As that Mars rules Aries in her seventh house, this also indicates problems in marriage. Since Uranus opposes the Ascendant and Moon and squares Mars, those problems should be considerable. This proved to be true since her marriage had ended in divorce.

The elevated Pluto in the tenth house square both her lights was an index to the dominating influence of her mother. The contraparallel of her third house Saturn to her Midheaven gave her the ability to work hard and accented the importance to her of basic security as it rules the fourth house (Capricorn on the cusp). The sextiles of Sun and Moon to Saturn were a helpful stabilizing influence.

The trines of the second house Mercury and Venus to her Midheaven would benefit her financially through the gift of gab (Mercury) in her career plus the ability to sell (Venus) that which was aesthetically pleasing (Venus). And the sextile of Jupiter to the Midheaven late in the seventh house or in the eighth house would give her even more success, financially and otherwise, in her career.

The developments of her life fit with this general outline so it was probable that the given and rectified times would not be very different. For many years she has been successful financially in the sale of women's clothing. This contrasted sharply with her personal life, where things were far from satisfactory. She was anxious to be remarried and had nothing but frustration in fulfilling this goal.

Fairly often miscarriages are found to be due to Uranus. On January 2, 1954 she experienced one on the Midheaven trine Uranus (but natal square). Note that Uranus is in the sixth house and does govern the Aquarian fifth house of children. As Uranus is so very accurate, the chart was set on this aspect, giving a natal Midheaven of 9 Cancer 25, an Ascendant of 8 Libra 09, and a Vertex at 22 Aries 12 in opposition to her Sun. This makes the rectified time seven minutes later than the given time.

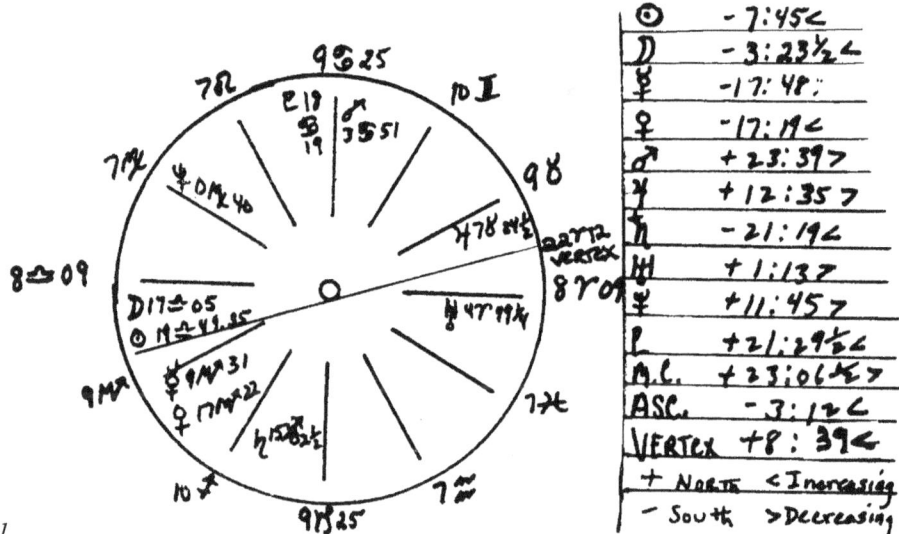

Figure 1

When the Midheaven reached the conjunction of Pluto at the beginning of July 1937, she had her first bad beating by her father due to having taken money from her mother (Pluto). In July 1940, on the Ascendant square Pluto, while away at summer camp, she injured her nose (Pluto). The nose as well as the reproductive system are shown by this planet; indeed, it is the planet of nosiness.

On the solar arc Sun trine the Midheaven in September 1948, her husband, whom she had married on April 6, 1947, made a favorable career shift to accounting. The powerful secondary progression Mars square the Ascendant timed an automobile accident (Mars) of her husband (Mars rules Aries in the seventh house), in which he cut (Mars) his arm. In June 1953 she left her home (fourth house) and children on Saturn opposite the Midheaven by solar arc (rules the fourth house and is ecliptic contraparallel the Midheaven natally). The trip was a fairly short one (Saturn natally in the third house).

On Ascendant arc Saturn square the Ascendant in October 1957 her husband went to California and failed to give financial support to her and the children. It was in about November 1958 that the exceptionally slow secondary progressed Uranus squared her Mars—these two bodies being the rulers of her seventh house.

Since she and her husband parted company she has had much legal battling (Mars in the ninth house of the law) to compel her former husband (Mars rules the seventh house) to give financial support to their children. The opposition of the Ascendant to Uranus (ruler of the fifth house) and the square to Mars make a powerful T-cross which accounts for the whole complex of the law, the children (fifth house), the divorce from her husband, and the erratic nature of the situation. Neptune in her eleventh house is both trine and parallel her Jupiter, which being near the end of the seventh house, has an eighth house influence. This has been a blessing to her in her dealings with friends and associates.

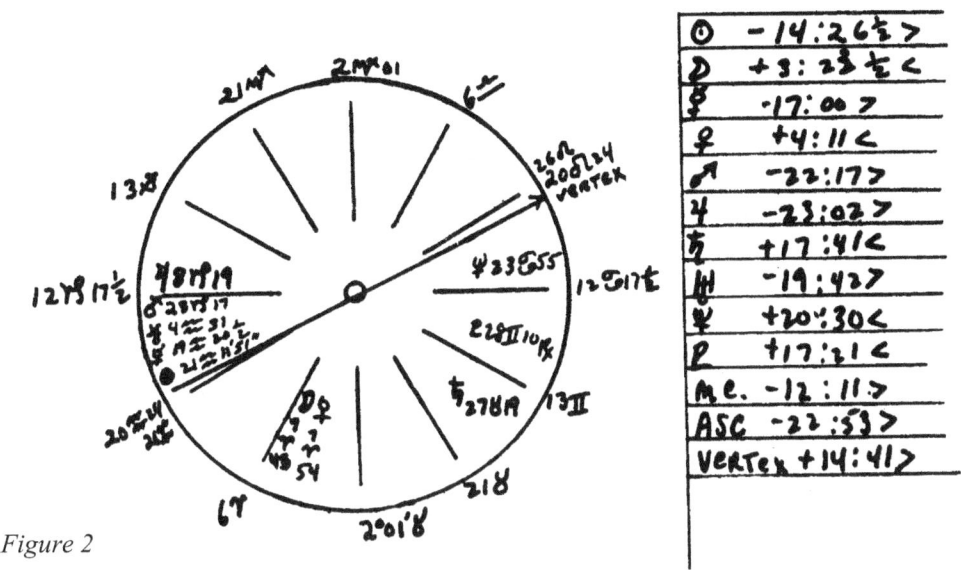

Figure 2

Thus, even though we have had no deaths of parents, this particular horoscope was not difficult to rectify. The parallel of the Moon to the Ascendant enables her to be very successful in her tete-a-tete (Ascendant) personal relationships with the public (Moon). Born just before a New Moon, she has a Balsamic Moon, which gives a curious sort of amorality. It also makes her very self-intent, especially as it is also in the first house. In all cases cited I use Campanus houses and limit the examples to those clients where my wife and I have had an opportunity to study the rectified chart for many years after its rectification as a cross-check on our accuracy. Her conception ©) and animation (``quickening'' or A) charts were also used and proved to be highly significant. The A chart is that of the emotions.

In our next example, the woman was born at 118W15, 33N54 on February 10, 1913 at a given time of 4:10 a.m., Pacific Standard Time. In my initial rectification, I moved the time back twenty-two minutes, the Midheaven being shifted back from 26 Libra 00 to 20 Libra 30, but this proved to be incorrect on checking with later events. (All charts shown—this one in Figure 2—are for rectified times).

The lady had been married twice. She is able to keep secrets, loves poetry, music, and astronomy. Two days before her second marriage, there was an attempt at suicide. She has been quite fond of animals, which have been emotionally important to her. She has research capabilities and interests. Her father died September 25, 1957, having been separated from her mother for many years. Her stepfather died November 25, 1947, and her first husband on December 8, 1954.

One feature of the chart is the very close opposition of Mars in Capricorn to Neptune in Cancer, probably from the first to the seventh house. Mars has a south declination of $22°17'$. By giving the Sun the same declination and finding its longitude, we can find the ecliptic equivalent of Mars' declination. It turns out to be 17 Capricorn 41. It is therefore possible that she may have Mars parallel her Capricorn Ascendant. Neptune at 20N50 is parallel 26 Cancer 40 so that unless the birth time is much later, it probably is not either opposite or contraparallel her Ascendant.

All of this is highly relevant since it is quite possible that this tight opposition (0°38' from exactitude) is square her Midheaven, which will have an important bearing on the position of that angle. If the Midheaven is 26 Libra 00 (given time) or some degrees earlier, she would have these bodies square her Midheaven and Pluto trine it. Since she has done various kinds of research professionally (Mercury type with Pluto contraparallel Mercury radically and Mercury as the vocational indicator) that part fits, but the squares of Mars and Neptune did not seem to fit her life.

There has been no real conflict, for instance, between her marriages and her career (Neptune in the seventh house square the Midheaven). The Midheaven at 2 Scorpio 01, which proved finally to be right, retains the trine of Pluto, but removes the out-of-sign squares of Mars and Neptune. It adds the square of Uranus and parallel to the Sun to the Midheaven. This last indicates the generally good relationships she has had with her male bosses. The Uranus is indicative of the many changes and ups and downs in her career.

She was assumed to have the given Capricorn Ascendant on the basis of her physical appearance along with the self-deprecating character so typical of Capricorn. Indeed, the rectified Ascendant at 12 Capricorn 17:30 is only 0°02' from the sesquiquadrate of Saturn, its ruler. As Saturn is natally in the fifth house, this could account for the fact that she has had no children (which would not have been true with an earlier Ascendant; note that Saturn is also square her Sun).

The buoyancy and breeziness of Jupiter at the Ascendant is much toned down because it is on the cadent side, it is a Capricorn Ascendant, and due to the close aspect of Saturn to it. She would have had the squares to her Ascendant of the closely conjunct Venus and Moon even if the time had been earlier. They should aspect it since she is not only attractive in appearance, but also since this is quite important to her. It must be realized that all major aspects to any one of the angles affect it and modify it. This is a major point made in my wife's book *Aspects to Horoscope Angles*.

Only with the rectified time does she have her Mercury-Sun conjunction opposite her Vertex at 20 Leo 24. This appears to explain her role (Vertex)—over which one has no conscious choice (Vertex)—of much Mercurial activity in her function (Vertex).

The following directions validated the chart: Midheaven opposite Saturn April 1938—separates from first husband. Ascendant conjunct Sun (co-rules seventh house) June 1946—second marriage. Solar arc Saturn trine Midheaven September 1947—major move to New York is important to her career. She returned home for the last time on September 30, 1937, but the exact date of leaving is not certain; it probably fits to the Ascendant arc Uranus trine Midheaven (but natal square) of early December 1937. The very same aspect by vertical arc at the beginning of January 1954 brought a difficult trip to Barbados as her husband was ill. Under Ascendant square Saturn in September 1950 her husband experienced financial stress (Saturn is natally square her Sun, which governs the seventh and eighth houses).

On converse solar arc Saturn square Ascendant in early May 1957 she had her two operations (late April and late May—Saturn natally in Taurus showing the thyroidectomy, and in September 1957 her father died). Note, too, the natal sesquiquadrate of Saturn-Ascendant. On Saturn opposite Ascendant in January 1958 we find the death of a kitten and a foot injury in early March 1958 (due to a fall—Saturn). She made a return trip to New York in early November 1957 on converse Ascendant sextile Uranus. A conclusive post-rectification test was the secondary progressed Venus trine Ascen-

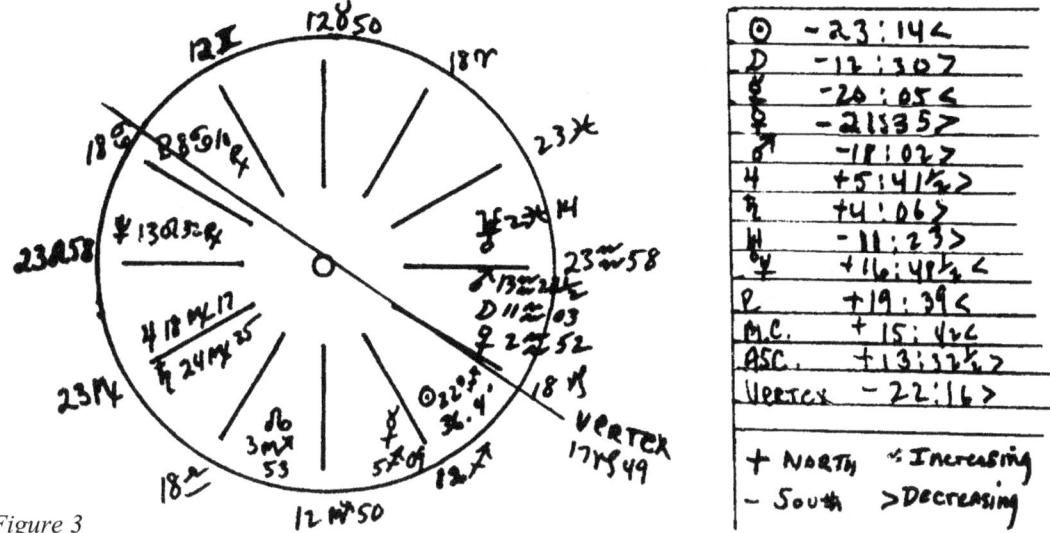

Figure 3

dant (but natal square) in August 1968. Venus rules her Taurus fourth house and is natally in her third house. At that time she found her dream house but was unable to buy it for financial reasons (Venus Moon is closely semisquare her Sun, which is nearly in the second house and rules Leo in the eighth house). This was a very powerful aspect since Venus was moving only eight minutes a year.

In our third illustration we made a considerable shift in the given time of birth, 9:50 a.m., Pacific Standard Time. She was born December 14, 1920 at 2E17, 48N43. As with our other cases in this chapter, thus far she has been married twice. Her parents separated when she was three-years-old. Her first marriage occurred June 16, 1947. He was killed in action December 13, 1950. On February 19, 1955 she married a second time. Her only child, a son by her first marriage, has been the apple of her eye (born March 29, 1948). She has been interested in astrology, history, interior design, and theater. She is a sensitive, imaginative, cultured and charming woman—very Neptunian. She has blondish hair, blue eyes and wide shoulders, i.e. the tapering down body structure typical of Leo. The given time gives a Midheaven of twenty-five degrees Taurus and an Ascendant of nearly three degrees Virgo. Thus, her physical appearance did not agree with her given Ascendant. From her appearance we would have to move the Midheaven backward to result in a Leo Ascendant.

Obviously, a major event in her life was the death in battle of her first husband. This could well be due to a stressful aspect of Mars, especially since it rules Aries in the ninth house (he was at a distance) and as it also rules, probably, over half of the last part of her eighth house. If the natal Midheaven is placed at 12 Taurus 50 she had Midheaven trine Mars (but natal square) at his death. When it was brought by secondary progression to the opposition of the Ascendant in late August 1934 she had scarlet fever—Mars natally in the sixth house. Since on her parents' separation she stayed with her mother, her mother played a major part in her life. Note that natally it is closely semisquare her Ascendant at 23 Leo 58 and is sextile her Midheaven.

But does the pattern of the chart fit her in other respects? The close trine of the Sun to the Ascendant, which it governs, accounts for the importance of her son as it is in the fifth house. The contraparallel of the seventh house Uranus to the Ascendant from the seventh house, which it rules, is an index to the short term of her first marriage and to some problems in her second one. The trine of the Sun to the Ascendant is one of the best things a woman can have for good personal relationships with men and thus is a major offset to the separative influence of Uranus.

In reading any chart one must not consider any one factor alone. A major question we must ask is whether she should have the aspects of Neptune opposition Mars conjunct Moon to her Midheaven, the aspects being close and Neptune being also in parallel to that Midheaven. Here we are confronted with a T-cross of a Neptune-Mars opposition with the Midheaven as we were potentially with the last example. The major discovery made by Vivia Jayne in her book on aspects to the angles is that afflictions to angles do not necessarily deny or deprive, although they spell out problems.

She would not be denied a career, but would be much frustrated in it (due to the tight squares). Indeed, she would be hard to satisfy (Mars-Neptune) despite fanatical intensity of desire (Mars-Neptune), and this has been quite true in her life. Of course, health problems are also shown by the strong sixth house emphasis (the Moon also being natally contraparallel her Ascendant). She has had more than her share of illnesses, having a constitutional delicacy typical of Neptune.

On Midheaven trine Neptune, but natal square, in September 1948 and the simultaneous opposition of Ascendant arc Venus to the Ascendant, she experienced a nervous breakdown (Venus, too, is natally in the sixth house of health). On Midheaven parallel Pluto in mid-1935, her mother was getting a divorce. On Pluto square the Midheaven in April 1955, she was both ill and had difficulties with some of her husband's friends (Pluto natally in the eleventh house). Due to the natal sextile, however, in both instances some of the difficulties were resolved. She had other problems in August 1941 when she endeavored to get work in the theater on solar arc Venus opposite her Ascendant (coming from the sixth house of employment). The sixth house has to do with illness as well as work; on secondary Venus opposite Ascendant in October 1938 her grandmother was ill.

While she has had frustration in her career, her good name and social and economic position have been protected due to the trine of Midheaven to Jupiter since Jupiter is at the end of the first house and nearly in the second house. There are no major aspects to her Vertex at 17 Capricorn 46. The square of the Virgo Saturn in her second house to her Sun has deprived her of a father since her parents separated when she was nearly three years of age. For that matter, her son (Sun in the fifth house) was also deprived of his father as shown by this same configuration. Her vocational indicator is her Mercury in Sagittarius late in the fourth house, thus indicating some of her vocational interests. The chart has proved accurate on other aspects that have occurred since its rectification.

While it hasn't been deliberate, it so happens that once more we have a woman who has been married twice. She was born May 2, 1925 at 41N10, 74W12 at a given time of 9:00 a.m., Eastern Standard Time. Her chart is shown in Figure 4 for the rectified time, 9:06:45 a.m., Eastern Standard Time. The given time put twenty-six degrees Pisces on the Midheaven. At first it was moved back to 24 Pisces 54, but this proved to be unsatisfactory. Her Cancer Ascendant with its Moon as ruler in late Leo plus the Taurus Sun seemed to fit well with her somewhat fleshy physical build. Provisionally it appeared probable that the time was not very far off.

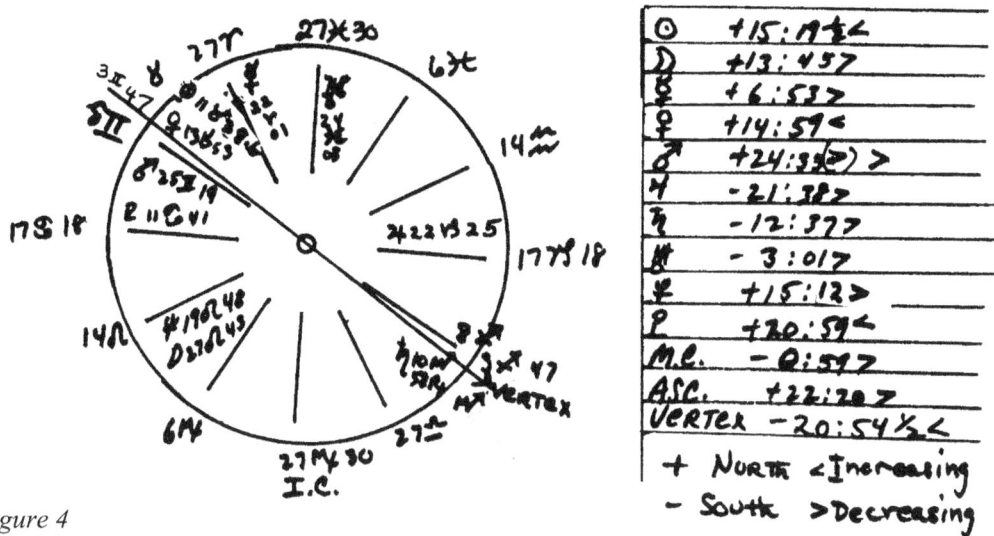

Figure 4

She has traveled and moved considerably, which fits the Uranus in her ninth house. Her relationship with her father was important but difficult (Saturn opposite Sun conjunct Venus). The Saturn in the fifth house also fit with her children and strong feelings of responsibility for them. The importance of the mother is shown by the late twelfth house Pluto conjunction with the Ascendant. When Pluto and Saturn are strong, as they are here (the trine of Saturn to the Ascendant doing much to resolve the opposition to Sun-Venus), then the authority and security due to the parents are of major importance. She would tend to expect too much, i.e. poor judgment of others, in particular a husband since her seventh house Jupiter does oppose her Ascendant.

Thus you see one of the most crucial things to do is to check to see whether the aspects to the angles fit with the life and character of the native. Having her Gemini Mars in the twelfth house square her Midheaven and Uranus not only would cause her to throw much energy (Mars) into her career (Midheaven), but with some frustration and also with some tendency to be involved in fights. Of course, she is very fixed since her Leo Neptune and Moon in her second house are parallel her Taurus Venus-Sun in her eleventh house (Neptune squaring Venus and the Sun widely), and is romantic.

The career is given some stability due to the sesquiquadrate of Saturn to it and also an ability to work hard (Saturn). Her Venus and Sun are only sextile the Ascendant from the eleventh, indicative of her capacity for friendship, but also they are in semisquare to the Midheaven. The hypothetical planet Pan is at 6 Pisces 12 so that its midpoint with the Ascendant of 17 Cancer 18 falls at 11 Taurus 45 and thus on her Sun; in addition this is 0°45' from a semisquare to her Midheaven. This really fits since she has been involved through her union activities in industrial disputes—Pan is a planet that puts one in the middle of controversial situations. Cupido, planet of union is at 18 Leo 40 and thus has its antiscion at 11 Taurus 20, exactly on her Sun.

The bearing this has on the rectification is the involvement of the Midheaven—she has been drawn into such situations via her career. It fits although one can certainly rectify a horoscope without recourse to hypothetical planets (for information on them see my book *The Unknown Planets*). The planet Lion is as important in timing deaths by direction as Saturn (male) and Pluto (female); Lion affects both sexes.

She has her Moon square her Vertex at 3 Sagittarius 47 late in her fifth house. The Vertex is the most karmic of the three angles and this may refer to her relationship with her daughter in particular. The aspects to the Vertex show those things which are fated and which one must learn to live with come what may.

Her Moon was just two minutes past the opposition to her Midheaven when her maternal grandmother died. Note that natally Pluto is semisquare that Moon. On the Ascendant arc Uranus square the Ascendant, her favorite (maternal) uncle died within one minute of exactitude (December 20, 1957)—Uranus does rule the sign in the eighth house. In early August 1957 she first had the Sun parallel the Ascendant and then in February 1958 Saturn was ecliptic contraparallel the Ascendant (by solar arc in longitude, Saturn's ecliptic intercept had the opposite or southerly declination from that of the Ascendant).

Her paternal grandmother passed away in February 1958—her Saturn (paternal) is natally in bodily contraparallel to her Moon (grandmother). She started on a new job under secondary progressed Mars (ruling Aries intercepted in the tenth house) conjunct her Ascendant in October 1959. A secondary Mars often leads, i.e. the event precedes the aspect, as here, for the progression was not exact until the end of November. This was her first (Mars) experience in lithography. In late August 1968 on Midheaven semisquare Uranus (natal conjunction) she went on a quick trip to Hawaii. On a flight to Phoenix her plane was forced down, which was quite upsetting—Midheaven parallel Neptune, which rules Pisces in her ninth house.

Her daughter wrecked her car on Midheaven opposite Saturn in the fifth house of children at the start of October 1970. The aspect hit in August, but Saturn is slow. We may not really separate her Sun from Saturn as they are rather closely in opposition; thus when eight months later she had Midheaven conjunct the Sun, she was laid off from her job due to union activities—the antiscion to Cupido and Pan/Ascendant midpoint were activated at nearly the same time. I should have noted that she was forced out of a position in July 1964 on Neptune opposite her Midheaven. From the foregoing and from accurately timed events since then, my wife and I assumed that her chart was accurate.

In the final example we have a woman born January 4, 1929 at 38N42, 77W01 somewhere between 6:00 and 8:00 p.m. This means that the Midheaven ranges from about 13 Aries 00 to 14 Taurus 30 and that the Ascendant ranges from about 27 Cancer 30 to 21 Leo 30, assuming that birth did actually occur within those two hours. Due to her physical appearance, fiery personality and pride it is rather probable that the Ascendant should fall in Leo. Midheavens were tried from 17 Aries 15 to 8 Taurus 45, which gave Ascendants from 0 Leo 40 to 16 Leo 59.

The first half of Leo is much more fiery and more direct than the last half, so an endeavor was made to limit the Ascendant to that part of Leo. Not enough attention is paid to the sign in which the Midheaven falls. It could be in the last half of Aries or the first quarter of Taurus. Since she had a fixed

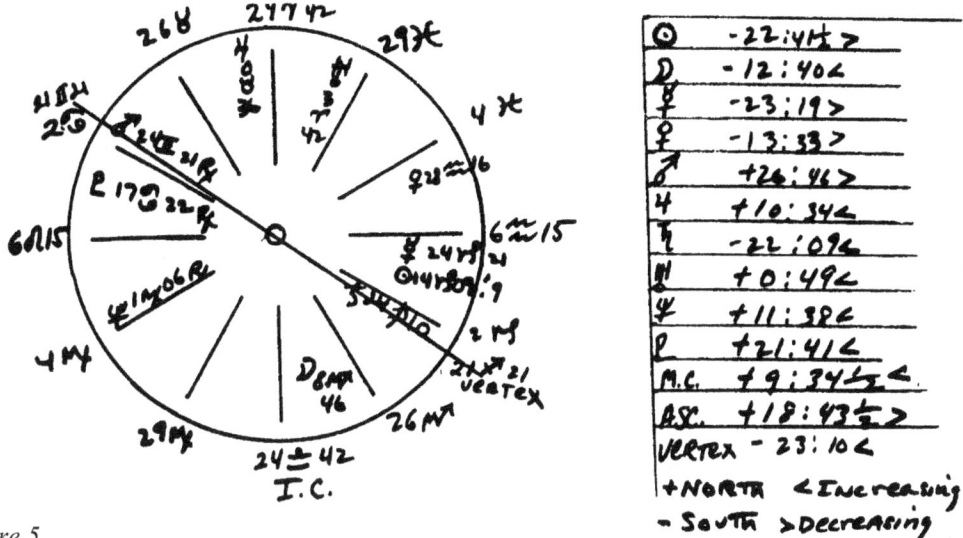

Figure 5

Moon in Scorpio, if she had both a fixed Ascendant and Midheaven, one would anticipate much stability in her career as well as in personality.

Her career had not been stable. She was an actress mainly, a dancer secondarily, but was much of the time compelled to make her living in secretarial work, which could mean that she had a sixth house Mercury square the Midheaven—a square since it was compulsion and not choice. This suggested that the Midheaven might be in about the last ten degrees of Aries. Indeed, the Vertex might aspect Mercury (element of compulsion in her function). As Mercury at 23S19 is parallel to 24 Sagittarius 09 (in ecliptic parallel to Saturn at 24 Sagittarius 10), the Vertex, too, should be in the last ten degrees of Sagittarius. The Saturn-Mercury combination (Saturn ruling the sign in the sixth house) would then describe the detailed secretarial work she was compelled to do.

A feature of this horoscope is the 0°11′ opposition of Mars to Saturn (with Saturn thus the Jonesian dynamic focus of the chart). Not only does such an aspect show one who blows hot (Mars), then cold (Saturn), but also one who works extra hard and really overdoes the expenditure of effort. This has been true of her to a marked extent.

She could, therefore, have Saturn sesquiquadrate the Ascendant, Mars semisquare the Ascendant, Saturn trine and Mars sextile her Midheaven, and Saturn conjunct and Mars opposite her Vertex. When the rectification was completed that is what she did have.

The harmonious aspects of Mars-Saturn to her Midheaven mean that she would best be able to resolve the difficulties of such an aspect via her career. Her late Aquarius Venus should be sextile her Midheaven due to the aesthetic nature of her career interests. One who is in the theater often has Neptune configured with the Midheaven, the element of make-believe. Neptune is trine her Midheaven and also parallels it. And, as it is at the very end of the first house, thus affecting the second house, she could make some money from acting (Neptune also rules the sign in the eighth house). Having a strong Mars-Saturn configuration plastered all over her angles, she often got involved in fights in her work (Mars ruling the sign in the tenth house and Saturn the sign in the sixth house). Her elevated Jupiter conjunct and parallel her Midheaven (and trine and parallel Neptune, too) enabled her to get jobs with ease so that she has never worried about losing them. As that Jupiter also squares her 6 Leo 15 Ascendant, she tended to be overly ambitious and optimistic about her career. Her angular fourth house Moon square her Ascendant indicated her personal trouble with jealous (Scorpio Moon) women and, earlier in her life, her family. They had moved often, too, when she was young—Moon in the fourth house. The Moon is semisquare the Vertex and contraparallel the Midheaven. The Moon-Vertex is indicative of strong karmic links with her family (especially her mother). The Moon-Midheaven aspect was important in showing the strong drive to appear before the public (Moon). The most important bodies for fame and recognition are Jupiter, Moon and Chronos. The aspect being an opposition indicated obstacles to be overcome in attaining recognition, Yet, Vivia Jayne has found, a so-called adverse aspect to the Midheaven by a benefic is preferable to none at all; some benefits will occur.

The Uranus in her ninth house showed long distance travel, which had been the case in her theatrical career. She started her career and went to Europe with a college group at the end of August 1949 on solar arc Uranus conjunct the Midheaven. She went on a summer stock tour at the beginning of August 1951 on the same aspect by vertical arc. Finally it occurred once again on Ascendant arc—a trip to Washington in early July 1955.

One could consider that these three aspects alone verified the accuracy of the rectification since Uranus is so accurate as to time and the events were fitting as to nature. A cousin was a suicide on Midheaven contraparallel Venus (it is at the end of the seventh and thus affects the eighth house and is natally opposite Neptune, ruler of the sign in the eighth and planet of suicide).

When the Midheaven opposed the Moon (mother-Moon rules the sign in the fourth house) her mother was hospitalized (twelfth) due to a serious operation. The same aspect occurred as a contraparallel (Midheaven moved by solar declination arc) in late 1946 at a time of great stress for her mother due to her father's financial setbacks. I should note that with Pluto opposite the Sun natally she had problems with men who had ties (Pluto) with other women (Pluto). This aspect, plus her Scorpio Moon, made her also somewhat paranoid.

4

Unknown Birth Times

It may be asked what one can and should do in the case of totally unknown birth times or where the hour is very vague such as the birth being given merely as having taken place in the morning. The relationships of the lights and major configurations in the chart to the pattern of houses becomes still more important in instances of this kind.

If the astrologer has a high degree of competence and knows considerable information about the native and his or her life, it is possible to rectify the chart. I would like to cite a case worked on by two very fine astrologers, Nicholas DeVore and Eleanor Hesseltine.

The native, a woman, had been born on October 13, 1899 and from the mother's very confused account, this was in the morning and might have taken place (because of the day of the week given) on the fifteenth. There was also conflicting evidence as to whether the gestation period was seven or nine months. The position of the lights and planet to the nearest half degree follows: Sun, 20 Libra 00; Moon, 9 Aquarius 00; Mercury, 27 Libra 00; Venus, 29 Libra 00; Mars, 15 Scorpio 30; Jupiter, 14 Scorpio 00; Saturn, 19 Sagittarius 00; Uranus, 5 Sagittarius 30; Neptune, 27 Gemini 00; and Pluto, 16 Gemini 30. The declination of Pluto is such as to bring it into contraparallel with both the Moon and Mercury, and even Jupiter, widely. While Saturn and Uranus are not conjunct, they are parallel. Saturn opposes Pluto, and both Saturn and Uranus are contraparallel Neptune. Therefore, there is effectively a multiple opposition (in longitude and declination) of Saturn and Uranus to Neptune and Pluto—a dominant configuration in the chart.

Her parents had so little love for her that they put her in a foster home. She grew up parentless. And she had more than the usual share of illness with which to contend in her life. Indeed, later in life her parents returned into her life and for many years she was extremely kind to her ailing mother.

From a careful study of her, Eleanor Hesseltine decided that her birth had occurred on the thirteenth rather than the fifteenth since on October 15, 1899, Mercury would have been in Scorpio instead of Libra, and Venus would have been only a matter of minutes of arc from the end of Libra, thus showing some Scorpio quality as well as Libra. This was an excellent example of reading the meanings of the planets in the signs. Having found the correct day, it was then a matter of approximating the correct time of day from a study of the planets in the houses.

Nicholas DeVore concluded that the multiple opposition of Saturn and Uranus to Neptune and Pluto might fall across her third and ninth houses and thus come by direction to her Midheaven in the younger part of her life. This was not correct but it was good astrology in that he recognized the importance of the dynamic relationship of the multiple opposition to her angles. Eleanor Hesseltine saw the multiple opposition coming to her Ascendant axis in her younger years when she had experienced so many difficulties. The twelfth house emphasis—Saturn and Uranus—fit her being put in an institution; the sixth house emphasis—Neptune and Pluto (Neptune was actually opposite the Ascendant)—fit the accent on illness.

This placed her Midheaven at about 19 Libra 00 conjunct her Sun (just in the tenth house) and also placed the Mercury-Venus conjunction elevated in the tenth house. This fit with her career in musical comedy as a dancer and singer and her appearances before the public. Indeed, she had always had quite good relationships with male bosses and important men (Sun radically conjunct the Midheaven).

The conjunction of Mars and Jupiter in the eleventh house of friends in square to the second house Moon showed her extreme generosity with her money and possessions with her friends—a trait that's a marked characteristic. The opposition of her Neptune to the Ascendant in late Sagittarius not only described her unusual directness and bluntness but also her love of religious and philosophical matters (last half of that sign). By direction all the main events of her life fit the major combinations of her planets with her angles so that the chart is certainly correct. I should say that few astrologers could have rectified such a chart.

Another technique one may use in rectifying unknown or very uncertain birth times is to add the solar arc (whose length is unaffected by such uncertainties) to the relevant planets for the major events of life—Saturn for the deaths of the father and of her man, Pluto and Neptune for the deaths of the mother and other women, and so on—until one has a whole set of such directed positions.

If, as a rule, the same degree, but in different signs, shows up frequently, this will often give the correct degree of the Midheaven (more probably) or Ascendant. And if one subtracts the same arcs this can have the same result—in this latter case the degree obtained can be that of the radical Midheaven which is being directed to an aspect of the Midheaven by solar arc in longitude or in declination arc, whereas in the first case (arcs added) it is the bringing of the planet to an aspect of the Midheaven or Ascendant. The foregoing technique is one of several that may be used when the birth time is uncertain.

If an unknown or very, very approximate time cannot be rectified what can one do? As is well known, one can make a solar chart and this is usually what is done. Or one may make a birth locality (Johndro) chart. However, the baseline published by L. Edward Johndro in his book *The Earth in the Heavens* was later changed by him from a moving baseline to a static one. That is to say, that if born at the beginning of spring (Sun at zero degrees Aries) and on the Greenwich meridian, then the Midheaven of the birth locality chart is zero degrees Aries. If born at the start of spring but, say, ninety degrees west of it, one must subtract ninety degrees from the right ascension of the Midheaven, giving a birth locality Midheaven of zero degrees Capricorn. But let us say the native was born ninety degrees west but not at the commencement of spring. Now the Midheaven of the place of birth is zero degrees Capricorn (as it is just ninety degrees of right ascension taken from the 360 degrees—or zero degrees—of zero degrees Aries).

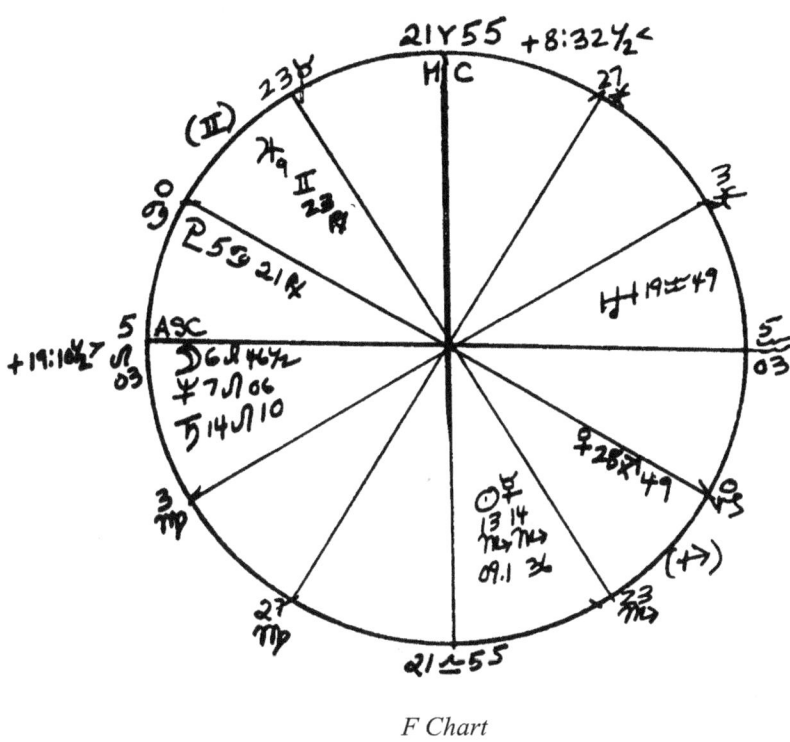

F Chart
November 5, 1917

Let us say the Sun was at fifteen degrees Gemini (to the nearest degree as the time of day is unknown). Now fifteen degrees Gemini is seventy-five degrees later than zero degrees Aries. Therefore, your birth locality Midheaven is zero degrees Capricorn plus seventy-five degrees, i.e. 15 Pisces 00 when found via celestial longitude. The right ascension of the Sun at 15 Gemini 00 is 73°43′. To find the birth locality Midheaven by right ascension instead of via longitude, add the 73°43′ of right ascension to the right ascension of zero degrees Capricorn, and thus to 270 degrees, which gives 343°43′ for the RAMC of the birth locality Midheaven. Primary solar arcs in true right ascension (DeLuce's equatorial arcs) are used with the Midheaven found by right ascension; the better known but more recent true solar arcs in longitude are used with the Midheaven found via longitude (at 15 Pisces 00). As Johndro pointed out, both methods are valid. Johndro corrected the way of finding his famous birth locality or Johndro chart in *Modern Astrology* in June 1950. Those who use his earlier baseline (moving) are wasting their time.

There are certain prenatal charts which one can do even if the time of birth is unknown,; indeed, even if the exact day of birth is not known. The one with which I have had the most experience is the F chart of fate discovered by Eleanor Hesseltine and me, with some help from W. Kenneth Brown, on November 1, 1952. The chart occurs at Moonrise or Moonset about three months before birth at a quarter Moon. The Moon must be applying to the square to the Sun as closely as possible. On an average the epoch occurs eighty-seven days before the birth epoch. The interval from the F to the B epoch may be a week or ten days longer or shorter than this eighty-seven day interval. In the case of a male the Moon will on an average be about a half degree above the Ascendant or a half degree below the

Descendant (i.e., cadent); for a female the Moon on an average is a half degree below the Ascendant or a half degree above the Descendant (i.e., angular). The half degree values are used before the chart is rectified. The only events not shown in the directions of an F chart are deaths. I hope other astrologers will test this chart which I have used often in the past twenty years when it appeared difficult or impossible to rectify an unknown time.

First, the chart must be validated before it is rectified, which is the subject of the next chapter. A case of such an F chart occurred on November 5, 1917 at 10:25:42 p.m., Eastern Standard Time (rectified) in New York City, 40N33, 73W57. Birth had occurred at an unknown time of day on February 7, 1918. Use the natal latitude and longitude for this chart unless at the time it occurred the mother was elsewhere. In the latter case, set up the F chart as though it had occurred at the birth place and then shift the Midheaven backward or forward in right ascension to the correct area, using then the latitude of the place of the F chart instead of the latitude of birth. The F chart indicates those ``blows of fate'' (karma) that we must strive to transmute.

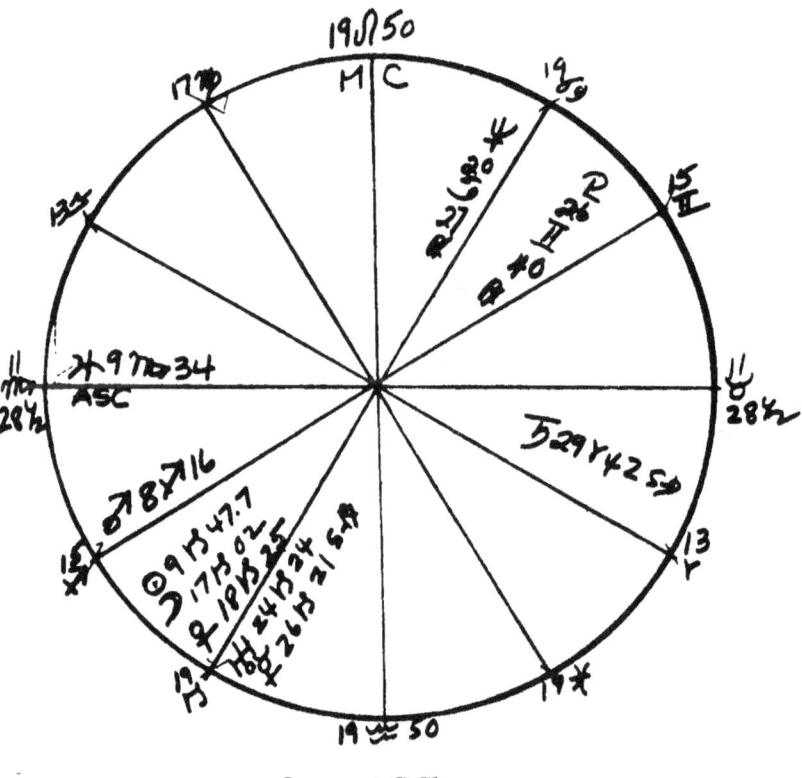

Incorrect C Chart
January 1, 1911
39N54, 75W08, 2:50 AM EST

The wide trine of Venus late in the fifth house to the Aries Midheaven is an indication of her activities as a commercial artist. The midpoint of the very close square of Saturn to Mercury (90°26′) is only nine minutes from a square to that Venus, i.e. Saturn/Mercury = Venus. One effect of this was that she worked very hard in very exacting detail work. If the Midheaven is moved by a very slow solar declination arc (instead of by simple solar arc in longitude) it squared Saturn in late December 1958, opposed Mercury nearly eight years later in early October 1966, and in that interval was sesquiquadrate Venus. During that time she was stuck in a low paying job (Mercury ruling Virgo in the second house). Afterward she did much better.

The Scorpio Sun's square to the Leo Ascendant is a wide eight degrees, so it is weak. She met her

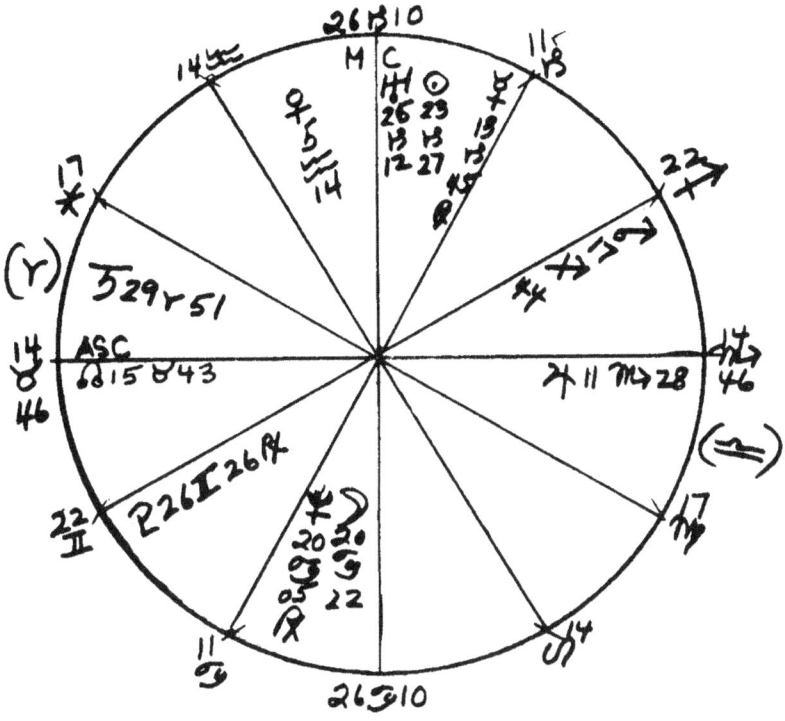

Correct C Chart
January 14, 1911
39N54, 75W08, 12:22 PM EST

future husband on solar arc Sun trine Ascendant in early March 1939. On Ascendant arc Sun trine it in late April 1946 he was released from Army service. On the Midheaven square Uranus (but natal sextile) in June 1945, she traveled (Uranus radically in and ruling the Aquarian seventh house).

The first time that the Midheaven squared Saturn and then opposed Mercury (late November 1939 to early May 1940) by solar arc in longitude she experienced stress with her future husband over career (Midheaven). At the beginning of May 1947 under solar arc Pluto conjunct the Ascendant she experienced an unusual trip with her husband. when the solar arc Pluto reached the parallel of the Ascendant (23 Taurus 58; the Sun and Midheaven at this longitude have the same declination as Pluto at 18N45), she changed her job (Midheaven) due to the underhandedness (Pluto) of her boss. She and her husband finally paid off the mortgage on their house in early 1956 as the fourth house Sun trined the Midheaven (by solar arc). In early July 1962 she and a woman collaborated on a book under solar arc Uranus trine Ascendant (from and ruling the seventh house). My wife and I forecast a successful job change for late September 1964 as the solar arc Midheaven made its conjunction to her Jupiter. She was satisfied with our reports based on this chart over a seven year period, a good test of its efficacy.

5

Horoscope Validation

Closely related to the technique of rectification is that of validation. This technique is used to test for the validity of a horoscope, a hypothetical planet, or a Node. Some investigators are convinced that the mean Node of the Moon, the one that is nearly always given, is valid, although one might well expect that the true Node of the Moon alone would be valid (they can be 1°46' apart).

Therefore, one can use directional tests to determine validity. And one must distinguish between, say, the geocentric Node of Mars and the heliocentric Node of Mars. Dobyns is convinced that only the geocentric Nodes should be used, but here again it is a matter of testing for validity.

The same question of validity must of course be raised in the case of any hypothetical planet. Actually if one is satisfied as to validity one then usually must rectify said planet in a number of different horoscopes in order to determine how rapidly the planet is moving along the ecliptic.

From my work, the work of my associates, and the work of a number of other capable astrologers, we have concluded that a number of hypothetical planets are valid. The importance of this is that, if we are right, skill in the techniques of rectification and validation make it possible to test reliably for the validity and accurate position of factors with which one cannot otherwise deal. This is not an easy thing to do in the first place. Second, if there is any serious question as to validity, then the factor must be validated by two or more groups of investigators independently. We applied such tests in 1956 to the eight hypothetical planets of the Uranian system of Witte and Sieggruen. These tests were independent of the supporters of the Uranian system. We were compelled to conclude that all eight bodies are valid.

In this chapter I am more concerned with the first kind of validation, i.e., whether a given horoscope is valid. A client may be unsure of which of two days or two years he or she was born. Before one can hope to rectify the chart, it must first be determined which of the two is valid. Or it may be that one is seeking to work with a prenatal (or postnatal) chart. Clearly one must be sure of validity before bothering to rectify.

The most brilliant application of both the validation and rectification techniques I have seen was a case handled many years ago. The man was born by the Hebraic calendar in one of three consecutive years, on a different day in December (depending on the year that was correct) and at an unknown time of day. Normally this would be hopeless. Fortunately the man was not young and had done much research to date the main events of his life. Indeed, his research convinced him that the first one of the three years was highly improbable.

The charts (solar) were set up for each of the two probable years and studied mainly in terms of sign position of the Moon and inner planets (including Mars and Jupiter) and in terms of the aspects between them. Being about a year apart they were quite different. From the study of him, his history and the two charts, it was concluded that he was probably born in the middle one of the three years.

Here, validation was based solely on sign position and aspects. From our study of the man we were convinced that he had a fixed sign on the Ascendant, each of us picking two fixed signs. Of the two each that we picked, we agreed on one, which later proved to be the correct one. It was then noted that his Neptune and Pluto were just about ten degrees apart and that two major stressful event sin his life were about ten years apart: the death of his mother (Pluto) and the birth of a child with a cord wrapped around his neck (Neptune). Then afflicting aspects (conjunctions, oppositions, squares) of these two bodies by direction (solar arc) with one of the angles timed these two events and gave an exact value of the Midheaven and Ascendant to test further. These positions proved to be right when subjected to the test of other directional aspects and their corresponding events. I don't think the man realized what good fortune he experienced to have had his horoscope validated and rectified.

In this case one validating step was skipped. It is an important step which is often essential. That is to say that one takes aspects by progression or direction to or by the lights (Sun and Moon) with other bodies. Let us say that Johnnie was born either on Sunday, August 3 or on Monday, August 4.

The Sun in the interval had moved nearly one degree which by direction is about one year. Aspects to or by the Sun will tend to differ by about one year. If one can find, say, half a dozen major aspects—preferably the hard aspects, but including parallels and contraparallels—it should be possible to say which of the two sets of six configurations fits the events of his life, and which of the two sets doesn't really fit at all. The two Moons will move much further apart than one degree so that aspects to and by the Moon may be an even better test for validity.

Therefore, in validation as contrasted with rectification, one uses aspects to or by the lights instead of to or by the angles. And one uses the lights since as a rule, aspects to or by them are considerably more potent than interplanetary aspects; although, of course, one may also use interplanetary aspects too for validation.

It is true that currently the prenatal or lunar epoch (I prefer the C or conception epoch as a name) is out of fashion. The main reason for this has been as follows. According to the Trutine of Hermes, the C Moon is conjunct or opposite the B (birth) Ascendant and the C Ascendant is conjunct or opposite the B Moon. Sepharial, who introduced the Trutine of Hermes into modern astrology and E.H. Bailey, who wrote a book on it, both insisted on the exactness of these Ascendant-Moon interchanges. Later, L. Edward Johndro, after studying 200 obstetrical cases from Flower Hospital in New York City, concluded that the interchanges were valid, but they need not be exact. The orb of admissible inexactitude he found to be that of any conjunction or opposition, i.e., not over seven and a half degrees. Johndro and his partner W. Kenneth Brown must have done 200 to 250 C charts and

Johndro was a first-class rectifier. Eleanor Hesseltine and I have done a similar number so that the four of us have done close to 500 C charts.

I mention this since one may set up a C chart with the above Moon-Ascendant interchanges. That usually occurs nine months before birth, but one many nonetheless have an incorrect C chart. Let us say that the one that has been done is nine months and six days before birth, but that the right one is actually fourteen days later or eight days short of nine months before birth. How can one tell this? How can the C chart be validated?

First, ask whether the planetary pattern fits the individual. If it looks all wrong, this alone is cause for rejecting it. Second, one applies directional tests, especially aspects to and by the lights. If it passes this test, it is probably a valid C chart. Third, one seeks to rectify the angles—if the chart should actually be wrong, one should be unable to rectify it. The final and definitive test is as to whether the astrologer can forecast via the chart. One example follows.

The native was born October 9, 1911 in Jenkintown, Pennsylvania at 10:53 p.m., Eastern Standard Time (given; rectified to 10:39:30 p.m.) at 75W08, 39N54. The Sun was at 15 Libra 43, Moon at 11 Taurus 28:30, Midheaven at 27 Pisces 09; Ascendant at 16 Cancer 14, and Vertex at 2 Sagittarius 35. What is mainly of interest here is the position of the Moon and Ascendant.

Ten lunar revolutions before the birthday is January 9, 1911 or nine calendar months before birth. Since the natal Ascendant was at 16 Cancer 14, the day of the C epoch (gestation interval being normal) would either be earlier (January 1 with the Moon in Capricorn opposite the B Ascendant) or later (January 14 with the Moon in Cancer conjunct the B Ascendant). According to the complex rules of E.H. Bailey, the January 1 epoch should be the correct one. It would be the C Ascendant in Scorpio in opposition to the B Moon. There are several reason why this version of his C chart does not fit him.

He does not look as much like a Scorpio Ascendant as a Taurus Ascendant. A number of investigators, including some non-astrologers, have suggested that the C chart Ascendant should have more to do with one's physical appearance than the B chart Ascendant since the pattern of the physical vehicle is initiated then. Second, the conjunction of Jupiter to the Scorpio Ascendant does not fit his temperament and personality projection.

There is a stellium in Capricorn (Sun-Moon-Venus in the second house, and Uranus conjunct Mercury in the third house). The third house Uranus-Mercury does fit his writing. But the New Moon conjunct Venus in Capricorn and in the second house would mean that he thinks and conceives mainly in terms of money, which is not true. As a matter of fact, the sextile of Jupiter and the Ascendant to the New Moon would make these ideas very successful, especially since Jupiter rules the sign in the first half of the second house.

Directional tests involving the Sun and Moon did not correlate to major events in his life, although one direction could have been significant—Sun contraparallel Pluto in the eighth house in late August 1944 some six weeks before the death of an important woman. But why the Sun? Therefore, it is appropriate to consider the other possible conception epoch of January 14, 1911.

As the Scorpio Ascendant does not fit, this chart is set up with a Taurus Ascendant (11°28′ before rectification, 14°46′ with the correct rectified value). The Moon is now in Cancer closely conjunct

Neptune in the third house opposite the Sun-Uranus-Midheaven conjunction in Capricorn and late in the ninth house. Such a powerful third-ninth house emphasis does fit the mentality, writing and publishing of the native, who is an innovative astrologer. Note the Mercury retrograde in Capricorn in the ninth house trine the Ascendant. He has had considerable success in the publication of his work (articles and books).

The Moon by solar declination arc (Moon moved in declination the distance the Sun moves in declination) was parallel his Saturn (ruling the last half of his eighth house) when his mother died in August 1965. The sudden trip to the funeral was timed slightly later that same month by Uranus trine Moon (radical opposition) by solar arc. In 1967 at the beginning of February, he had Sun trine Neptune (radical opposition) and in May of that year the Sun moved on to trine the Moon (also in a radical opposition), both by solar arc. His wife commenced an antique business in the home (Cancer on the cusp of the fourth house ruled by the Moon) at the time of the first direction, but was closed down by local (third house) authorities (Sun radically conjunct the Midheaven) at the end of May that year. The Moon signifies the woman who was affected.

In the late summer of 1953, the native was unusually tired and depressed on the Sun contraparallel Saturn by secondary progression, the effect being to cause him to withdraw from social contacts. At that time, too, he ended a business relationship and friendship with an older man (Saturn) at a distance (Sun radically in the ninth house). Note that the Sun is radically square Saturn. On the Sun by solar arc and secondary progression sextile Uranus, radical conjunction, in late March 1972, he arranged a successful and unusual astrological symposium (Uranus ruling the Aquarian eleventh house) in which he was the kingpin (Sun).

The planetary pattern of this chart fits the native, this being the first test for validity. Directions and progressions to and by the lights (hard aspects preferred) also fit his life events, the second test for validity. It was possible to rectify the angles of the chart in a satisfactory manner, the third test for validity. This chart has been effective in forecasting developments in his life and thinking—the latter since it is a conception chart—for many years, the fourth and final test for validity.

The results of any one test may not always be as conclusive and definite as one would wish, which is why more than one test for validity is often necessary for any careful and thorough astrologer. It might be added that extra care was devoted to validating this chart since C charts at or near noon are very rare. In the approximate 500 we have done, this has been the only chart of this kind. The Sun at the Midheaven (of a B chart) in a man's chart signifies that he tends to hold positions of authority. In a C chart such a position of the Sun should signify that the man is an authority as to ideas.

www.ingramcontent.com/pod-product-compliance
Lightning Source LLC
Chambersburg PA
CBHW081837170426

43199CB00017B/2763